Mindful Manipulation

How Perception, Expectation, and Behavior Connect to Create Reality

James J. Ranieri

Published by BookLocker.com, Inc., Bradenton, Florida.

Printed in the United States of America on acid-free paper.

BookLocker.com, Inc.
2014

First Edition

Dedicated to the memories of
my father, Dominic J. Ranieri, and
my uncle, Nick Marnell.

Acknowledgements

I would like to thank my readers and friends, editors, family and everyone who played a part in this work. Specifically, I wish to acknowledge the contributions of my wife and partner in life, Dr. Kate Ranieri, for her encouragement, guidance, patience and belief that I could complete this work. Thanks to our daughters, Emily and Francesca, for participating in my grand experiment to teaching them how to negotiate as children. Special recognition to Dr. Roland Dumas, for both contributing and serving as my compass to help me understand what I was trying to convey here. Dr. Jerry Talley for clarifying where we can and cannot negotiate and for contributing the majority of the content for "Not Everything is Negotiable." My appreciation to Steve Gingras, Jerry Clor, Lloyd Schafer, Edward A. Scott III, Esq., Ellen Bell, Esq., Michael Venturini, Philip Reiss and Jillian Bevacqua for contributing to the readability of this work. I extend a special thanks to my editor Sara Vigneri, who patiently facilitated my collection of thoughts and forged it into a coherent, pragmatic and humanist approach to negotiating.

Table of Contents

Food For Thought

Think of a kaleidoscope, like the one you played with as a child. Remember, when you manipulated it you created different, fantastic and curious images like the one on cover of this book? A kaleidoscope can hold much greater meaning than simply a child's toy. The dictionary defines it as:

> **ka•lei•do•scope** (kə-lī′də-skōp′) *noun*
> **1.** (General Physics) an optical toy for producing symmetrical patterns by multiple reflections in inclined mirrors enclosed in a tube. Loose pieces of colored glass and paper are placed between transparent plates at the far end of the tube, which is rotated to change the pattern
> **2.** Any complex pattern of frequently changing shapes and colors
> **3.** A complicated set of circumstances
> **4.** A series of changing phases or events: *a kaleidoscope of illusions.*
> **5.** A continually shifting pattern, scene or the like

So, my question to you is, given the definition, how is a kaleidoscope like a negotiation? Think about it.

In my mind, the process of turning a kaleidoscope is a perfect analogy to describe what happens in the negotiating process. The contents of the kaleidoscope, the tube, mirrors, colored glass and transparent plates are constants, but as the kaleidoscope is turned what we see changes. The same stuff looks different. Imagine two people using identical kaleidoscopes. Unless they are holding the instrument at exactly the same angle, receiving the same intensity of light and turning it at exactly the same rate, they will not see the same images.

The instrument and its contents are fixed. The people, circumstances and conditions are variable. Negotiations work similarly. It is, of course, more complex because the perceptions, expectations and behaviors of people are the variables in negotiations, which produce different results. Most of the time those differences are dramatic. When playing with a kaleidoscope we focus on the changing, distorting and mesmerizing images it produces. In negotiations we tend only to observe the tactics, assertions and demands, not what's driving them. The real issues are usually concealed like the kaleidoscope's glass and mirrors. We are drawn to what our senses perceive. This is a trap, which can easily seduce the unsuspecting negotiator.

Just we accelerate turning the kaleidoscope, so too the patterns of life are changing faster and faster in this complex and interdependent world we all share. What follows is a new look at an old game. The world is changing, man has evolved but our ways negotiating are stuck in the mud. They are outdated and inadequate. We desperately need new ways to deal with different people in a dynamic world.

Despite some refinements, we have been using the same tired approaches, techniques and tactics to negotiating since man was a cave dweller. That's a long time and a lot has happened. Mindful Manipulation is designed to build equitable and durable resolutions to today's problems; locally, regionally and globally. It confronts head on that we live in a 'flat', changing world and wrongheadedly attempt to use obsolete philosophies and skills to deal with our new realities.

Before you read on here's a challenge. Look at the image on the cover of this book. Can you see the faces? If yes, any guesses? Here's a hint, their works defines both extremes of the negotiating spectrum. If you don't know who they are that's OK; I'll tell you later. Have fun, read on and open your mind. The fifth theory of negotiation, Mindful Manipulation, is a fresh set of principles and practices that work to manipulate and influence mutually advantageous negotiated outcomes. It isn't what you think.

Introduction

What does a relatively enlightened, second generation Italian-America, leading edge baby boomer, dyslexic, former military aviator, engineer, sales executive, global business director, husband, father, son, brother, adjunct professor, who has taught and practiced negotiating for over 40 years know about the topic? Plenty. To understand and appreciate what I have to offer you might want to know a little more about me and what shaped my thinking.

I grew up, like most, very trusting and naïve, which was a result of a combination of youth and my hard wiring. Watching my father, Dominic, deal with street vendors, wrestle with car salesmen and even bargaining with the local grocers, I was both fascinated and horrified with his behavior and style. Dad was not an educated man in the traditional sense, but he was definitely street-smart. In fact, my three brothers and I knew he could buy a new car at a better price than anyone else's father in Chicago Heights, Illinois. He knew how to work a deal even when buying a suit for my eighth grade graduation from the school that served San Rocco Parish.

Needing a new suit meant a trip to Chicago's Maxwell Street, which at that time was dominated by Jewish garment merchants where the price tags were for the unknowing goyim (gentiles). To my father, the price tags meant nothing. He'd find a suit we both liked then launch a fierce bargaining with the proprietor. Once he had a good price, he said to my brothers and me, "OK, let's get the Hell out of here," and we walked out with the storeowner in hot pursuit, offering a lower price.

This tactical maneuvering was repeated time after time whether he was shopping for a car, clothes or washing machines. Occasionally, his haggling intensified when, with a boisterously loud voice, he used

1

name-calling, insults and off-colored remarks. Mortified, my brothers and I tried to hide in a corner or escape out of the store. But I learned some valuable lessons from these adventures with my dad. One lesson was that life is all about winning an advantage.

My family lived in Chicago Heights during the height of its prosperity. We lived in a small, but comfortable, ranch house. My dad, a master diesel mechanic, helped build the interstate highway system while Uncle Nick, who lived one block south of our home, worked for Ford Motor Company as a crane operator at night and owned and operated a small grocery by day, all to finance his son's education. Nick was the absolute opposite of my dad. To Dominic's brashness, there was Nick's gentle diffidence. Soft and kind, he was always the first to help without any consideration of what was in it for him. From my observations of and interactions with him, I learned a different lesson. For Uncle Nick, the relationship was the ultimate prize.

As I grew, I recognized that even though both men had very similar backgrounds, their personalities were completely different and were key to how they behaved in a bargaining situation. I now understand that winning and building relationships are not opposite approaches to negotiating. Winning and relationship are, in fact, inextricably linked toward closing a deal. Also, I now understand the personality of individual negotiators is a critical factor on the process and outcome.

The lessons learned from my father and uncle were seminal, but were only the beginning of my quest to understand how to deal with people. I was a typical middle class kid who grew up in the 'Happy Days' of the 1950's. Being active in sports and somewhat popular, I became fascinated by how some of the kids who were in the same social circles were more dominant and others more submissive. I observed that dominant kids tended to get their way much more than submissive kids. I questioned whether they were born that way or if personality is a function of their environment.

I have a learning disability called dyslexia. When you have dyslexia, it takes longer to make some connections and it's difficult to match the letters you see on the page with the sounds those letter combinations make. And when you have trouble with that step, it makes all of the next steps in learning harder. Reading, particularly aloud, is difficult and transposition of numbers and letters occurs all of the time. Dyslexia is caused by something not working normally in a region of the brain. As with most afflictions, my having dyslexia was both a curse and a blessing. It was a curse through my entire formal education, kindergarten through an MBA. I tried to make myself invisible or fake a coughing spell so the teacher would not call on me to read aloud. I would hide behind the kid sitting directly in front of me, or avert my attention to something else in the room. Reading was not only difficult, but time consuming. The dyslexia also impacted my psyche. I grew up in an era where learning disabilities were not fully understood. I stopped counting the number of times I heard, "Jim is a bright boy, but he just doesn't apply himself." It was much easier for my teachers to assign laziness as the cause of my substandard performance relative to my exceptional brothers.

Because my reading ability was so poor, I was forced to find other ways of learning. I discovered that I was highly conceptual and unafraid of experimenting. So, I began learning by doing.

During college I became involved in campus politics. The major lesson I learned as a novice politician was how to make deals with others. I learned to trade with people who wanted something from me and had something to offer in return. After college, I joined the military and became an aviator. I travelled extensively, was exposed to different cultures, value systems and world-views. I learned that people in other places lived differently from the way I was raised. Marriage and children taught me many more life lessons that furthered my skills in how to read people.

After the military I entered the world of business. I started my career selling for a global petrochemical company. It was there that I learned a name for what I had been subconsciously studying my whole life: negotiating. I was empowered to represent the chemical company and negotiate innumerable large and small deals, ranging from multi-year; seven figure international deals to the starting salary for a new hire. I taught my business colleagues how to negotiate using win-lose methods. I became a master process facilitator and problem resolver, skilled in both the heuristic and rational methods. I was trained to administer and interpret psychometric instruments. I found two of these tools, DiSC and the Myers Briggs Type Indicator (MBTI), to be particularly applicable to negotiating.

That's my story. On the surface my career and life experiences may seem to be a collection of unrelated events. But in my mind they all connect. I've studied, practiced and refined the craft of negotiating all my life. In this book I present theories, best practices and a bunch of do's and don'ts. I have lived what is written here. I have keenly watched how others negotiate and learned from their successes and failures. I have practiced negotiating by trial and error. I have learned from my many mistakes, adjusted and tried again. I have learned the vast majority of the don'ts by failing, sometimes miserably. Reality and experience have been fabulous teachers.

I hope you will learn from my failures and successes, but before you read on I want to share this; the classical methods of negotiating are old and tired. All of these theories have big pieces missing and at their core are suboptimal. I truly believe as stewards of this planet and our future that we should strive for equity in negotiations. That is no trivial task. The first half of this book deals with ways of achieving equity. Since not everyone shares the noble equity goal, we need to be pragmatic and prepare ourselves to defend our self-interests, securing what we need and deserve. The second half of the book deals with protecting those interests. Recognize that striving for equity and protecting self-interests are not independent variables. They are not mutually exclusive, but complement each other. In today's world they can and must coexist, so that we can have a chance at doing the same. So, let's start the journey with a bit of history, lest we repeat it. History provides context and therefore meaning.

The Classics

"For every complex problem there is an answer that is clear, simple, and wrong"

- H. L. Mencken

Negotiating has been practiced in varying degrees on this planet for about 200,000 years. Scientists believe that's how long modern man has been here. Man has negotiated as a way to trade, conduct commerce, execute agreements, buy or sell, make treaties, secure services and a plethora of other transactions. Civilized man has been negotiating fundamentally same way during that all time. Sure there have been variants and improvements to the process (science and technology have been added to the mix), but at its roots it is the same dance. So, unless the collective man is totally illogical or suffers from a serious mental defect the processes and tools we have been using must work, or do they?

Before I present a solution to a very ill defined problem, let's consider how we currently negotiate and what the shortcomings and consequences are of using these conventional methods. There are four classic approaches or theories to negotiation—structural, strategic, process and integrative. All of them are largely positional and tend to drive toward a win-lose outcome. They remain viable and relevant and are the price of entry. So, you would be wise to recognize these classics, both their advantages and disadvantages, to help you respond efficiently and intentionally with your negotiating partner. They have worked quite successfully in the past and will continue to be used in some variant by practitioners in the future. Some experts include Dr. Chester Karrass, Gerard Nierenberg, Roger Fisher, William Ury, Saul Alinsky and, of course, Niccolo Machiavelli. As promised, the kaleidoscope image on the cover contains the faces of Machiavelli and Alinsky, the bookends of the negotiating continuum.

Each of these experts draws on their traditions, assumptions and practices. To navigate a negotiation successfully, you must understand and apply the traditional, time-tested practices of the classics. Keep in mind, that while the classics are tactically efficient, strategically they fall short of having efficacy and sustainability in a complex, dynamic environment that requires relationship building as well as myriad types of gain.

The **structural** approach is based on the distribution of power between two negotiating parties. Structure can be derived from tangible, hard power or leverage, (such as capital) or social, soft power (such as legitimacy, authority, affability). There may be either balanced leverage (power-symmetry) between parties, or imbalance leverage (power-asymmetry) between a stronger and a weaker party. There is rarely perfect power-symmetry between the parties in a negotiation. This approach to negotiation predicts that the strongest will always win. History has demonstrated that those who have more power in a negotiation will only lose to those with substantially less leverage. Clearly, power is not necessarily the sole advantage in a negotiation. The structural approach also does not account for the emergence of a disruptive technology, a break-through strategy, such as rural Arkansas-based Wal-Mart's use of distribution infrastructure to dominate the retail industry, or a flawless tactical execution.

To illustrate, IBM owned the information technology market with its mainframe computers until the 1980s when the personal computer (PC) was introduced. It changed not only the market, but also the power structure with in it. Viewed as a disruptive technology, the PC threw IBM into chaos and facilitated the emergence of Microsoft, Dell, Apple and other industry giants. Another example of the flaws in a structural approach comes from the automotive industry. The Big Three (General Motors, Ford and Chrysler) reigned supreme in the automotive market after World War II because of their infrastructure and the size of the U.S. market. With the rise of the Japanese automotive producers, the industry experts predicted that the powerful Big Three would win the competition. History demonstrates the clear winner. With a strategy of providing products that worked at an affordable price, the Japanese manufacturers gained a foothold and eventually dominated not only the U.S., but also world automotive markets. It also demonstrates that the reliance on power inherent in the structural approach ignores other relevant variables including a cultural drive to compete or a technological superiority.

This approach also features the soft structural assumptions of power. For example, a young university professor walked into a Toledo car dealer with money to buy a car. Having done meticulous research on every aspect of the car including color, accessories, model and price, the professor felt empowered to know what would be the best price. Meanwhile, a salesman on the showroom floor knew the limits of how much he was authorized to sell the vehicle, but needed to discover what the buyer was willing to pay. The negotiation failed because the salesman assumed that because the professor was a woman, she would know nothing about the car or price--he foolishly thought he had power over her. Because of the salesman's assumptions the process was thwarted and he didn't even get to haggle.

The **strategic** approach considers how both parties, through each successive negotiating event (or games), can choose to be cooperative or competitive. Trust, as a degree of certainty about expected behavior of each negotiation partner, is always tested. Depending on the level of trust, people will cooperate to optimize the outcome (individual or collective) or not. While cooperation of both sides might yield a desirable result, the parties can never be certain that each will cooperate because each side works independently to optimize their own gain. This uncertainty emerges from two potential obstacles including 1) that decisions can be made simultaneously and 2) that concessions of one side might not be reciprocated. Thus, the parties have contradicting incentives to cooperate. If one party cooperates or makes a concession and the other does not, the non-cooperating party might gain more. Through repetitive interactions or games there emerges a reliable pattern of behavior, such as reciprocity. These patterns either serve to build trust or destroy it. The only way both parties can win (equal gain) is through cooperation built on trust. As kids learning how to play games, we quickly realized whom we could trust. We also learned that in many games there is always one winner and one loser. Both military strategist and economists have adopted this approach. The strategic approach, or Game Theory, popularized by John Forbes Nash often results in win-lose. A simple example of how game theory can be applied to everyday life is the game of chicken. Based on previous interactions two people enter into a contest to see who blinks. Both begin by thinking that the other will capitulate, but as the pressure builds one person blinks. The Cuban Missile Crisis was a real life example of a game of chicken with huge consequences and luckily, the Soviet Union's Nikita Khrushchev, did blink.

During the height of the Cold War (1947-1991) the Soviet Union had established a strong military presence in Cuba, which had declared itself as a Communist state and aligned itself with the Soviet Union. United States photoreconnaissance intelligence had proven that missile launch areas were being readied on Cuban soil. Further, shipments of Soviet built missiles were confirmed to be on the sea headed for Cuba. This posed a major threat to the United States security and reaction time to launch a retaliatory strike. In response, the U.S. Navy established a blockade of Cuba and readied for a possible nuclear response if the Soviets chose to run the blockade. At the last second, the Soviet fleet carrying the missile and purported nuclear warheads diverted, avoided engaging U.S. warships and returned to Russia. A multitude of reasons were speculated for the Soviet's decision not to run the blockade, including Khrushchev's concern that President John F. Kennedy did not fully understand the ramifications of his actions. Khrushchev blinked, the Russian missiles returned home and Kennedy won the day.

Haggling, also called horse-trading, best characterizes the **process** approach. Typical examples of this approach include buying or selling a car, dealing with a street merchant selling designer knock-offs on New York's Canal Street or getting your children to clean their rooms. The parties start from two opposing points and converge through a series of concessions. This process of discovery is called haggling. The process unfolds between fixed points, starting with divergence and ending in convergence. One party starts by making a high offer and the other responds with a low offer. Eventually, they meet somewhere in between the initial offers. The process approach is not always sustainable in complex negotiations because it is driven by concession-making ability and the relative power of the parties involved. The knowledge and practice of tactics and countermeasures weighs heavily in favor of those who have the greatest command of them. It is the practice that people most commonly and mistakenly associate as negotiating.

Haggling works when the price and the accompanying terms are not fixed. It attempts to discover both parties' realities by a series of offers and counteroffers. The practice of haggling can be at the expense of maintaining a good relationship. My father was a great haggler. It is an art form, in that you cannot simply bulldoze your way to a great deal, particularly if you need to buy or sell to the person with which you are engaged on a recurring basis. To be effective you need to be able to finesse the deal by determining the other parties' point of indifference. Haggling in some cultures is a way of life. In the U.S., it's not part of our DNA. The venues for haggling are somewhat limited to buying cars, houses, antiques, art or garage sale treasures.

The literature offers two definitions of the ***integrative*** approach to negotiation. The first refers to it as interest-based, principled or win-win negotiation. It is a set of techniques that attempts to improve the quality and likelihood of negotiated agreement by providing an alternative to traditional positional negotiation techniques. Positional negotiation assumes there is a fixed amount of value to divided between the parties, integrative negotiation attempts to create more value in the negotiation. It focuses on the underlying interests of both parties rather than random starting positions. It approaches negotiation as a problem solving intervention rather than a test of wills, and insists upon adherence to objective, ethical criteria as the basis for agreement.

Integrative negotiation requires a high degree of trust and relationship building. It may involve creative problem solving to discover possible mutual gains. This approach was popularized in Ury and Fisher's *Getting to Yes*. It assumes that the parties in the negotiation are rational, ethical and well intended. That is not always the case.

The second definition divides the ***integrative*** process into successive stages, from the pre-negotiation, first contact 'selling' stage to the final settlement. This "Tayloresque" approach is a formalized, scientific approach designed for negotiators to optimize their position in each stage. The outcome is analyzed by evaluating the performance of the actors at each stage. If sustainability of relationship and the agreement requires that the needs of both parties be satisfied in a negotiation, then this approach will not be desirable. By definition, this approach optimizes one party's position while the other party's position is subjugated.

Studying the classical negotiating theories I concluded that choosing the correct approach was not an either-or but an all-of-the-above decision. Further, I discovered that all of the classical theories are missing the same critical elements. This is the basis of the Principles of Mindful Manipulation and the secret to effective negotiating in the 21st Century.

A Case for Change

Most negotiations draw from ancient traditions, practices and assumptions embedded in classical theories. What worked in the past, however, no longer have efficacy and sustainability in a global community. Unless you suffer from psychoscherosis (hardening of the attitude, which causes a person to cease dreaming, seeing, thinking, and leading) or are a member of The Flat Earth Society, you surely recognize that the world of commerce is markedly different than it was even two decades ago. Companies are no longer either competitors or customers. Today, a competitor in one situation is a partner in tomorrow's situation. A seller is also a buyer and vice versa. Every negotiation event impacts future relationships as well as subsequent transactions. The demands are such that we must change the way we negotiate.

"There is nothing that is a more certain sign of insanity than to do the same thing over and over and expecting the results to be different"

- Albert Einstein

Furthermore, we now know that despite our global economy, humans remain culturally influenced and individually complex. It follows, then, that our negotiation behaviors must address the intricacies of both our new environment and the people that live in it. To do that, I'm arguing for change in assumptions, principles and practices of negotiations. Specifically, I'm arguing for a more civil, humanistic approach that philosophically grounds negotiating based on four distinct principles.

Don't think that I'm advocating a soft approach to negotiating. What follows is as tough and as practical as it gets.

The practices that I offer represent the best of classical, conventional schools of thought on the topic of negotiations that remain viable today. Think of the practices as the content for a survival skills course in negotiating. If you are not grounded in the practices, then attempting to use the principles will have a high likelihood of backfiring. A negotiator must use these practices to recognize if the Other (a reference to another party in the negotiation) is playing a win-lose game. The twist is that these practices are philosophically congruent with the principles.

This book is driven by the demands for new and better ways to negotiate, a renaissance of sorts. Based on insights gleaned from nearly forty years of industry experience, successful negotiation practice and teaching, theoretical applications drawn from negotiation, personality and human communication theories, this book confronts these new realities with new tools. I believe that the time has come for a fifth theory of negotiating, Mindful Manipulation, with its principles and practices that are in sync to navigate the commercial and personal issues we all face in the 21st Century.

The remainder of this book follows a logical sequence for learning and doing. In Part One I make my biases, suppositions and assertions transparent. Part Two discusses each of the principles in great depth. Part Three defines the still relevant classical practices. Here's my promise and my warning to you. If you are a skilled negotiator and appropriately apply these principles, you will create more durable and equitable resolutions to your future negotiations. If you are a negotiating novice and apply these principles without an understanding of the classical practices, you may make yourself easier prey to someone to exploit you.

What's Different?

The problem with the old ways of negotiating is that the people involved were largely treated as interchangeable parts. Any discussion as to variability in perceptions, expectations and behaviors as they relate to negotiating were either non-existent or simply mentioned in passing. The old schools fail to identify what the true trade offs are when we negotiate. The conventional theories about negotiations focus on the results and ruses while completely avoiding the how, the methods and the means to achieve those results. But the manner and method of achieving results is much more significant than acknowledged. The 'what' and 'how' need to be balanced. Lastly, they tend to lead people to believe that everything is negotiable. That, in fact, is not true.

I have developed four counterintuitive, unconventional and avant-garde principles and a set of time-tested traditional negotiating practices that will enable you to be successful in any situation where negotiation is applicable. I call it Mindful Manipulation. In this context, mindful means being aware, wary and thoughtful in a negotiation. Manipulation means to influence, navigate or maneuver the negotiation process. The word manipulation has a negative and sometimes sinister undertone, but that is not intended here.

Mindful Manipulation is the thoughtful practice of understanding the Other's perceptions and expectations, then influencing and shaping them through civil, consistent and purposeful behaviors to create advantageous negotiated results. Graphically, it looks like this.

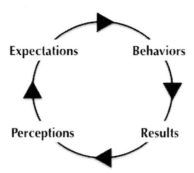

Mindful Manipulation is the caring, pensive and considerate art of shaping perceptions and expectations. It is not sinister or devious, but honest and at the core of the human condition when it comes to securing what you need. Mindful Manipulation is the pragmatic, humane and elegant methodology for achieving that balance of what and how. It's far different than anything else you may have read about negotiating. It is an effective way to practice negotiations regardless of the intent of the Other. Mindful Manipulation is a significantly new, counterintuitive, value driven approach to negotiating. It is a twist on Teddy Roosevelt's adage, "Speak softly and carry a big stick," but applied to all negotiating, not just diplomacy. The principles will guide you to speak softly, while the practices are a big stick available should you need it. Said differently, the implied strategy is if you mess with me, then I'll mess with you. Practicing Mindful Manipulation ensures that you will get what you really need in an ever-changing world regardless of the game that the Other plays.

So What

In addition to the four new principles, Mindful Manipulation also equips you with a self-defense arsenal of weapons should you need them (i.e. the big stick). In the pages that follow you will come to understand your negotiating self, learn how to mitigate your vulnerabilities and capitalize on your strengths. You will learn how to read people, mindfully manipulate their weaknesses, expectations and behaviors, play into their comfort zone, build trust and neutralize their power, not necessarily to exploit them, but to build better, more balanced agreements.

I'll help you understand that winning cannot be accomplished without impunity. There are always consequences and trade offs. I'll make you consciously aware of the trade-offs that you are making in terms of risk and reward, gain and relationship. I will make the connection between your cognitive preferences, particularly your innate basis of decision-making and your negotiating default 'soft' wiring.

I will provide you with a philosophy and a framework to facilitate the process of how to conduct negotiations that is both pragmatic and humane. I'll a share a philosophy anchored in remaining calm and focused, acting with civility, persuading by engaging, and staying on the same page. Additionally, you will be exposed to a flexible problem-resolving model, and some key facilitative behaviors and actions.

I will define the domain or turf where negotiation is applicable and appropriate so that you will not waste your time trying to achieve the impossible through the negotiating process. By understanding what types of issues are appropriate for negotiation and which are not, you will be able to avoid the frustration created by impasse and deadlock.

Lastly, I will share with you the best of what is relevant from the traditional classical theories of negotiation to act as a negotiating survival manual. I'll discuss the behaviors, tactics and countermeasures that work before, during and after a negotiation. Time tested and powerful, these actions will keep you from being exploited. The book will enable you to read the negotiating situation and respond effectively and efficiently. Practicing Mindful Manipulation will allow to you to increase the upside and minimize the downside when you negotiate.

Part I: Assertions, Suppositions & Biases

"Once we know that life is difficult once we truly understand and accept it then life is no longer difficult."

- M. Scott Peck

Before I advance into an explanation of the Principle and Practices of Mindful Manipulation, I need to ensure that we are on the same page by defining some operating assumptions underlying this work. I will share the embedded assumptions, suppositions, assertions and biases that have influenced all that follows. First, I'll:

- Define negotiating as I see it, because you need to be clear about what it is and what it is not.
- Share my beliefs on how compromise and its fit with negotiating
- Differentiate needs from wants
- Discuss winning and losing and their impact on negotiating
- Define trust, who to trust, how to build it and why it is so important to negotiating
- Discuss the absence of a universal standard of conduct
- Show how expectations drive the negotiating process
- Provide you with a few insights about this book

On Negotiating

So what is this life dance called negotiating, or this game without agreed-upon rules? Webster defines negotiation as dealing or bargaining with another or others in the preparation of a treaty or contract in preliminaries to a business deal. The Oxford English Dictionary (OED) definition is holding communication or conferencing with another for the purpose to settle matters of mutual interest either through agreement or compromise. Here's my definition: **Negotiating is a process that can temporarily resolve issues between people and groups of people.**

It's very important to understand what negotiating is, and what it is not before we look at how to do it. Negotiation should not be confused with arbitration and mediation. It does not require a disinterested party to facilitate the resolution of an issue. In the realm of tasks that we do, some are technical and specific, with right and wrong answers. Other things we do are more forgiving; there are many answers that can work, but to be successful, others must agree and support the answer. In the technical sphere, you need the skills, abilities and tools required for tasks like solving an equation or writing a computer program. A skilled person can do the task without agreement from others, and the correct answer is definitive. The vast majority of things we do, however, require some give and take and some participation and agreement from others, because everyone must support the solution. Those that require agreement of participating individuals are what we refer to as negotiations. Like medicine, law or research, negotiation is a practice, part science and part art.

There are three key words in the definition; resolve, temporarily and people. Let's look at them in reverse order. **People** -- you can only negotiate with people. This fact makes negotiations complex and messy. I find it amazing that the classic theories of negotiation either avoid the people issue or minimize the importance of understanding the Other. Both Webster and the OED reference another or others. At a high level, when you are dealing with someone else for something that you need, you are negotiating. Since people are different and we can only negotiate with other people, we need to deal more effectively with the human issues in negotiations. Human behaviors and beliefs are multi-faceted and extremely complex. Throughout history, people and groups have largely been out-of-sync with one another. These conditions, attitudes and perspectives are forged by our cognitive preferences, our gender, our ethnicity, our culture, our values and what was going on in the world when we grew up. During the course of this book, I will attempt to highlight some of the relevant differences, and to make sense out of the 'people stuff' as it applies it to the negotiating process.

Temporarily -- agreements, deals or contracts are all made under a defined set of conditions. If the deal is struck, it defines a state of 'equilibrium' where the parties can interact as agreed. If one or all of the conditions that define the circumstances surrounding the agreement significantly change, then just as in physics or chemistry, the equilibrium is disturbed and a new state of equilibrium is created. So, the idea of a permanent solution is an oxymoron. All solutions, like structures, are temporary and will eventually fail. It is naïve and wishful thinking to believe that we can create a solution, system, organization or structure that will endure forever.

Negotiation is, at its core, problem ***resolving***, not problem solving. Solutions tend to have an aura of permanence. But the reality is that equilibrium is only reached until something changes. Life is dynamic, not static, and as things change, our resolutions to past problems may come under pressure. Negotiating only works when the parties involved share at least some common ground. If there is no common ground or common interests, you cannot negotiate, so don't even try. If absolutism dominates the issues because the problem is steeped in morality and beliefs then it is a classical situation with no common ground, no room for compromise or give and take. It is deadlocked from the onset.

We are going to focus on a set of problems that are narrower than the large and inclusive 'problem-resolving' domain. We are not going to try to resolve the Middle-East crisis or to get your teenage son to behave better. The focus is on situations in which two parties have aligned interest in an agreement, but also have interests that are in conflict. A simple example is purchasing a new car. The customer and the salesperson have an aligned interest in concluding the transaction. Both will have their needs met and will gain from the transaction. They are in conflict, however, because the buyer wants the lowest possible price and the seller wants the highest price. A conversation in which the difference is resolved is a negotiation. If both sides come to common ground then both will benefit from the concluded transaction. When a union is on strike, both management and union members want a mutually beneficial resolution. They may differ on the terms of specific contract language, benefits or pay, so they engage in conversation to find a resolution—a negotiation. Sounds easy enough, so what's the problem with how we negotiate now?

Since negotiations are always people centric, it is prone to unpredictability and variations. Better understanding of people and new skills can dramatically improve results and predictability. There are rational and emotional components of problem resolving. Because negotiation is a people process, it does not lend itself to a linear or algorithmic approach. There can be no numbers to plug in and crank out a solution with statistically predictable results. Negotiating requires that we use a heuristic model rather than a formulaic one to optimize desired results for both parties. Heuristics are iterative and dependent on trial and error. To be effective at heuristic problem solving requires both a different mindset and markedly different skill set. This different mindset is woven into the principles. The skill set is of a more facilitative nature than what we traditional consider negotiating skills.

On Compromise

It is important to understand how compromise and negotiating fit together. The Oxford English Dictionary (OED) explains that to compromise is "to arbitrate and settle differences." Implicit in this definition is the process of give and take that usually results in one or both parties not achieving all that is needed or wanted. At best, compromise is suboptimal. Here is a rule of thumb that describes the relationship between compromise and negotiation, "you can have negotiation without compromise, but you cannot have compromise without negotiation." If two parties practice 'positional negotiating', or present demands that are markedly different, there is no way to reach agreement without compromise. Positional negotiation starts with solutions instead of problems. If we can identify the problems in the form of needs, then we can most likely get to agreement without compromise. The worth of the compromise is governed by the degree of reciprocity the parties exhibit without sacrificing their real needs. This requires an understanding of the differences between a need and a want.

On Wants and Needs

Separating wants and needs is not only a semantic argument, but also critical in negotiations. It is a subtlety that many do not grasp. This may be true not only for yourself, but your negotiating Other. The fundamental but significant difference between a want and a need is the number of possible solutions. Wants usually have one solution, whereas needs tend to have multiple options for solutions. For example, wanting a new BMW is markedly different than needing transportation to and from work. In the latter, a car is only one of multiple options that will satisfy the requirement for transportation. Taking public transportation, walking, quitting your job, telecommuting or car-pooling are options that can potentially satisfy that need versus buying a new BMW. The want is further restricted because of the word new. Needs are indicative of pain. They define a problem. Needs can be satisfied with multiple solution options, and these options create fallbacks. Wants do not, because they are solutions. The Rolling Stones' Mick Jagger and Keith Richards offer sage advice in the lyrics of their 1968 hit song, *"You Can't Always Get What You Want"* The song counsels that you might not get what you want, but you should try to get what you need. That's a major difference in mindset; shifting from solution to problem focus. Take heed.

When you hear someone say they want something, always ask them what they really need. It opens the door to a multitude of options that they might not have considered. This is absolutely crucial to both problem-resolving and negotiating. If you ask someone what he or she wants, it will usually only generate one specific option. Watch the words that you chose. Eliminate the word want and substitute need in its place. Practice by playing a mental game with yourself. Be aware and mindful of your word choices.

Remember that if you and the Other's needs and wants are satisfied, there will be little compromise and the resultant resolution may be durable. If only the needs of both parties are satisfied, the resolution may be practical, but may not endure. But if either party's needs are not satisfied, then the resolution is doomed to failure and usually backfires.

On Winning and Losing

Winning and Losing are both logical and emotional. They coexist in the concrete and the abstract. As a military aviator I personally participated in an extremely frightening example of how win-win, win-lose and lose-lose played out in the Cold War. For 40 years, a singular strategy called Mutually Assured Destruction (MAD) was the driver for peace. MAD was the brinkmanship driven concept that in a nuclear war, if one side initiates, the other side's retaliation would be so massive and devastating that neither side would survive, let alone win. This is a perfect example of a win-win driven by the fallback of a lose-lose, where win-lose was not a possibility. Using the military criteria of acceptable loss, win-lose was not an attainable end state because no one wins in a full nuclear exchange. A limited nuclear option was not viable either since retaliation would be massive.

Two diametrically opposed ideologies, capitalism and communism, competed for world dominance. Without the consequences provided by MAD, there would be no way that leaders on each side would agree to an equitable preservation of the status quo. Without the consequences of a war that would result in mutual annihilation, forty plus years of peace would not have occurred. The win-win common ground was to avoid total mutual destruction, which was the lose-lose. I fully recognize that this is a rather grim view of humanity, but history is full of examples where acceptable loss fueled grabs for power and dominance, adherence to dogma and ideology, and atrocities foisted on another people or the world at large to gain supremacy.

The rule that drove MAD may apply to us as well: that is, without consequences, nothing works. You cannot allow people to act with impunity. If you do, then they will. You must have a lose-lose. Let's look at Nordstrom, the retail chain renown for exceptional customer service. Once Nordstrom had a no questions policy on all returns of any merchandise. One consumer tested the policy and demanded a refund for a set of tires based on dissatisfaction. Nordstrom issued a full refund even though they didn't sell tires. If there are no consequences of behavior, then people will exploit the system. Nordstrom's no longer has a no questions refund policy.

Strikes, war, divorce or litigation may be the only potentially lose-lose fallback options to drive a mutually acceptable, win-win result to a negotiation. The lose-lose scenario need not be employed, but it needs to exist. Consequences of behavior must be balanced. The annals of business are loaded with examples of failed attempts to focus exclusively on the positive consequences (rewards) to build a better company, partnership, client base, organization or service. Yes, some thrive for a while but largely due to a sound business strategy or superior offerings rather than the fact that it may be a great place to work. Focusing exclusively on people as a strategic differentiator is unsustainable.

The following table is my attempt to represent in a summary fashion how winning and losing play out. They are listed from the left to right, most to the least preferable outcomes from my perspective in a 'once and done' negotiation. It is offered to ground the discussion and define the continuum of the negotiating domain. It ranges from Machiavelli's, *The Prince*, a guide for the Haves to maintain power and control to Saul D. Alinsky's, Rules for Radicals, written for the Have Not's on how to take it from them and everything in between. The table identifies how attributes such as Order of Preference, Thought Leadership, Position of Power, Strategy, Source of Tactics, Information Sharing, Trust and Relationship/Gain factor into the equation by Intended Outcome. A short list of examples is provided for each Outcome. Given this range of potential outcomes for negotiations, shouldn't the seasoned negotiator be prepared to deal with all of them? The point is that people play different games to get what they desire. Often the game is not transparent. Negotiating success is dependent on reading behavior, interpreting intent and responding appropriately. This means that you must be facile at playing across the game spectrum.

Intended Outcome	Nothing to Win	I Win You Lose	We Both Win	We All Lose	You Win, I Lose	Nothing to Lose
Hierarchy of Preference to Me	1	2	3	4	5	6
Position of Power	Very Strong	Strong	Balanced	Balanced	Weak	None
Strategy	Positional	Positional	Collaborative	Positional	Positional	Surprise
Tactics	Standard	Standard	Problem Resolution	Standard	Standard	Radical
Information Sharing	None	Little	Required	Little	Little	None
Trust	Little	Little	Much	None	Little	None
Gain or Relationship Driven	Protect. My winning is not to lose	Gain	Both	Both	Relationship	Your Losing is My Winning
Application	Protect: -Power -Control -Image -Markets -Territory	Voting Litigation Business War	Business Marriage Scientific Development Economic Development	War Strike Divorce Business Stalemate	Voting Litigation Business War	Revolution Terrorism Sabotage Suicide
Examples	Syrian Revolution, pre-Apartide South Africa	Russian invasion of Crimea, US Invasion of Iraq, Anything Donald Trump does	They're largely a matter of perception and perspective	111, 112, 113 U. S. Congress, the War on Drug, the War on Poverty, the War on Anything	Fighting in Ahfganistan for the last 2000 years. Punctuated by Russia and the US experiences	Syrian Revolution, pre-Apartide South Africa

I believe that the following **WARNING** summarizes my experiences rather succinctly. You will periodically see **WARNINGS**, but also **CAUTIONS** and **NOTES** throughout the book. They have been added for emphasis on important points about the conduct of negotiations. If not heeded, **WARNINGS** can have a devastating impact on a negotiated outcome. Overlooking a **CAUTION** can have severe impact, and **NOTES** contain important, good-to-know information about negotiating and people. Most, if not all that you encounter in this book are there because of mistakes that I have personally made. So, here's my warning about playing win-win all of the time.

WARNING

You cannot play win-win with someone who is playing win-lose with you, unless you force a lose-lose. That may cause a change in their strategy

When we negotiate, the pie is sometimes limited and the negotiation becomes about how to divide it. This is the realm of positional or distributive negotiation. Win-win resolutions can occur even if there is a fixed pie, but both parties must exhibit a willingness to collaborate. Negotiators can enter the positional arena that is driven by a win-lose mentality without true collaboration. One way to ensure that the pie will be divided equitably is to have one of the parties cut it and allow the other party to choose the piece that they want. It is critically important to avoid applying the rules of positional negotiation to all negotiating situations. The problem with the positional approach is that it doesn't relate well to the dynamics of today's environment. Few negotiations in today's business environment are once and done. The negotiators must always remember that nothing is permanent, power tends to shift and there will always be a tomorrow.

Positional negotiations are generally characterized as being short term in focus and competitive in nature. It's driven by a win-lose mentality characterized by the buyer wanting to buy at the lowest possible price and the seller wanting to sell the highest price. Negotiations conducted in this arena usually wind up in a zero sum game. That is, if I get more pie that means you will get less. Contrast that to negotiations where the party's intent is to create mutual gain by capitalizing on synergies. They tend to be characterized by a more cooperative approach, where increasing the mutual gain is the operative strategy. Expanding the pie and sharing the incremental value creates a win-win result.

It is important to understand that win-win, like win-lose is not a result, but a mindset. It's a way of seeing the world, a lens to view situations. Neither mindset is wrong nor right, they just are. The reality of today is that to be effective you must be able to play win-win, win-lose and every other game on the continuum. The choice of the game you play is not an either or, but all of the above. You must be able to interpret the game of the Other and respond accordingly. The following table illustrates some of the opposing characteristics of win-win and win-lose. Look at the characteristics and determine what direction you lean.

Win/Lose Mindset	Win/Win Mindset
Looks for the 'Right' Answer	Looks for Innovative Answers
Linear Thinker	Holistic, Systems Thinker
Conceptual	Perceptual
Past/Future timeframe Focus	Focused in the present
Solution Oriented	Problem Focused
Rational	Intuitive
Controlling	Facilitative
Analytical	Big Picture
Absolute truth	Relative truth
Limits alternatives	Recognizes multiple alternatives
Uses rewards and consequences	Uses tasks as self motivating
Categories are mutually exclusive	Category boundaries are gray and fuzzy
Objective	Subjective
Hierarchical	Egalitarian
Promotes competition and conflict	Promotes cooperation and harmony
Values results and individual achievement	Values collaboration and process
Short term focus	There is always a tomorrow
Driven by measures and rank	Driven by growth and development
Exclusionary	Inclusionary
Looks for differences	Looks for similarities
Suspicious	Trust

"Human nature is not black and white, but black and grey."

- Graham Greene

Why not play win-win all of the time? The problem with that approach is one of trust. Being able to achieve a win-win is based on mutual trust. I'm not talking about the warm fuzzy, high school BFF (Best

Friend Forever) kind of trust, but practical trust. Here are the questions you need to answer about trust; what is it, to whom do you give it, how does someone earn yours and how do you build it with others?

On Trust

"It is not from the benevolence of the butcher, the brewer, or the baker that we expect our dinner, but from their regard to their own interest."

- Adam Smith
The Wealth of Nations

First, what is trust? At its core trust is having confidence that someone will behave as you expect. It's not judging good or bad behavior, but predictable behavior. It is a subjective process at best, and for many of us deciding to trust someone is based on our beliefs about the true nature of humanity. Who we trust comes from the answer to this question, is man good or evil by nature? Of course, no one knows the answer to the question and it cannot be proven either way, but many people go through life believing that man's basic nature is one way or the other, which drives how they view others and subsequently how they grant trust.

WARNING

Most promises are not kept

Trust is the predictability that someone will deliver on a commitment or behave as anticipated during a negotiation. It is not a measure of goodness of virtue, but simply whether events will unfold as expected. Predictability is prone to error. There is always risk in trying to predict. If you need to add goodness into the equation of determining if you should trust someone, then I offer Pascal's Wager as guidance. Pascal, a seventeenth-century French philosopher, mathematician, and physicist, devised a philosophical argument known as Pascal's Wager or Pascal's Gamble to support a belief in the existence of God. His point was that even if there is a possibility that God does not exist, you lose nothing in believing. On the other hand, if you don't believe in God, and God does indeed exist, then you will suffer eternal damnation. The argument encourages people to err on the side of caution and believe in God.

Adapting Pascal's Wager to the natural state of man's goodness, we tend to believe that man by nature is basically good or basically evil. This belief guides our decision to trust people or not. Some assume that the Others involved in a negotiation strive to maintain a harmonious relationship, do not exploit situations and do not solely act in their self-interest. Those who believe that man is fundamentally good are making a bet that if they are wrong the results may yield tremendous gain for the Other and potentially a catastrophic loss for them. Others believe that people are always driven to optimize their own gain, protecting only their self-interests at the expense of others. So, what is the best philosophical approach concerning the nature of man in negotiations? Like Pascal's Wager it is a rational and safe bet to act as if people are less than good, and believe that people will put their own interest first. The consequences of believing to the contrary are infinitely more severe than trusting that man will usually do what is right. It is naïve to pretend that everything and everyone is good and wonderful. Do not expect or assume good intent from the Other. The logical negotiating approach is to suspect everything and everyone until proven trustworthy, particularly when you have had limited experience with others. If you gratuitously trust people then you are inviting disaster. Make them earn it.

WARNING

In desperate times, people do desperate things

So, how does one determine if someone is trustworthy or not? By watching their behaviors. Refer to the matrix below, on the horizontal axis are *behaviors* ranging from 'same' to 'different'. On the vertical axis are *values* ranging from 'same' to 'different' and again applying the binary standard.

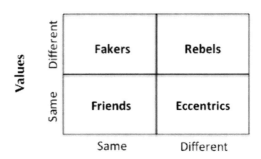

Behaviors

If people behave and think like us, we assume that we share values. We refer to them as friends or kindred spirits. At the other end of the spectrum, if a person neither shares our values nor our behavioral norms then we think of them as rebels, mavericks, radicals or some other less flattering generalization. If people share our same thoughts and values, but act differently, then we generally refer to these people as eccentric, strange or weird. Finally, if people who do not share our values and thoughts but act very much the same as we act, then we categorize them as fakers or phonies.

WARNING

Be careful where you place your trust, particularly when it's placed with relatives and friends

Here's the interesting part. Which of these people do we trust? Clearly the people who behave and think like us. Which other category would earn our trust? Surprisingly, it's people who behave like us, but may think differently. Why? We cannot see thinking or values. We only see their behaviors and we interpret them as indicative of how they think, what they believe or reflective of their values. Arguably, you can say that over the long term you will be able to discern values by observing behavior. But we generally make quick decisions about people based on what we see, such as their behavior. So we trust people who behave like us. Again, trust in the purest form is about being able to predict behavior.

"*Appearance is usually far more important than reality.*"

- Jonathan Haidt

Let me offer a personal illustration. I am an engineer with an MBA and retired from a large corporation. I am a former military officer, have had one wife, two adult children, three grandchildren, belong to the 'right' organizations, live at the right address and behave like the majority of people with whom I have worked over the years. Most people I know and have worked with are very conservative and classify themselves as such. I, however, consider myself to be independent without political affiliation. In a nutshell, I would describe myself as fiscally conservative, but socially progressive. The interesting thing is that most of my work colleagues have no problem sharing their politics and opinions openly with me. I rarely reciprocate. They believe that I think and value the same things they value, because I act like they act. Here's a life lesson; be careful laying your cards on the table by expressing your opinions, people who share your behaviors may not always share your beliefs. If maintaining trust with them is important, then expressing your point of view may breach their trust in you. Putting you life out on Facebook may be fun, but dangerous.

Let's look at how trust plays out in the context of the negotiation. In the following graph the horizontal axis measures the differentiation between offerings of either information or technology, from low to high. On the vertical axis is the need for affiliation between the parties involved, again from low to high. Transactional is the operative mode when low differentiation and low need for affiliation are required. Business is awarded strictly on price; need for trust is generally very low among those involved. If we change the affiliation parameter to high with a similar offering, then the operative mode switches from transactional to relationship based. The need for trust is now high since the buyer trusts that the seller is going to act in his or her best interest. This is the nature in most mature markets with repeat sales to the same customer base. The differentiator is not the product, but from whom you buy. In situations where new technologies or market leadership is truly superior and highly differentiated the need for affiliation is reduced because the technology is paramount. Finally, if both affiliation and differentiation need to be high the parties involved are in a partnership relationship. There is a mutual dependence on one another to maintain trust.

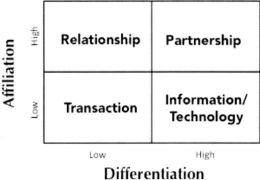

Differentiation

If trust is breached when operating in the relationship mode, then the mode switches quickly to transactional. This is because all that was promised, stated or claimed prior to the breach and in the future is now suspect. If trust is breached in the partnership mode the party that is wronged will move to either the transactional or technology/information mode depending on their primary drivers and the severity of the breach. Trust is fragile. You must be constantly attended to it to maintain it.

The answers to how someone earns your trust and how you build trust with others are the same. Understanding, consistency, alignment and adaptation are the keys to building trust. Understanding the other is paramount in developing a trusting relationship. Honoring your commitments and keeping your word are indicative of consistency. Adapting and aligning your behavior, language, mannerisms and style to be compatible is the hard part. It requires attention, mindfulness and conscious effort. For most of us, this is not a natural skill set.

On Standards of Conduct

"Man is a beautiful machine that works very badly"

- H. L. Mencken

Unless people are focused, trained well and highly disciplined, they will tend to act somewhat unpredictably in negotiations. In life there are no guarantees, and most warrantees are limited. As with all human behavior and interactions, there are no absolute standards in negotiations. Negotiations can only occur between people or groups of people, like organizations, countries or religions, and these people are different and view their world differently. It is because of this human condition that there are no true universal principles or standards.

Some might say that a consistent standard when it comes to dealing with people is the Golden Rule. Almost every religion and culture has some version of it. The problem is it assumes that we all share a common way we want to be treated, which is clearly not true in other cultures and rarely true in our own country. Some say, "do unto others before they do unto to you," while others may say, "always abide by the Golden Rule." Though the Golden Rule in some form must be a universal code, "do unto others as you would have them do unto you" is merely a nice sentiment. It doesn't express the universality to be an absolute. The perspective is myopic in that it's derived from the actor's point of view.

It might be more universal or absolute if it were rewritten as "do unto others as they would have you do unto them." The focus shifts from you to the Other. Some referred to it as the Platinum Rule. This approach would be great if you were Yoda, the Buddha, Jesus or someone who could look into the soul of another and understand what they need. Regrettably, the vast majority of people who have temporarily visited this planet cannot do a Spock Vulcan Mind-meld, so there is no universal standard of conduct. In the absence of such a universal standard absolutes are arbitrary at best.

As an example, imagine I am negotiating with you and I do something that catches you off guard, nothing illegal or immoral, but something to exploit the moment. Later, you find out that you were exploited, not badly, but taken advantage of none-the-less. Because of your own lack of preparation for my twist on the situation you now deem my actions unfair, exploitive or unethical. What standard can we apply to evaluate my conduct? Regrettably, there is no such standard to be used as the basis of evaluation. The only standard that is relevant at all is the law of the jurisdiction where we conducted our transaction. However, law has anomalies and biases and is usually a very broken system that should only be engaged as a last resort.

Law is an inconsistent standard as well. It not only varies by locale, but also by intent. Let's take a look at the differences between Roman and Germanic Law: the latter is prevalent in the western world. Roman Law judges were trained in the law orally. It wasn't written anywhere. Germanic Law was codified and built on precedent. The law is broken once a standard is exceeded. Simply exceeding the speed limit, whether purposeful or not, is all that is required for conviction under Germanic Law. Whereas, under Roman law you would need to consciously decide to drive too fast and therefore purposefully breaking the law to be convicted. Roman Law still has vestiges in the Catholic Church, but has been replaced in most Western societies by Germanic Law.

Even laws are not absolute. For example, O. J. Simpson was found not guilty in criminal court but guilty of wrongful death in civil court. And President Bill Clinton challenged the definition of 'sex' during the Monica Lewinski scandal hearings. Many other layers of human beliefs and rituals that influence our behavior add more complexity. Take 19th century Europe--there were no civil laws in Europe forbidding usury, the loaning of money for profit, but church law prevented Christians from issuing the loans and benefiting from the interest. That's one of the reasons that many Jews in Europe became wealthy in the 1800's. Practicing usury with gentiles was not forbidden for Jews under Jewish law. The action, or rather, inaction, of Christians when it came to usury would seem to indicate otherwise. It was not the civil law, but their beliefs that influenced their actions. The differences in values, perceptions and worldviews become even more extreme with the layering of cultural, religious, ethnic, gender and nationalistic norms of behavior. To better understand the Other, we offer the following discussion on each of these layers to act as a framework to view and appreciate the elements of human diversity in negotiations.

On Expectations

**What we negotiate is the Other's
expectations, and they ours**

The critical negotiating skill is one's ability to manage and manipulate the expectations of Others. We do this either subconsciously or consciously (which will be discussed further in the "Best Practices During a Negotiation" section). Being aware and avoiding our normal behaviors that subconsciously, unwittingly and negatively impact expectations is tremendous. These undesirable behaviors generally occur in the beginning of a relationship, when we are trying to impress in sell mode or just practicing wishful thinking.

Let me share a personal example of how expectation setting occurs. I was married nearly forty years ago. My new partner in life, like me, was an Air Force officer with her own significant responsibilities as a charge nurse in the base hospital. Very shortly after we got married, I was getting ready to go to the squadron for mission planning and training activities, when I discovered that none of my uniform shirts were ironed. Prior to our marriage, I would either iron the shirts myself or take them to the base cleaners to be laundered and pressed. Upon my discovery that I had no shirts ready for wear, I unwittingly blurted out, "I have no uniform shirts to wear." To which my new partner in life responded, "Well whose shirts are they?" I said, "Mine of course." She concluded the discussion with a simple, "Well."

Had Kate, my wife, said "Let me get one ready for you honey," I would have appreciated the loving gesture. Had she done so, she would have more than likely assumed the responsibility of being my laundry service in perpetuity. She didn't offer. Instead, she set our collective expectations for what has turned out to be a very egalitarian relationship with few gender and role boundaries. In expectation setting, there are no do-overs and a Mulligan is rarely offered.

CAUTION

Selling is the practice of determining 'if' you will do business, and negotiating deals with the 'how' you will do business. They happen simultaneously and are inseparable. Don't ever think otherwise

Sales people use a time-honored and legal practice called puffery. Puffery paints a better-than-reality picture of a product or service. It deals only with the benefits of the offering and either ignores or greatly diminishes any costs associated with it. Look at any real estate description—is it dishonest or unethical? Did you ever hear the saying, buyer beware? It fundamentally acknowledges that the practices of puffery and high pressure selling are common. Puffery is encoded in the DNA of most sales people. In many cases it is mistaken for the 'secret sauce' of selling. It is the quintessential 'product push' mentality. Promises made are either explicit or implicit and set up what is referred to as the 'over promise, under deliver syndrome.' Whether promises are implied or explicit, the results are the same. How does this apply to negotiations? What we offer as puffery during the selling process usually impacts the negotiating phase of reaching agreement and can bite you in the behind.

Puffery is purposeful. Wishful thinking is usually not--that stems from your view of the world, depending on whether you are an optimist or a pessimist. Optimism may work against you in negotiations because optimists tend to be wishful thinkers. While a noble attribute, optimism unwittingly and unintentionally sets up the 'over promise, under deliver' dilemma. The motivation may be completely different from a pessimist who practices puffery, but the results are usually identical: disappointment and distrust. Optimists tend to aim high. By their nature or programming, they see only blue sky. Be aware that even in a beautiful cloudless blue sky, turbulence can occur at any moment.

On the Relationship of Perceptions, Expectations, Behaviors and Results

Let's first look at the end state, **results**, as it relates to negotiations. Results are shaped by the decisions we make in coming to agreement; the concessions, demands, strategy, tactics and information we choose to employ in the process of determining how we will do business. These actions that drive our behavior and effect our results are driven by our **expectations** of what we believe is the desired end state. Using a principle of Newtonian physics that for every action there is an equal and opposite reaction, we can extrapolate that for each action one party takes in a negotiation, there will be a response, or a **behavior**. The response will either manifest itself in an overt behavior by the other party and/or an internal shift in perception by the Other.

All actions or behaviors in a negotiation serve either to confirm or refute our **perceptions** of reality. Based on these perceptions, our reality is either reinforced or discredited. If reinforced, we tend to dig in and feel reassured. If refuted, we tend to spiral out of control temporarily, become confused and start searching for a new reality. Here's how these element of perceptions, expectations, behaviors and results relate. We enter the negotiating arena with expectations of results based on our perceptions. We observe behavior in a negotiation, interpret it, and that either reinforces or alters our perceptions. If our perceptions are confirmed, it reinforces our expectations and drives our behavior toward the expected end. If it does not confirm our perceptions, then confusion occurs and expectations are adjusted. This adjustment, either up or down, drives our behavior, which impacts the results.

The following graphic attempts to describe the relationship and interactions among the elements of:
-   **Perceptions**, an interpretation of the situation based upon observations of results, or collective experiences, preferences and values
-   **Expectations**, what we can expect given what we perceive to be occurring

- **Behaviors**, what we do, how we act or react to try to realize our expectations
- **Results**, the consequences of our behavior

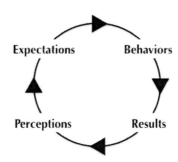

The way to affect results is to influence perceptions that create expectations that are then manifested in behavior, which drives results. Here's a great example of how <u>not</u> to create expectations. I am by nature a wishful thinker, an incurable romantic and a cockeyed optimist. I travelled a lot during my career. Any time there was a possibility of catching an earlier flight to get home I would broadcast the news home and hope for the best. I would rarely get to take advantage of the earlier flight for sundry reasons. So when I arrived home as originally scheduled, I was late because I had set new expectations of an earlier arrival time. When I discovered the following quote by Tom Peters, I tried it and now live by it: "Under Promise and Over Deliver." This strategy has worked for me. It leads to an occasional pleasant surprise rather than the usual disappointment.

So what are we actually negotiating; ideas, goods and services, sharing the wealth? In my mind, we are always negotiating perceptions and expectations. The rest follows as a natural result. The practice of negotiation is going about the business of manipulating, exploiting, persuading, proving, convincing and changing the Other's perceptions and expectations. It's expectation engineering. Expectation setting is theoretical, while engineering is the practice of applying theory to life. A great negotiator is great at perception and expectation engineering and, in most cases, re-engineering.

On Expectations Set By Others

How to set goals should be a core competency of management. Caution, 'Aim High' goal setting does not try to accomplish 'Mission Impossible.' It shouldn't be a 'no brainer' either. The goals that management sets should be the reach and stretch variety, but they must also be achievable.

CAUTION

People will generally strive to achieve the goals or targets set for them, and that's all

I have conducted negotiation simulations for years. The results that I have seen correlate with what I have experienced as a sales executive; people will set their own goals to achieve the goals set for them, and that's all. I'm not talking about the silly annual process of performance evaluations, but more granular goals at specific negotiations.

On This Book

This work is the distillation of over thirty years of studying and executing negotiations. It is contrary to conventional wisdom, but does have elements of the tried and true techniques of the craft of negotiating. I have attempted to give credit to those who instilled, defined and planted their thoughts into my mind. Through this long journey many of these thoughts have become mine. If recognition of another's idea has been missed between these pages, I apologize. It is not intentional. This book is not "Negotiating for Dummies," nor is it a doctoral dissertation. It is intended to be practical for a seasoned, experienced person, who negotiates. The principles and practices that will be presented follow no sequence or hierarchy, but they do interrelate. Much time is dedicated to understanding the Other, which is code for your negotiating counter-part, adversary or competitor. I have tried to simplify the discussion on negotiations without making it simplistic.

Of the books written about negotiating, some are good. Others have offered some sort of mechanical model or philosophic approach that guarantees a successful outcome if used properly, a magic potion or a silver bullet to win in negotiations. Some are more theoretical and lack practicality, espousing, for example, "I only play win-win." This book is not like that. It is an answer, not the answer; an alternative theory about the conduct of negotiation that is in step with the world we live in. It provides practices to refine the conduct of negotiations practically. As a result of using them, you will be able to build more enduring resolutions to problems, secure what you really need, and not deprive the Other of their true needs.

Understanding alone will not ensure success in negotiating theatre; there must be pertinent, relevant practice accompanying knowledge. Knowledge without application is mental masturbation. Application without knowledge produces rote, unguided behavior and has a limited shelf life or little chance of continual success, particularly when the context changes.

The Principles that I will discuss next are contrary to or missing in conventional negotiating wisdom and practice. Some may call them counterintuitive; others may call them soft, but I think they represent common sense. They may appear to be deceptively simple, but they are not. Following them is not easy. In fact, using a humanistic approach is more complex than using the other theories of negotiation. That is as it should be since they deal with an extremely complex organism, humans, that the other schools of thought simply ignore. Unlike previous books advocating a more human approach to negotiating, this work makes the assumptions that everyone is not rational and that win-win, albeit the desired approach, it is not the only approach to negotiating. Next I will present Mindful Manipulation as a resolution to better navigate the issues we face in the 21st century. You must recognize that the world today is interdependent and the win-lose mentality of the past no longer has efficacy. A new mindset must drive us to create more durable, equitable and human resolutions. If we do not adapt to the current environment with the institutionalization of new practices then the consequences will result in more polarity and division.

Part II: The Principles – Mindful Manipulation

Confronting the Problems with the Classics

The Fifth Theory of Negotiating

Today, we live in a perilous world where power, economies and most other things are constantly in flux. The way that things are gained and redistributed is rarely fair and equitable. The civilized, industrial world isn't getting smaller; in fact, it's growing. There are few places, if any, where you can hide from reality, start over, or insulate yourself and those you love from the formidable realities of globalization. It's everywhere. So, build a bridge and get over it. You need to have the ability to get or keep the things that you need for living. The trick is not to deprive the Other of what they need.

In a negotiating situation, there is a range of approaches. On one hand, you can capitulate and appease the other person's terms. You could just accept the asking price of a new car; the path that my Uncle Nick tended to follow. At the other extreme, you can say anything to convince or coerce the other person to agree to your point of view, even if it's a completely bogus story. In both cases one person loses and one person wins. The loser realizes that they have lost and carries a decent amount of hostility toward the winner, to the point of avoiding future dealings with that person or their employer. That is more philosophically aligned with my dad's view of the world. He fought for almost everything.

Most of us are not born with the ability to negotiate. Yesterday's negotiating skills are woefully inadequate to deal with today's realities. Today's negotiator must be a very strong problem resolver, facilitator and have an intimate understanding of people. Not just skin pigmentation and genital plumbing differences, but diversity of thought that includes cultural, generational, gender, preferential hard wiring and behavioral differences. It doesn't stop at understanding; today's negotiator must be able to effectively and efficiently deal with these realities to earn the right to advance to negotiating table.

WARNING

The Principles are offered to create more durable, equitable and mutually beneficial agreements. If you rely on them solely without an intimate command of the defensive Practices, then you will make yourself easy prey to be exploited

Because negotiations are always people centric, it is prone to unpredictability and variations. New skills and a better understanding of the Other can dramatically improve results and predictability. There are rational and emotional components of problem resolving. Mindful Manipulation helps navigate the rational and emotional terrain of the human condition more effectively. Because negotiation is a people process, it does not lend itself to a linear or algorithmic approach. Negotiating requires a heuristic model rather than a formulaic one to optimize desired results for both parties. Heuristics are iterative and dependent on a trial and error approach. To be effective at heuristic problem solving requires both a different mindset and markedly different skill set. This different mindset is woven into the principles. The skill set is of a more facilitative nature.

The lessons Dominic and Nick taught me served as my inspiration for the principles. The first lesson was that two men with such a similar background were so dramatically different. Not only on how they view relationships, but most everything else as well. Uncle Nick and my dad had remarkably similar life experiences; they were both first generation Italian-Americans (their parents emigrated from the same province in Italy), neither had a formal education beyond the eighth grade, they grew up in the same Italian neighborhood, attended the same church, belonged to the same clubs, neither served in the military during World War II, they married sisters, they worked hard, and both raised families. But they were vastly different. Their worldview wasn't even close.

> *"The shoe that fits one person pinches another; there is no recipe for living that suits all cases."*

- Carl Jung

The first principle acknowledges that ***People Are Different***. Negotiations can only occur between people or groups of people, organizations, countries or religions. At a high level, the genetics and the experiences that define people are never exactly the same. Layer on culture, gender, generation and perception differences and it's a wonder that the results are even close. The more similar the experience base and value set, the closer the outcomes will be. But there is variation in everything. I offer identical twins as proof. They may share a lot of traits, beliefs and physical characteristics, but they are usually far from exact duplicates. In fact, scientists will tell you that neither man nor nature creates anything that is exactly the same. They may be similar but not exact. Variability is a fact of life in nature, manufacturing and human beings. Later in this book we will broach sources of variation in humans that make them different to serve as a planning framework. We will establish that people and groups of people are different and view their worlds differently. Pretending these differences do not exist, or my way is the only way, is a prescription for disaster.

Now, back to my story about Dominic and Nick. Dad was all about gain. He liked to gamble and liked to win. His view was that everyone else did too. To him life was a game, but he was just better at it. Uncle Nick was all about making people happy and solely tended to the relationship aspects of life. This gain/relationship dichotomy served as the genesis for the second principle of Mindful Manipulation.

The real trade-offs are ***Relationship and Gain*** in the give and take of negotiating. As with all capital, we expend it to capture or secure something else. Gain is one form of negotiating capital. It is tangible, logical and concrete capital. Relationship is the other form of capital in negotiations. It is made up of feelings such as empathy, trust, affability and caring. You can think of it as human capital. I discovered years ago that most people tend to make emotional decisions for logical reasons. Depending on who is involved, the emotional and logical criteria and relative balance can vary greatly. Some of us tend to lean to the more emotional side and others tend to the more logical end. We all have default settings called preferences. We instinctively gravitate to them. Some try to keep everyone happy and will trade gain to accomplish that end. Others will gladly reap gain at the expense of relationship. Every trade-off in negotiations can be distilled into either gain or relationship categories. It is wise to learn to balance how the relationship and gain are traded.

Back to Nick and Dominic. Nick was always gentle, kind, and non-confrontational. He usually capitulated in situations that required taking a stand. He would sing *"Que Sera Sera"* (Whatever Will Be Will Be), a song popularized by Doris Day in the 1950's. In stark contrast to Nick, Dominic was tough, combative and loud. When he went after something he wanted, he aggressively pursued it and usually got it no matter what it took. Nick and Dominic were two men with two completely different sets of rules and ways of navigating through life.

Negotiation has been described as a game without rules. Life is full of examples where people attempted to justify the means in quest of a grander end; attempting genocide to achieve ethnic cleansing, dropping the atomic bomb on Japan at the end of World War II in the Pacific, blowing up clinics and killing doctors to stop abortions. Albeit the aforementioned travesties are not ubiquitous, people do try and succeed by behaving in ways that are less than legal, ethical, moral or humane to get what they want, and others just go along for the ride.

The third principle, ***Ends and Means,*** defines a way that we could conduct ourselves in a negotiation that is both ethical and practical. It's not soft. Negotiation has often been referred to as the Game of Life. However, this game does not have an agreed upon set of rule or a step-by-step instruction manual. The codes of conduct range from 'the ends justify the means' to the Golden Rule. I will offer you a behavioral model to consider, but it is not intended to be an absolute or the only way to behave in negotiations. They are guidelines, rules of engagement or a code of conduct to assist in navigating the heuristic process of negotiating with people. They are not soft, but pragmatic, effective and humane.

Dominic attempted to negotiate for everything while Nick didn't even try to play the game. The fourth principle, **_Not Everything is Negotiable_** limits the realm of what's negotiable. It warns of the perils of trying to fit a round peg in a square hole, using negotiations as the strategy to resolving everything. It is critically important to understand when negotiation is an appropriate intervention. It is even more important to know when negotiation is not applicable to a problem or situation. Negotiation is different from traditional problem resolving because in negotiations, full disclosure rarely occurs as a matter of course.

In the following chapters we will take a deeper look at each of the Principles; Chapter One – People are Different, Chapter Two – Relationship and Gain, Chapter Three –Ends and Means, and Chapter Four – Not Everything is Negotiable.

Chapter One – People Are Different
A Kaleidoscope of Possibilities

The world was a different place in 1992.

In 1992, the Twin Towers still stood in New York, the financial markets were heading toward the rosy Clinton years, the internet and real estate bubbles had yet to burst and Enron was a darling energy company that could do no wrong. Everything Enron touched turned to gold.

And it was under this hubristic prism that Enron foolishly entered into a negotiation for a power plant in India that would foretell the company's spectacular demise nine years later.

Case Study: *Enron and Dabhol Power Company*

U.S. energy giant Enron adopted a strategy to diversify it portfolio by expanding its growth abroad in emerging countries. In 1992, Enron began negotiations with the state government of India and the Maharashtra State Electricity Board (MSEB). Enron proposed a colossal project for the construction of a $3 billion, 2015-megawatt power plant. Enron chose the town Dabhol, Maharashtra, situated on the Indian Ocean as the site of their project aptly dubbed the Dabhol Power Company.

To ensure a successful deal, Enron needed a long-term purchaser of electricity to lock in long term debt financing and generate a sufficient return to investors in the project. This meant that MSEB, the only potential buyer available, would have to enter into a long-term contract with the Dabhol Power Company. Within a week, a memorandum of agreement was signed assuring that the Dabhol project would charge no more than 2.40 rupees (7.3 cents) per kilowatt-hour to MSEB.

Since a huge volume great of liquefied natural gas (LNG) would be required to power the plant, Enron chose to import gas from a joint venture they had with Qatar, 1200 miles away. As the largest project ever undertaken in India, Enron proposed splitting the project into two phases. Phase 1 would produce 700 megawatts and would use locally produced natural gas. Phase 2 would produce 1,300 megawatts using the natural gas imported from Qatar.

Three issues emerged early in the process:

– *The Indian government estimated that the project would produce an excess capacity of electricity for years. The plant would be too costly in comparison to the more traditional sources of fuel, such as coal, already in use. In response, Enron launched a successful campaign to promote the positive environmental impact of its project.*

– *Enron's projected 27 percent ROI to its shareholders was deemed unacceptable by India's central government and the government of Maharashtra--they considered a 20 percent return as more reasonable. Eventually, they agreed on 25 percent ROI.*

– *Mounting public opposition to the project rose over the electricity tariff, government official bribery and the fact that the project was closed to competitive bidding. What was Enron's solution? Ignore the opposition and continue financial negotiations.*

In 1993, MSEB signed the power purchase agreement with Enron and the Dabhol Power project began.

Public opposition continued to increase and activists filed suit in the India High Court challenging the legitimacy of the project. In 1995, the Shiv Sena Party and the BJP made their opposition to the project as a primary election issue *alleging that the proposed electricity tariff was excessive and would penalize the poor. The Shiv Sena and BJP coalition won the elections and launched an investigation into the project, resulting in MSEB backing out of their power purchase agreement with the Dabhol Power Company. Enron and its partners had already been invested $300 million and were incurring daily losses of $250,000 because of delays.*

Dabhol and its partners initiated arbitration proceeding against MSEB and the Maharashtra government. The government countered by launching legal action to invalidate the arbitration action alleging that the contract had been illegal. Maharashtra's government officials responsible for the investigation made it clear that they had no desire to renegotiate the contract but Enron managed to persuade them to reopen negotiations. A review panel was appointed not only to attempt renegotiations, but also to hear complaints from opponents of the project over the electricity tariff, the capital costs of the project, the payment plan and also the effect on the environment.

The deal was renegotiated. MSEB gained a 30 percent partnership; the electricity output of the plant was increased to 2,500 (post phase 2). Capital cost was reduced from $2.9 billion to $2.5 billion and the tariff was lowered from 7.03 cents to 6.03 cents subject to the cost of fuel and inflation. In 1996, the Maharashtra government agreed to the renegotiation proposal submitted by the review panel. The Indian government gave their approval and extended their guarantee of Maharashtra's obligations. Enron dropped their arbitration proceedings and Maharashtra dropped its counter suit.

Even with a new deal, the project seemed to hit a wall. Several organizations including unions, activists and other public interest groups filed legal actions in the courts in an effort to stop Enron. The courts ruled that the project could not proceed until all these suits were heard. The courts finally dismissed the last suit in late 1996.

In mid 1999, phase 1 of the project was completed and the plant began to operate. Enron had obtained financing of $1.9 billion for phase 2 which was targeted to be on line by the end of 2001. More problems arose when MSEB was no longer able to pay for the electricity it had committed to buy. By 2001, MSEB had accumulated a debt of nearly $50 million forcing the Dabhol Power Company to shut down and file suit against MSEB, the central government and the government of Maharashtra. That same year Enron declared bankruptcy, shaking up the U.S. markets and harkening the beginning of the end of our faith in the U.S. financial system.

What Went Wrong: Enron's strategy to diversify through international business development used the same practices in India as they used in North America. The project collapsed not only because of the economics of the deal, but also because of a philosophical divide about the relationship between technological advancement and Indian national identity. The Enron project was made possible due to a shift in India's national policy away from government ownership of assets in the energy sector toward private investment. The power sector was a symbol of progress and technological advancement and the heart of India's economic soul, literally fueling the economic growth of postcolonial India. Opening the power sector to foreign investors was controversial; Enron intensified the controversy by proposing to invest in India with a project of such magnitude.

The deal collapsed because Enron failed to assess or grossly minimized the importance of the cultural differences between the Indian people and their own management. Enron's negotiating style ignored that people are different.

[1] The case study above contains excerpts and direct quotations from the Enron the case studies published Enron Negotiations Debacle in India by the Negotiating Experts (http://www.negotiations.com/case/negotiation-project-india/) and Enron in Maharashtra: Power Sector Development and National Identity in Modern India, April 16, 2002 The Lauder Institute, Professor Emily Thompson

Cross Cultural Implications to Negotiating

Perhaps you think it's noble to treat everyone equally, but unless you are dealing with people very much like yourself this approach will ultimately prove ineffective in negotiations. The Enron-Dabhol Power Company negotiation was an exemplar of a failure to understand the Other. What happened in India was not an isolated issue.

During the 1970's when the Japanese Economic Miracle was in full stride, American executives packed Boeing 747's flying to Japan to see what was really going on. Other than mandatory calisthenics, workers singing the company song and the proliferation of quality circles, these executives saw very little differences in Japanese business practices. When American executives flew into Tokyo to conduct business they were greeted by their Japanese hosts, asked when they were returning to the U.S., entertained and made to feel at home. Dinners, late night entertainment and cultural tours abounded. Then when the date approached for the American executives to head home, a fresh Japanese negotiating team replaced the entertainment hosts. With the deadline looming, the hard bargaining started. Driven to get a deal done, the over entertained Americans tended to make substantial concessions that were suboptimal and unplanned. The American executives unwittingly placed themselves at a negotiating disadvantage because they didn't understand this Japanese cultural dance.

North American culture doesn't require negotiating for basic subsistence--a disadvantage when negotiating with cultures that do. Sure, we haggle with the car dealers or when buying a house, but that's about it. We live in a largely fixed price economy. We don't argue the price per pound of chicken breasts in the grocery store, but this negotiating practice is much more common outside the U.S. Despite inherent differences across various cultures, we apply our cultural norms to everyone else—we assume others will think and act like we do. But it is absolutely imperative to gain insight into the societal norms of other people's behavior, belief systems and how they value goods and services, prior to negotiating internationally.

On a recent business trip to China, I spent some time walking through the free markets in Shanghai looking for deals. I saw five pairs of Hugo Boss dress socks. One merchant offered the socks for 15 Chinese Yuan Renminbi, or roughly 50¢ per pair. They were knock-off, but it's a great deal anyway, one that is too good to pass up, right? I said no, and walked away. The street vendor followed me and kept lowering his price with each of my successive steps away from his stall, until he finally looked at me and said: "I see you know the game." I left the market with ten pairs at 15¢ a pair. I was on his turf, playing his game and by his rules.

Geert Hofstede, a noted Dutch social psychologist, developed a framework to evaluate and assess different cultures. In his book, *Cultural Consequences*, he offers tremendous insights on how to deal with foreign cultures using six categories to assess potential similarities and differences. These dimensions can help determine where the rules of the game are similar and where they are different and by how much.

Culture is multi dimensional. It can be view from multiple perspectives; nationality, organizational, occupational and gender. Hofstede defines culture as the collective programming of the mind that distinguishes one group or category of people from another. This programming is both conscious and unconscious. Hofstede likens his explanation of culture to software. Humans come with a fairly similar operating system. Then countries, organizations and occupations add on their own distinctive, and proprietary differentiated applications. The operating system runs in the background, but the applications are what you see. Country and gender level programming, which is largely unconscious, begins at birth and continues through puberty. Organizational and Occupational level programming is largely conscious and starts when a person joins the organization or discipline. Let's take a little deeper look at each level according to Hofstede.

Country – The 7 billion plus people in the world are distributed into approximately 200 nations. The United States State Department recognizes 195 and the United Nations 193. Understand that there are dozens of territories and colonies that are sometimes referred to as a country but don't count because they're governed by other countries.

Included in this category are Puerto Rico, Bermuda, Greenland, Palestine, Western Sahara, Northern Ireland, Scotland, Wales and even England. Some nations are more culturally homogeneous, and others are not. Larger nations like Brazil, China, India and Russia are a collection of culturally different regions. Even North America (limited to the U.S., Canada, and Mexico) has been further divided into arguably nine to eleven separate sub-cultures.

In spite of these shortcomings assessing national cultures can be fascinating, enlightening and useful. Research by Hofstede has shown that the values held by a majority of the population create cultural differences. Values are defined the general preferences for "one state of affairs over others," and not "cherished moral convictions." Citizens attain these values in through largely unconscious programming in their earlier years. These values are remarkably durable. They do change, but slowly within spans of generations, catalyzed by changes in their collective experience. I will discuss the nuances of this change process in the U.S. as it applies to negotiations in the next section on Cross-generational Implications to Negotiating.

Organizational -- We work for most of our lives. Many of you have and are working for an organization, a company, a government, a not-for-profit. Organizational programming begins when you're hired. Most cultures are rooted in practice, but are strongly influenced by values and occupational thinking, such as an engineering, financial, consulting, technology, service, military or entrepreneurial mindset. Many times people self-select into organizations that reflect themselves. Many companies select candidates for employment based upon a combination of can they do the job, will they be motivated to excel in it and do they fit the organizational culture. Historically, the least evaluated criterion and the one most prone to failure is the same, fit within the organization.

Occupational -- Different occupations require different ways of thinking. When you study and become an engineer, lawyer, physician, nurse, soldier, artist, chef or computer technician each requires degree of mental programming. Occupations all have heroes, values, convections, beliefs and rituals.

Gender -- The degree of gender differentiation in a country is highly dependent on its national culture. Because it is so intertwined with the national culture gender programming starts at birth and is an unconscious process. Arguably globalization and social media are having a significant impact on extending the programming of gender and societal roles well past puberty. A more detail discussion of this phenomenon will happen shortly in the Cross-gender Implications section of this book. Even tough traditional gender roles, values and behaviors are changing; recognize that they must be evaluated within the context of each individual country.

Hofstede's work statistically analyzed each country and ranked them according to each of the dimension or attributes. His work studied 76 countries (95 countries in the Indulgence versus Restraint attribute) according to the following dimensions.

1. **Power-distance relationship** defines the importance of the hierarchical organization in the culture. What does rank mean and what are the benefits of rank? Is the cultural structure pyramidal or flat? Is there an aristocracy or is it egalitarian? Answering these questions gives insight into the organizational layers, power structure, decision-making process and time required to get something done. You can't just walk into a room and say *Take me to your leader*, you need to enter negotiations with a prior understanding of how their authority structure works.

2. **Uncertainty Avoidance** refers to the need for rules and laws to allay anxiety; when uncertainty is rampant in society, regulations help to create a sense of control and well-being. Unlike risk avoidance, uncertainty avoidance deals with an amorphous feeling rather than a concrete threat. Assessing the levels of uncertainty avoidance within a culture will help you gauge the degree of formality and the rituals required to negotiate.

3. **Individualism versus Collectivism** compares individual rights, freedoms and accomplishments to those of the collective society. Does the culture favor individualism over rights of the family, tribe or nation? The U.S. leads the world when it comes to a focus on the individual versus collective, with Australia, Great Britain and Canada trailing right behind. And because differences in individualism versus collectivism greatly impact the laws, norms and behavior of that culture, it is vital to determine this factor before negotiating.

4. Hofstede emphasizes the importance of **Masculinity versus Femininity** and how gender roles affect the norms and values of a society. For example, does the culture favor 'masculine' values like competitiveness or wealth accumulation, or 'feminine' values like nurturance and relationship building? By examining the traditionally male or female behaviors, roles and practices accepted within that society, you could assess how masculine a culture is. For example Japan scores highly masculine, while Nordic countries score toward the feminine side. Determining a country's masculinity versus femininity requires looking at what drives values the structures and systems within the country,

5. **Long-term versus Short-term Orientation** -- Is the cultural orientation strategic and long-term, or short-term and tactical? For example, during the Vietnam War, the U.S. skewed short-term while North Vietnam favored long-term, eroding the will of the U.S. government to stick it out. So while the U.S. military was much more powerful than the combined NVA and Viet Cong, the lack of a sustaining will to win ultimately caused an unanticipated and disappointing end to the conflict. But long versus short term orientation differences are not limited to war--the short-term orientation strategies that drive Wall Street, for instance, work in direct contrast to the planned, long-term economies of more socialistic governments like China.

6. **Indulgence Versus Restraint** is a relatively new dimension. It's rooted in what is referred to as the Well-being versus Survival dimension. At the core of this dimension are three attributes; happiness, life control and importance of leisure. Happiness is an overall measure of how the country rates itself on the happiness scale, ranging from very happy to not happy at all. Life Control is a measure of the societal belief on the degree of control a citizen has over their life choices. Importance of Leisure is determined by determining the relative ranking of the importance leisure time in relation to family, friends, politics, work, religion and service to others. The results of measuring these attributes were correlated and countries ranked on an Indulgence versus Restraint scale. According to Hofstede, Indulgence refers to "a tendency to allow relatively free gratification of basic and natural desires related to having fun and enjoying life. Restrain reflects a conviction that such gratification needs to be

curbed and regulated by strict social norms. Because they're manifested in behavior, differences in this dimension are probably the biggest potential pitfall to unconsciously stumbling in international negotiations. If you don't hear or feel the music you can't do the dance.

I have created a tool, the *Cultural Landscape*, to help graphically identify potential areas of conflict and alignment. Since similarities rarely create conflict and differences and changes usually do, I applied the tables in Hofstede's *Culture and Organizations; Software of the Mind* to the *Cultural Landscape* and plotted the rankings of the countries I wanted to compare. I then looked for differences and similarities between or among the cultures. Generally the rankings are from 1 to 76, the number of countries review in the assessment. The attributes range from high to low or measure the relative polarity if the choice is binary. As an example, if you look at the Individualism versus Collectivism attribute, the higher the ranking the more the country favors Individualism. The lower the ranking the more the country favors Collectivism.

Let's look at the *Cultural Landscape* below. It visual depicts how the United States ranks relative to each of Hofstede's attributes. Interpreting the results on the graph show that the United States of America has:

- A relatively low Power-Distance Relationship score relative to other countries. This means that hierarchical relationships are less important in the USA versus most other countries.
- A very low Uncertainty Avoidance need. That means relative to the rest of the countries evaluated the culture in the USA generally doesn't see the need to create laws, controls, regulations and rules to create a sense control, allay anxiety and have an atmosphere of general well-being.
- The USA ranks first in the preference for Individualism versus Collectivism.
- The systems, values, norms and structures are highly Masculine versus Feminine.
- The USA has a relatively Short-term Focus.
- The culture strongly prefers Indulgence versus Restraint.

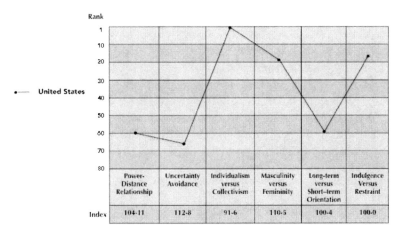

This looks pretty accurate to me. How about you? To this point all we have is a nice picture of what the culture of the USA generally prefers. Let's take it a step further to extract more intelligence and meaning from the tool. Let's overlay the *Cultural Landscape* of the United Kingdom, also known as Great Britain, (a composite of England, Wales, Scotland and Northern Ireland) we see that the pattern below is remarkable similar for the US and the UK. The exception being that culture of the UK values a somewhat longer-term focus. This alignment of patterns may explain why the relationship between these two countries has been relatively amicable for the last 200 years. Yes there are style, ritualistic, ceremonial and other differences, but at the core both countries' values are highly aligned. So far any surprises?

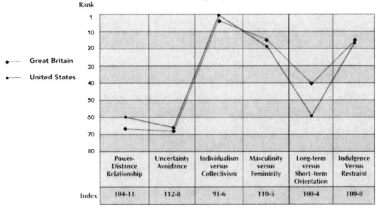

Let's now layer on Germany, Italy and France to the US/UK (Great Britain) *Cultural Landscape*. There are areas of relative alignment in the Individualism versus Collectivism and Masculinity versus Femininity, but not as dramatic that between the US and UK. There are major areas of divergence in the other four attributes. The composite of these attributes or preferences create a country's worldview. Differences in that composite may become areas of dispute and conflict. This may partially explain why Europe has been in turmoil for much of history.

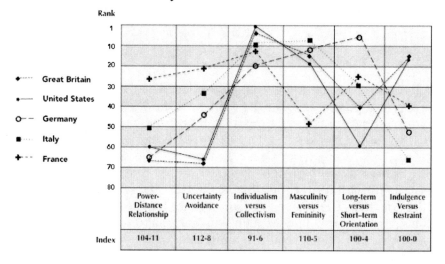

Note in the next graphic that that Italy and Germany have relatively similar patterns. Like the UK and US they follow the same pattern, but differ somewhat in magnitude. Could this be a possible contributor to alliances made during World War II?

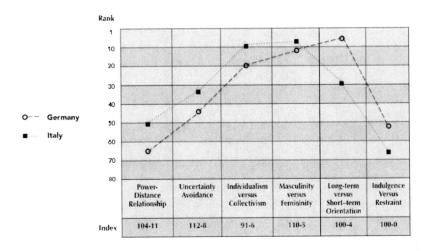

Look at the *Cultural Landscape* comparing the US and China, which areas are shared and which are divergent?

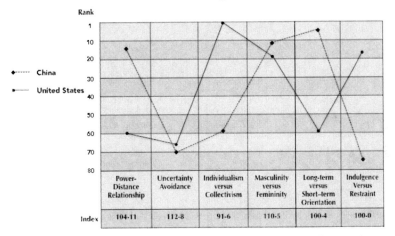

Employing the *Culture Landscape* to assess US and Russian cultures tells another story. Unlike the US/China Cultural Landscape, there are no areas of alignment between the two composite cultures to build common ground. Unlike China, Russia has a high need for uncertainty avoidance. Another interesting difference is that the Russian culture has a higher preference for Feminine values, structures and norms than either China or the US. If you were a US Company negotiating with a Russian company how would you interpret this graph? What actions would you take to ensure the differences in culture have no to minimal impact on the results of that negotiation?

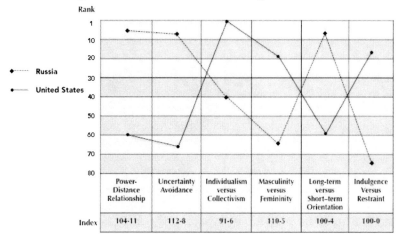

	Power-Distance Relationship	Uncertainty Avoidance	Individualism versus Collectivism	Masculinity versus Femininity	Long-term versus Short–term Orientation	Indulgence Versus Restraint
Index	104-11	112-8	91-6	110-5	100-4	100-0

Finally, let's compare China and Russia. Note that four attributes are similar, two almost dead on, and the other two are markedly different.

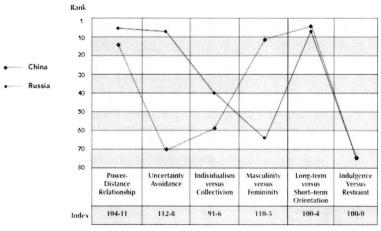

	Power-Distance Relationship	Uncertainty Avoidance	Individualism versus Collectivism	Masculinity versus Femininity	Long-term versus Short–term Orientation	Indulgence Versus Restraint
Index	104-11	112-8	91-6	110-5	100-4	100-0

Hofstede's six attributes and the *Cultural Landscape* are presented as food for thought. If you are involved in negotiations that are cross-cultural, cross-organization or cross-occupational, I strongly encourage you use these six attributes and the *Cultural Landscape* as a framework to understand and analyze the differences and similarities in cultures. Then assess the possible impact on the negotiating process. This exercise will help to void needless conflicts initiated by unwittingly violating cultural behavioral norms. Avoiding the unconscious gaff and faux pas can pay big dividends at the negotiating table. I recommend using this tool not only at the national level of assessment, but the organizational and occupational level as well. Look for similarities as areas of opportunity to build common ground. Examine cultural preference differences as areas to create mitigating actions. Although there is no published organization or occupational indices like Hofstede's National Culture, a reasonable hypothesis can be created as a working model. Creating and testing *Organizational* and *Occupational Landscapes* as part of the negotiating preparations might prove to be insightful, informative and very useful.

Cross Generational Implications on Negotiating

The next 'difference' in people that we'll examine is by the generations in the U. S. workforce. They are called generational cohorts. It's a group of people who have experienced the same events within the same time period and the same culture. The time periods are approximate, so there may be some ambiguity to what generation you belong. In today's popular culture we know these cohorts as Traditionalist, baby boomer, Generation X, Milliennials and Gen Z. Developed as the theory of generations by the sociologist Karl Mannheim in the 1920s, it's based upon the theory that groups of people are bound together by the sharing of the experience of common historical events. These experiences create value systems.

The value systems that we adhere to as adults are actually set into place during our childhood. According to sociologist Morris Massey, at the University of Colorado, there are three distinct periods of human development, which influence our value system. Around age seven, we go through a period of massive, unfiltered information absorption and it is during this Imprint Period that we learn right from wrong. Between the ages of eight and thirteen we experience the Modeling Period where we mimic the people we look up to such as our parents and teachers. The last stage, between the ages of thirteen and 21, is called the Socialization Period. This is when we pull away from things we learned in the earlier phases and move toward people who we independently connect and relate to. Experts agree that the end of the Socialization Period locks the value programming process in place.

Each generational group in this country experienced a collective set of circumstances that was different from the preceding generation. Differences in culture, the economy, trust in our government, religion, and family all have a tremendous impact on how each generation defines its collective worldview. This worldview then shapes our value set, which in turn steers our behaviors. These differences among generations have the potential to create conflict because the core of trust is based on behavior.

The differences among the generations currently in the workforce in the U.S. are significant enough to create confusion and suspicion.

Questioning the motivations, capabilities and work ethic of a different generation has a tremendous impact on the negotiating process, since trust is at the core of business negotiations and relationships. Building on the work of Ira Wolfe in *Geeks, Geezers and Googlization* about the motivations, capabilities and work ethic of each different generation, I contend that these differences have a tremendous impact on the negotiating process. Let's take a look at the generational variety currently in the workforce:

Traditionalists. Born prior to 1946, Traditionalists tend to value loyalty, authority and respect and constitute about six percent of the workforce population, according to a 2012 report by the Bureau of Labor Statistics. But their numbers, and influence, are rapidly diminishing. Most Traditionalists are products of World War II and the Great Depression and their values were forged as a result of these circumstances experienced in their youth. They believe that if you don't do anything wrong, you have nothing to worry about. Most still avoid debt and are wary of using credit to get what they want. Traditionalists respect authority and believe that everyone has their role in the hierarchy of the workplace. They also tend to make judgments of status based on race, gender, sexual orientation, ethnicity, income and education.

Married Traditionalists tend to stay with their partners even if they cannot stand each other because they believe that marriage is permanent. Most don't remarry if their spouse dies, although men are more likely to try marriage again because they likely need someone to manage the cooking, cleaning and 'domestic stuff.' Many still live in the first home they purchased because they bought it with that intention. Traditionalists are joiners, and as this generation fades away we will probably witness a decline in clubs and fraternities like the American Legion or the Elks. Following the code of their emigrant heritage, they stick to their roots and traditions, and many cities still have vestiges of these close-knit communities (like Chinatown or Little Italy).

Value Turn-ons: They trust in God and country and believe in saving for the future, honoring family and hard work and the value of education as a vehicle to move up. They also believe in structure, tradition, hierarchy, belonging to organizations, assimilating into American culture and sacrificing for the common good.

Value Turn-offs: Slackers, cross-ethnic and cross-religious liaisons, people that don't stay where they 'belong', people who didn't pay their dues.

Impact on Negotiations: They tend to stick close to their core beliefs and behaviors and do not trust anything that diverges from that core. They truly believe that society was better in the good old days. Technology, slang, cursing, immodest clothing and lack of professional demeanor lend an aura of distrust. They aren't big on formality of business relationships--a handshake will suffice. Since women were traditionally in the workforce as secretaries, teachers, nurses or factory workers, male Traditionalist generally will not negotiate well with women. Subordination to a woman, person of color, or perceived lower social strata may be insulting.

Baby Boomers. Born between 1946 and 1964, their parents taught them that the key to success is to work hard and pay your dues. Boomers currently represent the largest percentage of the workforce, comprising nearly 39 percent of employed Americans.

Baby Boomers were the first television generation. During the 50's and early 60's children watched shows on TV that value programmed an entire generation into a specific mindset. Shows like *The Adventures of Ozzie and Harriett, Leave it to Beaver, I Love Lucy, Father Knows Best* and *The Donna Reed Show* created illusory images and expectations of the quintessential American family. But in most cases, the dynamics portrayed in these programs juxtaposed the reality at home during the Vietnam War. Raised on the values of their Traditionalist parents, but growing up among the free love, counter-culture, anti-war movement sparked by the war, Boomers developed an antithetical belief system. For example, Boomers believe in hard work, earning your way, paying dues and belonging to organizations but they also embrace sexual promiscuity, drug experimentation and challenge authority.

Traditionalists raised their Boomers with the hopes of seeing them make a better life for themselves. However, this value system of 'you can do anything,' led to a generation of self-indulgent flower-power Boomers who then grew up to overindulge their own children. Boomers want to believe in heroes, like their Traditionalist parents, but paradoxically are distrustful and wary of icons. This transitional Boomer generation is chock full of contradictions.

Value Turn-Ons: They value materialism, accumulation of wealth, social status, tradition, lots of toys, security, recognition, having their opinions validated, feedback, personal rewards and public recognition.

Value Turn-Offs: Phonies, meaningless traditions and values, being a cog-in-the-wheel, waiting for rewards, being ignored, aging.

Impact on Negotiations: Status and rank are important. Since they were the first instant generation, bureaucracy and waiting frustrates them. Boomers often struggle with the relationship versus gain trade-off in negotiations. They utilize technology with varying degrees of competency, but most still prefer face-to-face communication.

Generation X. Born between 1965 and 1980, Gen X'ers represent over 33 percent of the U.S. labor market. They tend to strive for work/life balance and professional and personal growth.

What started off as over indulgence by the Traditionalists to their Boomer offspring was totally eclipsed by the Boomers' cultivation of the Gen X'ers sense of entitlement. And while Boomers were the first generation raised with TV, Gen X'ers were completely immersed in television culture. MTV, Sesame Street, The Simpsons were a big part of the values portrayed to this generation during their childhood, and a far cry from *Father Knows Best*. Their Boomer parents lived with free love, while Gen X'ers witnessed HIV/AIDS and the safe sex movement.

This generation popularized tattoos as body art, body piercings, night wear as outerwear and flip-flops as the footwear for all occasions—setting the stage for a more casually dressed workforce. And because of an unfriendly labor market, many have settled for McJobs—menial, low-paying, dead-end jobs that rarely satisfy their post-college expectations. They were the leading edge of an entire generation of emerging technically savvy kids, resulting in the first real computer generation.

Value Turn-Ons: Quality of work life, keeping the balance between personal and business, autonomy to act, technical toys, personal development and growth, flexible organizational structure, lasting relationships.

Value Turn-Off's: Being micro-managed, bureaucracy, they distain too much form (process) with little substance (results), hypocrisy and flashy suck ups.

Impact on Negotiations: Gen X'ers want to be recognized for who they are and what they contribute, not rank or station. They are not big on rituals and tend to be more balanced in their approach to problem resolution. With a focus on work/life balance, they are likely to acknowledge personal or family issues and tend to be more tolerant when these issues affect business dealings. They prefer texting to telephone calls.

Generation Y/Millennials. Born between 1981 and 1994, Millennials are the most recent generation to enter the labor pool. Sometimes referred to as Americas Next Great Generation, they currently comprise 22 percent of the workforce. However, their influence will grow substantially in the years to come.

Beginning with the Traditionalists, self-indulgent parenting values have passed from one generation to the next. Each iteration has ramped up the level of self-absorption. Milliennials live in a world where no one keeps score, because they were told that everyone is a winner!

Yet, Milliennials spent plenty of time playing co-ed team sports like soccer or basketball. And while their Gen X parents may have hidden the scoring sheets, the kids always knew who really won. Therefore, Milliennials are performance driven and value a team-oriented environment. A Stanford University Baby Boomer might have invented the first video game Pong, but Millennials have taken video games to an art form. Contrary to the lessons taught by the 'no one loses' in soccer illusion; video games have winners and losers. In the more violent versions, the winners usually kill the losers.

Value Turn-Ons: Being part of a winning team of bright creative people, tangible rewards that add credibility, being a hero, making contributions that have major impact.

Value Turn-Offs: Cynicism, sarcasm, condescending behavior, being discounted because of age, lack of techno-savvy
Impact on Negotiations: Milliennials react strongly to bullying. They are risk takers who get frustrated by Traditionalist and Boomers who block them from achieving their goals.

Raised in a fast-paced world, this generation has trouble waiting, frustrated by rituals and intolerant of bureaucracy. Therefore, they may tend to react abruptly without thinking through the consequences. Thanks to three generations of indulgent parenting values, this generation is convinced that they have everything 'pretty much figured out.' They prefer using technology as their primary method of communication.

Generation Z. Born between 1995-2009, or 1997 to 2013, this generation is just starting to enter the workforce. The first generation that was raised entirely in the presence of the Internet and in a virtual reality world, these digital natives might also be referred to as Generation@, Net Generation or iGeneration.

You could also call them the Left Behind Generation thanks to 2001's No Child Left Behind Act (NCLB) that held educators accountable based on student aptitude on standardized tests. NCLB resulted in an educational system that taught to the test and spawned a generation always looking for the "right" answer. With a focus on teaching test taking instead of developing critical thinking skills, one might speculate that NCLB has intellectually dumbed down an entire generation.

They might also be referred to as the Pluralist Generation, or Plurals, because they represent the most diverse ethnic composition of any generation and the last generation to see a Caucasian majority. In 2012, Plurals are 54 percent Caucasian, 24 percent Hispanic, 14 percent African-American, 4 percent Asian, and 4 percent mixed race/other. Research indicates that Plurals exhibit positive feelings about the increasing ethnic diversity in the United States and are more likely than older generations to have social circles that include people from different ethnic groups, races and religions. Plurals are the least likely generation to believe in the American Dream because they are growing up in a period of economic decline. They are expected to be the first generation to earn less than their parents. Traditional domestic gender roles have been blurred and muted thanks to the increasing fragmentation in families.

Value Turn-Ons/Turn Offs/Impact to Negotiations: Too early to predict.

It's important to realize that disconnections in behavioral patterns can set up a dynamic where either trust is breached or suspicion about the Other will prevent trust from ever being established. Behavioral differences in generations tend to be pronounced and consequently the negotiator must find ways to cope and adapt to different styles in the workplace. This is also true for men and women coexisting in the workplace and specifically in negotiating situations.

Gender Implications on Negotiating

Our society rewards compliance to the standard of behavior that we collectively define as normal or acceptable. However, normal behavior is in a constant state of evolution and the boundaries of acceptability will continue to change. In fact, the perception of 'normal' may fluctuate depending on a person's gender. For example, your friend tells you of a negotiation where this person named Chris walks into the room, slams a pile of papers on the table with a thud and says 'I don't have a lot of time so we need to keep this short and sweet.'

What if I tell you Chris is a woman? Does her behavior make her seem pushy or bitchy? Now what if I tell you Chris is a man? Do those same behaviors now seem assertive, but normal? Subconscious expectations of appropriate behavior our interpretation of what is normal. As enlightened as we may think we are, when a man looks at a woman, it conjures certain images and standards in his mind. It's the same for a woman looking at a man. It is impossible to deny that gender differences and preferences exist. They just do.

Adam Grant's *Give and Take* highlights this difference in negotiating tendencies between men and women. He points to research by Carnegie-Mellon's Linda Babcock that says women tend not to ask for more may exacerbate pay inequality. Babcock's work looks at beginning salaries for men and women. Initially companies offer basically the same salary regardless of gender, but men tend challenge the opening offer by asking for more. Women tend not to ask for more money and wind up accepting a job at a lower salary than their male colleagues. The same tendencies apply to merit and promotional increases. So pay inequality may be largely an artifact of negotiating practices. Over a career it becomes a substantial difference.

In 2013 *Lean In* by Facebook's COO Sheryl Sandberg hit the New York Times Best Sellers List. Whether you agree with its views or not, the book has started an important conversations. The point of the book is that in spite of the multitude of gender biases that still operate all over the workplace, excuses and justifications won't get women anywhere. Instead, Sandberg advocates that women believe in themselves; give it their all, "lean in" and "don't leave before you leave." Translated it means don't doubt your ability to combine work and family. Leaning in promotes assertiveness, juggling work and family, stepping forward, succeeding professionally and then putting yourself better position to ask for what you need and to make changes that could benefit others. Ultimately, then women will attain equal pay for equal work and more women in the highest executive positions in the private and public sector.

March 2014 Slate ran an article by Katy Waldman, *Negotiating While Female: Sometimes It Does Hurt to Ask.* It chronicled a woman who subscribed to the tenets of Lean In. She was offered a position at a college and assertively counter offered by asking for more. As a result of her counter offer the job offer was rescinded. How could this happen? After all in negotiation training we are all taught that worst-case scenario is that someone will say no to our counter offer. Waldman talked with Babcock to dissect what happened. "It's not that women can't negotiate, but they have to be much more careful about how," Babcock told the Slate's Waldman. "Men can use a wide variety of negotiation approaches and still be effective. But women generally need to pull off a softer style." "We're used to seeing women being less aggressive, more soft. And when people don't behave the way we expect them to, there are often negative consequences: You'd see similar social penalties if a man in a business context broke down and cried." The generational norms of the Other, who experiences the behavior, will influence the response that will impact the eventual outcome of the negotiation.

So, do men really have the advantage at the negotiating table? According to a 2005 Harvard Business Review article, while gender does not predict negotiating performance there are certain environments where gender will play a role in negotiating outcomes. The two situations identified in the article are when the "opportunity and limits of the negotiation are unclear" and when "situational cues" are ambiguous. The more ambiguous a situation, the more likely those expectations of behavior will be based on gender. Men outperformed women in competitive environments (positional negotiations) in which payoffs are determined by comparing relative performance (i.e. men stepped up their performance level; it wasn't that women succumbed to the pressure of the competitive situation). Whereas women outperformed men when the when they assumed the role of agent or advocate (facilitator) rather than playing the role of principle or advocating for themselves. Said differently, men are better at distributive or positional negotiating while women are better at brokering agreements for others.

Women also hold the cards when it comes to purchasing power. Tom Peters presented data during a talk I attended in 2004 illustrating the percentage of final purchasing decisions made by women:
- Women make 83 percent of all consumer purchases
- Women buy 94 percent of home furnishings
- Women plan and purchase 92 percent of vacations; 70 percent of adventure travel decisions and plans come from women
- The primary decision maker when purchasing a home is a woman 91 percent of the time
- 80 percent of D.I.Y. are initiated by women
- Women purchase 51 percent of consumer electronics
- While women buy 60 percent of cars, they are involved in the decision to buy 90 percent of all cars
- Women open 89 percent of bank accounts and investments
- Women make 80 of health care decisions

If you consider that consumer purchases have historically constituted 75 percent of the U.S. economy, you can estimate that women make the primary decisions for approximately 62 percent of the entire economy.

There are also gender differences when it comes to negotiating skills. The May 2006 cover story of World Business explains that women have the potential to excel in negotiating because of these traits:

- The ability to put themselves in their counterparties' shoes
- Comprehensive, attentive and detailed communication style
- Empathy that facilitates trust-building
- Curious and attentive listening
- Less competitive attitude
- Strong sense of fairness and ability to persuade
- Proactive risk management
- Collaborative decision-making

Bottom line, while neither gender is innately better at negotiation, men and women will approach negotiation differently and if you are facing someone of the opposite sex in a negotiation you would be a fool to ignore the differences. For example, women might take for granted what impact their appearance can have on a man. While we might like to think we are enlightened enough to see past someone's outer appearance, the reality is that sexuality is part of the human condition. Pretending as if sexuality doesn't exist and expecting that we must conduct ourselves in some puritanical, self-deprecating way is absurd. That said here is some advice when negotiating with the opposite gender.

IF YOU ARE A WOMAN, READ THIS!

I am going to let you in on a secret. Most of the men I speak to (especially those of the older generations discussed earlier in the chapter) have trouble focusing on a woman's intellect or savvy when the following obstacles are in his path:

– Revealing or sexy clothing
– Aggressiveness
– Acting coy, or dumb
– Speaking loudly or with a shrill tone
– Tears (or other obvious displays of emotion)

Yes, I can see you rolling your eyes. You are having trouble believing that men can still be so knuckle dragging and caveman-like. I'm not here to lecture anyone on political correctness. I am just here to help you level the playing field and increase your power with the person on the other side of that negotiating table. And if you are a woman, and he is a man, you will be judged on how you dress, how you speak and how you behave. What's your game plan? Accept the fact that this is not an opportunity to enlighten him on feminism or discuss gender inequality. Dress conservatively, adopt a calm demeanor, speak firmly but softly and keep all emotions checked at the door. That way, you can dazzle him with your intelligence without distraction. And remember to play into your natural advantage as a woman--build empathy, trust and openness and you will be unstoppable during a negotiation.

MEN, THIS IS FOR YOU

Do you assume you will have the upper hand when dealing with the fairer sex? Then you are exactly the person that needs to read this. Perhaps you are from a generation that has trouble seeing women in certain roles, or perhaps you are just the type of guy who likes talking business over beer and can't seem to relate to a woman. So if you end up in a negotiation with a woman follow these rules:

Avoid condescending behavior. Finishing sentences, restating what someone just said to legitimize the thought and speaking on behalf of someone else are all traditionally aggressive behaviors. It comes across as pulling rank, implying that because the person speaking is a woman you consider her subordinate and feel you must validate and legitimize her thoughts, words or actions. The reality is that by behaving in this fashion, men actually accomplish the exact opposite.

Don't save the day. Acting as a protector instead of as a peer is not well received. No one asked you to be a big brother or father. The fact is that women don't need or want protection. Most women view this type of behavior as just another way to demean and control them. Treating healthy, strong, confident and intelligent women as if they need to be saved symbolically annihilates their self worth. So does this means you shouldn't open the door for a woman? Most women tell me they enjoy when a man is courteous and mannerly such as pulling out her chair at a restaurant. However, the principle point is not whether the gesture is good or bad, but how is it being received. If it is not appreciated or welcomed, simply don't do it. It will set up a negative dynamic.

Avoid hugs. Since kissing or hugging hello is not the norm in the U.S., stick with a handshake. However in some cultures, particularly European, a polite social embrace between people who are friendly is not only acceptable, but also encouraged. Different countries vary on the dynamics of the actual embrace, but generally the man approaches a woman and either gently embraces her or lightly touches her shoulders, she reciprocates and air kisses one or both cheeks. But no matter what country you are in, lips are not part of the equation.

Don't gawk. Some women have likened gawking to being mentally undressed by a man. Gawking at body parts, no matter how appealing or on display they may be, is at best distracting and at worst a form of sexual harassment. Stay focused and concentrate, being distracted puts you at risk.

Cognitive Preference and Behavioral Implications on Negotiating

Negotiation is a process of discovery. Assuming comparable negotiating skills and leverage, the person who discovers the most about the other person will usually experience a more advantageous outcome. Keeping a positive balance between getting and giving information while maintaining a civil, non-adversarial, problem-resolving environment is a delicate but important proposition. Information is the currency of a negotiation. Generally, the more of it you have, the better you will do. The Greek philosopher Epictetus said, "We have two ears and one mouth so that we can listen twice as much as we speak." Sage advice.

Questioning is a way to engage in dialogue without having to provide information. The power of the perfect question is awesome. However, asking too many questions can be construed as an interrogation. The nature, pace and force of the questions also can send undesirable signals and alienate others. As we'll discuss later, just as empathy has an impact on sales effectiveness, so too does the perception of genuineness of the questioner. Questioning (and its complimentary skill, listening) requires control of ego and the practice of selflessness. It is difficult to learn to question effectively without creating a negative environment unless you are operating in your comfort zone or extremely skilled at questioning and listening.

An important take away here is that people make decisions by different means. Failure to recognize this fact results in communication breakdowns and then distrust. Disconnections occur when the communication process breaks down because people are not appreciative of different information processing types and are consequently no longer on the same page. At this point, further dialogue and negotiation cannot progress until the parties regroup and recalibrate where they are. It is absolutely essential that parties involved in negotiations stay on the same page and move through the process at the same rate if the negotiation is to be successful. It is important to note that a person's information processing preferences can be exploited by intimidating them with facts or concepts.

There are four negotiating dynamics that are crucial to successful problem resolution. They coalesce to form very the essence of critical negotiating behavior. Most of us have a default setting that forms our natural negotiating behavior preferences. Crack the code of your own defaults and those of the Other and you will be better able to leverage yourself during negotiations. I've found that psychometric instruments, particularly Myers-Briggs Type Indicator (MBTI) and DiSC, can offer great insight into the preference and predictability of people's negotiating behavior. Although I am not expert, I have also found that the newly emerging, Big Five correlates relatively well with MBTI. The Big Five will remain a topic for another time. I use these tools not to attempt psychoanalysis or to pigeonhole the Other, but to gain insight to them so that communication and relationship building can be more effective with them.

The only person that can validate your type is you. MBTI is not a test. It is an instrument that based upon your responses to questions reflects your clarity of preference for a particular characteristic. I recognize instruments like MBTI have been misused, inappropriately applied and sometimes reduced to parlor games. What follows is intended to assist you in determining how basic personality preferences impact these four critical negotiating dynamics. In Chapter Two: Relationship & Gain I will explain how these innate preferences impact your default settings for trade-offs and the type of information you prefer. There is a greatly expanded discussion of the instrument in the Resources Section of this book.

To help determine your negotiating dynamics or preferences, ask yourself these four questions:

1. How do you share information?

Do you prefer to talk before you think, or to think before you talk? If you are an extrovert, then you may be disclosing valuable information without even realizing it. The consequences of this can be devastating to the outcome of a negotiation. Conversely, if you are introverted and tend to keep your thoughts to yourself you may be perceived as calculating, indifferent, manipulative or cold. By not providing any information, you may shut down the conversation before it starts.

2. *How do you process information?*

In addition to the amount of data we provide and collect, how we collect and provide it is critical element in successful resolution. Are you a conceptual or a detail person? Do you subscribe to the motto, *In God we trust, and all others bring data*? Do you make a decision and support it with selective facts that reinforce that decision? Do you go with your gut feeling or believe only the facts? Do you provide information in the form of concepts, anecdotes, stories and metaphors, or do you stick to the facts and nothing but the facts? We all have preferences on how we process and provide information in order to make decisions. In the negotiating forum, these preferences manifest themselves by the speed with which we decide and what we use to make decisions. Sometimes speed is good, other times it's not. Decisiveness is usually considered a positive attribute. There is an old idiom Paralysis through Analysis, which has a very negative connotation. It means that people who study a problem, topic or issue to an extreme wind up being immobilized by the analysis and never take action So is being a quick decision maker good or bad? Should you trust your gut or trust the data?

3. *What is more important to you, winning an argument or making sure everyone is happy?*

Exhibiting too much ego and strength without enough empathy will paint you as an intimidator, bully or steamroller. Conversely, if relationship is your default, then you might be viewed as weak, soft, ineffective, or working for the other team. No drive and no empathy in the negotiating arena will render you easy prey, while focusing too much on what you can gain can similarly sabotage the negotiation. If someone perceives that you have made a gain at his or her expense, it impacts the relationship. The reciprocal is always true as well. Finding a balance between relationship and gain is one of the few laws that govern the negotiating process.

4. Can you make decisions under pressure?

Does the pressure to get the job done ever effect what you decide? Does the immediacy of the situation cause you to react prematurely? Does dealing with an ambiguous situation drive you absolutely crazy? Does your mother believe that she can set her watch by your punctuality, or do you have a lost or broken wristwatch? People have different tolerances of the pressure created by deadlines. They also have different tolerances for dealing with ambiguity. These differences can have dramatic impact on negotiating outcomes. Time pressure drives people to act prematurely, while ambiguity is intolerable to a highly structured person.

MBTI is a psychological instrument and should be treated as such. What follows is a very brief description of MBTI and is not intended to stand-alone, but to arouse curiosity for further exploration. If you are interested in pursuing more information on cognitive preferences, then engage a qualified MBTI administrator. So, now that you have perspective on your negotiating preferences, it's time to look at yourself and the Other. We'll use here is MBTI because it ties directly to the negotiating attributes. DiSC does correlate with and support some of the attributes as well. If you have taken the MBTI recall your type and use what follows as a review. If not, apply these short hand questions to yourself and others as a first attempt to gain insight. Answer these four questions about either you or the person that you're working with:

When communicating, do you/they:
Talk to think	Then maybe	E
Think to talk	Then maybe	I

When evaluating situations, you/they get their data from:
Their senses	Then maybe	S
Their intuition (gut)	Then maybe	N

When making decisions, do you/they primarily decide based upon:
Logic and the facts	Then maybe	T
People & relationships	Then maybe	F

Looking at how you live, do you/they prefer:
          Organization and structure   Then maybe   J
          Refining and perfecting   Then maybe   P

You should have four letters that indicate your preference. Pay particular attention to the Sensor/Intuitive and the Thinker/Feeler preferences. We'll be using them in Chapter Two to determine some default settings. If you want to dive deeper into type, then look at the corresponding typology in the Resources Section to see if it fits. Once you have a fix on and validate your type read the explanation of the impact on negotiation. It's OK to be unsure of a preference. Many times they are not clear to us. This quick tool is designed to simply get you to start thinking.

The following clues are offered to help you understand type preference further:

Extroverts (E): Have no problem looking you in the eye, tend to act first and think later, focus on the outer world of people, things, and activity, get energized by interaction with others, love to talk, participate, organize, and socialize, get impatient with slow, tedious jobs and complicated procedures, prefer to figure out things while they are talking.

Introverts (I): Need to break visually or look up and away when talking with others to collect thoughts, get energized by reflection, thought, and contemplation, direct their energy and attention inward and receive energy from reflecting on their thoughts, memories and feelings, need space and time alone to recharge their batteries, want to understand the world, prefer to figure out things before they talk about them.

Sensors (S): Are concrete. Identify relevant facts and act based on experience. They determine realistic constraints, devise and implements incremental solutions. Sensors question and challenge radical new approaches, rely heavily on their five senses to take in information, gravitate to information that is real and tangible - what is actually happening. They observe the specifics of what is going on around them and are especially attuned to realities, are practical and realistic, tend to focus on details and may ignore the big picture, tend to be literal in their words and would rather act than think.

Intuitives (N): They are dreamers and try to consider all possibilities. An intuitive likes to brainstorm alternatives, solve multiple problems at the same time , consider the future and identify trends and patterns. They trust their hunches and intuition. Focuses on conceptual information, sees the big picture, but often tends ignore the details, strives to be attuned to seeing new possibilities, focuses on the future and would rather think than do.

Thinkers (T): Assess the logical consequences of a choice or action, then decide based on logic and reason. Critiques and analyzes to identify what's wrong with something so they can solve the problem. Strives to find a standard or principle that will apply in similar situations, follows their head rather than their heart, values truth over tact and sometimes appears to be blunt and uncaring about the feelings of others. Have strongly held principles, values fairness over everything. Analyze the underlying issue and dissect the problem, debate or argue to surface all opinions. They create or apply models and question the fundamental assumptions. They tend to speak objectively.

Feelers (F): Are 'People' people and decide on the basis of their feelings and personal likes and dislikes. Use subjective information, like to consider what is important to them and to others involved. Appreciate and support others and looks for qualities to praise. Strive to create harmony and treat each person as a unique individual. Want others to like them so they find it difficult to say no or disagree with others Need and value kindness and harmony and is distressed by interpersonal friction, feel rewarded when they can help others. Empathetic, involves all parties, considers effects of decisions on others. They use values to evaluate options, get buy-in from stakeholders and tend to speak subjectively in people terms.

Perceivers (P): Spontaneous, hate to be boxed in by deadlines or plans, tend to postpone action and seek more data, gather more information before making a decision, feel confined by plans and final decisions, prefer to stay open to new information and last-minute options, works at many things at once, prefer flexibility and tend to react well in emergencies when plans are disrupted (sometimes they create the emergency). Tend to run late.

Judgers (J): Structured, like to live in a planned, orderly way. Seek to regulate and manage their lives. Want to make decisions, come to closure and then move on. Tend to be organized and like to have things settled. Are energized by accomplishing tasks and getting things done, focus on completing the task, want only to know the essentials and take action quickly, sometimes too quickly. Like to feel that people can set their watches by their punctuality.

Personal and Business Motives

So far we have discussed how cultural, gender, generational and cognitive preference difference can impact negotiations. These factors form the basis of a person's perception and the way they view the world. You can get a better understanding of what drives their expectations in negotiations by examining their situational experiences and their personal and professional motivators. This insight provides a tremendous advantage on how to approach the negotiation that is about to take place.

Personal motivators have been touched on in the cognitive preference discussion and will be discussed further in Chapter Two. The factors discussed in these sections are the backbone of personal motivation. Personal risk tolerance and other factors such as the relative need for money, control, power, authority, recognition and affiliation create a more complete picture of the Other. An assessment of what they require for a negotiation to be personally successful is an invaluable exercise in preparing for a negotiation. Think of the exercise yielding a Balance Sheet or Profit and Loss statement to help paint a personal picture of the Other. As with all assessments, treat them as assumptions that need to be thoroughly vetted and tested.

Business motivators are probably clearer than personal motivators. The functional role, position of authority and incentives that the Other is faced with in a negotiation has an incredible impact on the results. Too often we do not consider these dimensions when assessing how best to proceed in a negotiation. You should always consider the

Others functional role, their position in the organization and what incentives and disincentives have been put in place to drive results.

The Planner in the Resources Section of this book provides guidance on how to proceed with both the personal and business motivator assessment. Use it. It will pay great dividends.

Summary – People Are Different

People are different. Understanding the implications of culture, gender, generational and cognitive preferences is imperative in the conduct of successful negotiations. It is not only the managing the differences that can be a point of contention in a negotiation, but also managing agreement. All too often I have observed parties in a negotiation engaged in violent agreement and unaware they are arguing the same point.

Try This:

Envision someone with whom you have negotiated. Using the following Radar Chart, plot the differences between yourself and that person. Starting at the three o'clock position, in this case dealing with Age, and ask "How similar or dissimilar where we?" then place an "X" on the corresponding radial ... the farther from the center the more alike, the closer to the center the more dissimilar. Continue around the chart until you have addressed all of the criteria.

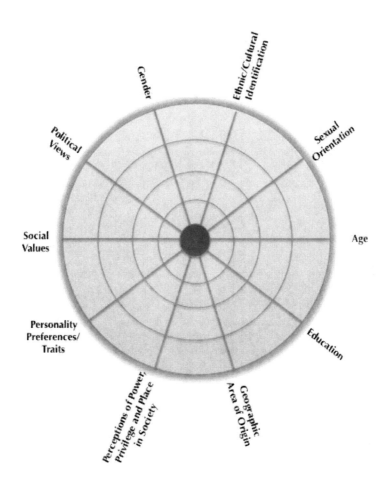

How similar or dissimilar were you to the other person?

How did the negotiation work?

What do you think the impact of these differences will be if you're in negotiations?

Chapter Two: Relationship & Gain
Of Takers, Giver and Matchers

Whether conscious or unconscious the only tradeoffs in negotiations are relationship and gain. This dynamic tension between these two components has always been in play in negotiations. My purpose in discussing it is to ensure your trade offs are being made consciously. Let's look at how the need for power (gain) totally dominated personal bonds (relationship) in the formation of the social media giant, Facebook.

Case Study: The Founding of Facebook

The Story: It is a matter of public record that four people, Mark Zuckerberg, Eduardo Saverin, Chris Hughes and Dustin Moskovitz, founded Facebook in a Harvard University dorm room in February 2004. As of 2013, only one of these co-founders remains with Facebook, Mark Zuckerberg. The question that I will attempt to answer is why does only one remain? Before we go there, here's a bit about each of the co-founders:

Mark Zuckerberg, CEO and Chairman, is the face of Facebook. Zuckerberg enrolled at Harvard University from Phillips Exeter Academy. By his sophomore year, he had developed a reputation as the go-to software developer on campus. He built a program called CourseMatch, which allowed students to choose their classes based on the course selections of other users. He also invented Facemash, which compared the pictures of two students on campus and allowed users to vote on which one was 'hotter'. The program became wildly popular, but was later shut down by the school administration after it was deemed inappropriate.

Based on his reputation, three of his fellow Harvard students— Divya Narendra, and twins Cameron and Tyler Winklevoss— sought him out to work on an idea for a social networking site they called Harvard Connection. This site was designed to use information from Harvard's student networks in order to create a dating site. Zuckerberg agreed to work on the project, but dropped out to work on his own social networking site with Dustin Moskovitz, Chris Hughes and Eduardo Saverin.

The group ran the site—first called The Facebook—out of a dorm room at Harvard until June 2004. After his sophomore year, Zuckerberg dropped out of college to work on Facebook full time. The company had relocated to Palo Alto, California. By the end of 2004, Facebook had 1 million users.

In 2005, Facebook received a huge boost from the venture capital firm Accel Partners. Accel invested $12.7 million into Facebook, which at the time was open only to students of Ivy League schools. Facebook then granted access to other colleges, high school and international schools, pushing the site's membership to more than 5.5 million users by December 2005. The site then began attracting the interest of other companies who wanted to advertise with the popular social hub. Not wanting to sell out, Facebook turned down offers from companies such as Yahoo! and MTV Networks.

Facebook seemed to be going nowhere but up. However, in 2006, the Facebook mogul, Zuckerberg, faced his first big hurdle. The creators of Harvard Connection claimed that Zuckerberg had stolen their idea, and insisted he needed to pay for their business losses. Zuckerberg maintained that the ideas were based on two very different types of social networks, but after lawyers searched Zuckerberg's records, incriminating Instant Messages revealed that Zuckerberg _might_ have intentionally stolen the intellectual property of Harvard Connection. Zuckerberg later apologized for the incriminating messages. Although an initial settlement of $65 million was reached between the two parties, the legal dispute over the matter continued well into 2011, after Narendra and the Winklevosses claimed they were misled in regard to the value of their stock. Zuckerberg faced yet another personal challenge when the 2009 book, The Accidental Billionaires, was published, and then became the basis of Aaron Sorkin's critically acclaimed film, *The Social Network*, which received eight Academy Award nominations. Zuckerberg objected strongly to the film's narrative.

In spite of the criticism, Zuckerberg and Facebook continue to succeed. *Time* magazine named him Person of the Year in 2010, and *Vanity Fair* placed him at the top of their New Establishment list. *Forbes* also ranked Zuckerberg at No. 35 Most Wealthy. His current net worth is estimated to be $9.4B. He has a 28.2 percent stake in Facebook.

Eduardo Saverin is now a major investor in Qwiki, a next generation search engine. He was born in Sao Paulo Brazil. Saverin held the role of chief financial officer and business manager. A lawsuit filed by Facebook against Saverin and a countersuit filed by Saverin against Facebook was settled out of court. Though terms of the settlement were not disclosed, the company affirmed Saverin's title as co-founder of Facebook. Saverin signed a non-disclosure contract after the settlement. His current net worth is estimated to be $2.8B. He has slightly less than a 2 percent stake in Facebook.

Chris Hughes is the founder and executive director of Jumo. His current net worth is estimated to be $850M. He has no stake in Facebook.

Dustin Moskovitz, currently the co-founder of Asana. He is the youngest U.S. billionaire. Born in Washington D.C., Moskovitz met his fellow co-founders at Harvard. Moskovitz was an economics major before dropping out of college to relocate to Palo Alto, CA to work on Facebook full-time. Serving as both Vice President of Engineering and Chief Technology Officer, Moskovitz led the technical staff, oversaw the major architecture of the site and was responsible for the company's mobile strategy and development. He left Facebook in 2008 to start Asana, a company that builds project management software to help companies collaborate. His current net worth is estimated to be $2.7B. He has a 7.6 percent stake in Facebook.

The details of the original agreement among the co-founders are not known, but one would assume that there would be some relative equity in the distribution of shares. While all four co-founders are living large, looking at the arithmetic begs the question: How is Zuckerberg's net worth and stake in Facebook so much greater than the other three co-founders combined, and why have the other three co-founders left Facebook?

What Went Wrong:

Power and control, which are forms of gain, always come at the expense of relationship. Zuckerberg's pattern of trading relationship for gain extends beyond the three co-founders of Facebook. The Winklevoss twins and Divya Narendra (they engaged him to work on the Harvard Connection), Sean Parker (of Napster fame and Facebook's first president who had a huge role in developing Facebook and helped Zuckerberg to gain power and control), and Owen Van Natta (responsible for putting the huge enabling deals together to fuel Facebook's growth), all are very wealthy because of the Facebook experience, but they were also casualties of someone else's need for power and control.

While it's difficult to have empathy for someone who made millions of dollars on Facebook, everyone save Zuckerberg seemed to have received the shorter end of the stick. Sadly, Facebook is not an isolated instance for grabs of power and money.

The power struggle within Twitter was every bit as brutal as the struggle within Facebook. Even my family was affected by the problem power grabs at the expense of relationships. Several of my family members were involved the founding and building of a highly successful restaurant chain in the 80's. My uncle, who was a minority shareholder and non-founder of the enterprise, wound up with a disproportionate higher share of the control and the treasury of the business. The one-time partners don't speak to each other anymore.

Moving from the world of billionaires to the real world, the article "What Makes a Good Salesman" appeared in the July-August 2006 edition of the Harvard Business Review. Because of the high cost of training and turnover, the authors advocate the use of an evaluation tool to assess perspective salespersons. As depicted below, at its core there are two dimensions that differentiate good sales performers from mediocre to poor ones. The two dimensions are Exhibiting Empathy and Ego Drive. Research studies found a correlation between salespersons scoring high in these two characteristics and superior performance.

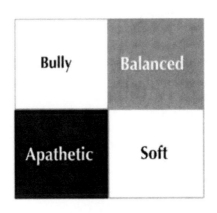

The argument that good sales people need to possess both perceived empathy and strong ego drive readily translates to negotiating. The classic trade offs in negotiating are Gain (Ego Drive) and Relationship (Perceived Empathy). The truly effective negotiator, like his Other, needs to create the perception that he has a sincere commitment to the negotiating relationship, while working towards his own needs. Again, the operative word is perception. Make no mistake; all trade-offs in a negotiation can be classified either as gain or relationship. Where would you place Mark Zuckerberg, or any of the other co-founders? I contend that Zuckerberg simply played the gain game better than his 'friends'.

Regrettably, most of us have an unconscious default setting of either gain or relationship. The problem is not that we have a default, but that this default is largely unconscious. In the extreme, the consequences of defaulting to gain, like a salesperson with too much ego strength and little to no empathy, is that you may be viewed as an intimidator, a taker, a bully or a steamroller. Conversely, if relationship is the default setting, then you might be viewed by your own organization as weak, ineffective, a giver or working for the Other's team. No drive and no empathy for a salesperson would leave them unemployed, and in the negotiating arena it would render them easy prey. Most of us are somewhere in the middle, but we tend to lean one-way or another; leaning toward gain or relationship, defaulting to getting more or to maintaining harmony. Defaulting to relationship or gain is neither bad nor good. It is what it is. Whatever your default, recognize that there are consequence. Trade relationship and gain consciously, not unwittingly. The issue as it relates to negotiation is one of balance or equilibrium between relationship and gain.

Many times the default is set by the organization that we represent. The organizational decision criteria is generally clear and usually set to maximizing gain for the owners. The individuals and their defaults are there to execute. Early in my business career I was involved in litigation over breach of contract for the supply of energy. As background, my company negotiated long-term contractual agreement for the supply of natural gas a few years earlier. Then, due to international tensions, specifically the overthrow of the Shah of Iran, the energy landscape changed abruptly. Our supplier was now stuck with an underperforming deal supplying methane to us at a grossly lower price relative to the market. The supplier asked for relief in the form of a price increase, but we refused. My company's perspective was prudent; a contract was a contract and we were entitled to preferential pricing versus the market. The company chose gain over relationship.

Did the natural gas supplier simply accept our position? No, they chose to breach the contract and pay the remedies stipulated in the contract. Why? Because paying the remedies was financially much more attractive than continuing to supply at a grossly reduced price relative to what the product was worth on the market. They too chose gain over relationship. The financial metrics companies' use tends to drive this choice. Gain is equal to profitability; relationship is categorized as 'goodwill,' which is an expense. Some of us who were involved advocated price relief, which in retrospect would have been more financially advantageous for my company. Sometimes the gain/relationship default of the negotiators may be at odds with the organization. Being in this situation can be risky. It can be both uncomfortable and career impacting.

Contrary to popular thought sales, not prostitution is the world's oldest profession. Before any service is delivered it must be sold and negotiated. What makes a great sales person? What defines a good negotiator? What is the difference between selling and negotiating? Do these two activities happen sequentially or in parallel? Are they separate and distinct or intertwined? How do the promises made when trying to persuade someone to buy get resurrected and used as weapons against you when it's time to bargain? These are tough, but critical questions to answer, because we are all affected by the selling/negotiating process daily. Even though most people treat the disciplines of selling and negotiating as if they are completely separate and distinct phases, in fact, they are not. They are inextricably linked to the same end result: closing a deal. So, what *is* the difference between selling and negotiating? In my mind, the difference is huge. Selling and negotiating are flip sides of the very same coin, and they happen simultaneously, but they require different skills.

Selling answers the question if someone is going to do business with you. Negotiating involves working through the details of how the two parties will do business. Selling is persuading someone to do business. When you are selling, you must prove that you do what you claim to do and try to determine if you are compatible with the customer. In negotiating, you and your customer are agreeing on terms and conditions and developing principles for engagement, resulting in a handshake, a formal contract or something in between.

Always negotiate for something that has significance, financial or otherwise. Pick your battles. There are some things that are not worth negotiating. Think about it, why do businesses design systems where people are out of the transaction? It is to discourage or eliminate the potential for nickel and dime bargaining, or nibbling. Businesses limit the capabilities and authority of their representatives. Does it make sense? It certainly does if you want to stop customers from negotiating. You cannot negotiate with a computer, can you? The gain versus relationship trade-off is at play here. The customer is not able to negotiate, which is a gain for the provider of services. Blocking customers from negotiating, however, negatively impacts relationship from the perspective of the receiver of the service.

Always be conscious of the fact that the Gain/Relationship trade-off is in play. Don't delude yourself; if someone perceives that you have made a gain at his or her expense, it will impact the relationship. The reciprocal is always true as well. In addition to defining **'what'** is being traded in negotiations, **'how'** it is traded will differentiate those that do it successfully and those that do not. Before we move on we need to address one way the **'how** is accomplished, compromise, and where it fits into the negotiation continuum.

Conventional wisdom leads us to believe that the word compromise can be substituted for negotiation. On the surface it is a seemingly cooperative approach to resolving positional differences, but the approach can be fraught with pitfalls. The terms negotiating and compromising are neither synonymous nor interchangeable. Compromise is simply one strategy to achieve agreement in a negotiation. Compromise is the hallmark of positional negotiating and is integral to its success. ***Mindful Manipulation*** postulates that compromise occupies only a small part of the negotiating landscape. Mastering the art of compromise is essential to being able to negotiate effectively. ***Mindful Manipulation*** advocates that the parties involved embark on a problem resolving path rather than one that is positional and focuses on discovering the Other's absolute bottom line. Compromise only works if both party's needs are met and the wants are traded. If the true needs of each party are not met then the negotiation will ultimately disintegrate, creating a result that systems thinkers' call "built to backfire." This process of separating wants and needs is not a trivial task. It takes great skill and patience. It requires the practitioner to play dual roles of negotiator and facilitator.

MBTI Dominant Functions and Implications to Negotiations

The MBTI functions are the Sensor (S), iNtuitive (N), Thinker (T) and Feeler (F) preferences. Based on our type, these functions prominently play out in our personalities. Each type has four levels; Dominant, Auxiliary, Tertiary and Inferior. Our Type combined with our Source of Energy (Extrovert/Introvert) and our Orientation to the World (Perceiver/Judgmental) determines the relative persistence of these functions.

I talked about the dynamic tension between relationship and gain in negotiations. Further, I stated that the Thinking and Feeling functions are an indicator of our default hard wired preferential settings. If we look at the dominance of the function, we can get a reading of just how strong that default. Yes, all Feelers have a proclivity to trade gain for relationship, or what Dr. Adam Grant would categorize as a *Giver*. The reciprocal is true for Thinkers. They tend to default to gain and in Grant's terminology would be *Takers*. The table below shows just how dominant that proclivity. The higher your type on the chart then, the higher your proclivity to defaulting to gain. The majority of types reside in the middle. They have a default, but it isn't as pronounced as those on the extremes of the continuum. They innately seek balance between giving and taking; Grant calls them *Matchers*. Note that even if you are a Matcher, you have a preference toward giving (Relationship) or taking (Gain). It may not be as pronounced as those extremes, but it exists. Every one has a preference. No one is so perfectly balanced and non-judgmental that they are always neutral.

MBTI Type and the Gain/Relationship Default

MBTI Type	Thinking Feeling Default Continuum	Dominant	Auxiliary	Tertiary	Inferior
ESTJ	Gain	Thinking	Sensing	iNtuitive	Feeling
ISTP		Thinking	Sensing	iNtuitive	Feeling
ENTJ		Thinking	iNtuitive	Sensing	Feeling
INTP		Thinking	iNtuitive	Sensing	Feeling
ESTP		Sensing	Thinking	Feeling	iNtuitive
ISTJ		Sensing	Thinking	Feeling	iNtuitive
ENTP		iNtuitive	Thinking	Feeling	Sensing
INTJ		iNtuitive	Thinking	Feeling	Sensing
ESFP		Sensing	Feeling	Thinking	iNtuitive
ISFJ		Sensing	Feeling	Thinking	iNtuitive
ENFP		iNtuitive	Feeling	Thinking	Sensing
INFJ		iNtuitive	Feeling	Thinking	Sensing
ESFJ		Feeling	Sensing	iNtuitive	Thinking
ISFP		Feeling	Sensing	iNtuitive	Thinking
ENFJ		Feeling	iNtuitive	Sensing	Thinking
INFP	Relationship	Feeling	iNtuitive	Sensing	Thinking

Moving from the Thinker/Feeler functions to the Sensor/iNtuitive Functions we can rearrange the table to determine what types have a stronger need for specific forms of information. For example, lets look at the ESTP versus the ENTP. ESTP's have more gravity that the other functions and therefore have a much stronger preference for these forms of information, because the S and N are dominant.

When making your case and attempting to persuade or manipulate the Other to your point-of-view, it becomes increasingly important to demonstrate alignment with the Other. This is more a case of process than content. Presenting information in an Other-friendly form is critically important to both the selling and negotiating process. Intuitives tend to work from a general case or concept and apply specifics or details to that concept. Sensors tend to work in exactly the opposite way.

MBTI Type and the Need for Concept/Details Default

MBTI Type	Sensing iNtuitive Default Continuum	Dominant	Auxiliary	Tertiary	Inferior
ENFP	Concepts	iNtuitive	Feeling	Thinking	Sensing
INFJ	↑	iNtuitive	Feeling	Thinking	Sensing
ENTP		iNtuitive	Thinking	Feeling	Sensing
INTJ		iNtuitive	Thinking	Feeling	Sensing
ENFJ		Feeling	iNtuitive	Sensing	Thinking
INFP		Feeling	iNtuitive	Sensing	Thinking
ENTJ		Thinking	iNtuitive	Sensing	Feeling
INTP		Thinking	iNtuitive	Sensing	Feeling
ESFJ		Feeling	Sensing	iNtuitive	Thinking
ISFP		Feeling	Sensing	iNtuitive	Thinking
ESTJ		Thinking	Sensing	iNtuitive	Feeling
ISTP		Thinking	Sensing	iNtuitive	Feeling
ESFP		Sensing	Feeling	Thinking	iNtuitive
ISFJ		Sensing	Feeling	Thinking	iNtuitive
ESTP	↓	Sensing	Thinking	Feeling	iNtuitive
ISTJ	Details	Sensing	Thinking	Feeling	iNtuitive

So what are the implications of functional dominance to negotiation? Understanding functional dominance gives you a better insight into what makes the Other tick based on information preference (facts or concepts), and how they will make decisions (trade relationship or gain). This relative strength of the function provides a more precise look into what drives a specific type. Understanding this nuance can assist in manipulating the conversation to make it resonate more with the Other. Choice of words, tone of voice and non-verbal communications can be altered to accommodate the specific needs of the Other.

Summary – Relationship and Gain

All trade offs in negotiation can be categorized as attempts to reap gain from or to build a relationship with the Other. Our nature dictates that we all have a default. The default varies in strength from person to person and is controllable with training and discipline.

Try This:

Answer them honestly and quickly. Do not over analyze your responses. Do these statements describe you, yes or no?

- I am unbiased even if it might endanger relationships with people.
- I think about humankind and its destiny.
- Objective criticism is always useful in any activity.
- I trust my reason rather than my feelings.
- Believe that the facts speak for themselves.
- My actions are frequently influenced by emotions.
- I help people while asking nothing in return.
- I tend to sympathize with other people.
- I value justice more than mercy.
- I empathize with the concerns of other people.
- I'm touched by stories about people's troubles.
- I stand firmly by my principles.

Based upon your responses, do you think you are more likely to trade relationship for gain or gain for relationship? What is the impact of this preference on your negotiations?

Chapter Three: Ends & Means

The Dependent Variables

Case Study: Removal of Saddam Hussein from Power in Iraq

The Story: *The world is a hostile place and strong defense is an absolute necessity for survival, but what happened in Iraq is just another episode in a long line of failed U.S. foreign policies. These policies tend to over rely on military power to "protect our national interests." A partial list of political maneuvering doomed to fail include: Setting up puppet governments destined to fail (Vietnam, Iran, Iraq), using nuclear weapons in war, and assassinating foreign political adversaries and allies. What follows has nothing to do with Republicans or Democrats, but offers the illegal removal of Saddam Hussein as yet another attempt to impose the American will on the rest of the world.*

What Went Wrong: *The invasion of the sovereign State of Iraq under the pretext of finding weapons of mass destruction (WMD) turned out to be an entirely false premise. The real agenda was to remove Saddam Hussein from power. That "end" was accomplished, but the means were clearly not justifiable. This invasion is particularly suspect in light of the fact that Hussein was empowered by the U.S. to serve as a buffer to the Iranian threat caused by the deposal of the Shah in favor of an Islamic fundamentalist cleric, the Ruhollah Mostafavi Musavi Khomeini (known in the West as Ayatollah Khomeini). What may have really happened was that Hussein pissed off the U.S. by failing to show proper deference and particularly his disrespect to the Bush dynasty. Serving as vice president under Ronald Reagan, George H. W. Bush (41) acted as the primary envoy to gain Iraqi (Hussein) support of U.S. interests. Hussein's invasion of Kuwait and George H. W. Bush's failure to depose him, set up a dynamic that would fester until September 11, 2001 when George W. Bush (43) would attempt to vindicate his* *father's reputation by finishing the job that his father began by removing Hussein from power.*

When bullying and negotiating with the vast majority of our allies failed to garner support for military action, President George W. Bush (43) and his fellow so-called "Chicken Hawks" (Rumsfeld, Cheney and Wolfowitz) decided to go it alone. It's important to note that none of the "Chicken Hawks" ever served in the military and Bush "43's" service record is highly suspect at best. To add credibility to their plans, they manipulated General Colin Powell, then Secretary of State, playing him as a shill. Like the rest of the American people, he too was duped. They executed a vendetta against the Iraqi leader with Operation Iraqi Freedom. Conjecture has it that George W. Bush perpetrated this action to pay back Hussein. In "W" Bush's mind, the American People blamed his father for failing to extricate Hussein from power during Operation Desert Storm and subsequently causing the senior Bush's loss.

At the end of the day, a puppet Iraqi Government executed Saddam Hussein and neither a terrorist threat nor WMD's were ever found. Saddam Hussein may have been a ruthless, brutal dictator who perpetrated atrocities on his enemies and many innocent Iraqi's, but he was not guilty of the crimes that formed the justification for the second invasion of Iraqi and his subsequent execution. Personal retribution was achieved at a great financial cost to the United States and great human suffering for the combatants on both sides and for a multitude of innocent Iraqi civilians.

Leaving the arena of war and world politics, is there a way we should conduct ourselves in business negotiations that is both ethical and practical? The following behavioral model is not intended to be an absolute or the only way to behave in negotiations, but to serve as a guide, code of conduct or principles of engagement to assist in navigating the often turbulent process of negotiating with people. At first blush this may look like soft stuff, but it is not. It is pragmatic, effective and humane. Using and practicing these behaviors will set you up for success. In today's dog-eat-dog world the following principles of engagement are true differentiators; they really work.

The Venn diagram above shows the three sets of behaviors that can help you effectively navigate the human terrain during a negotiation. Think of them as a touchstone to keep you on course. They are complimentary and work synergistically. The more these practices overlap the bigger the sweet spot. They are not exclusive or limited to the practice of negotiating. ***Be Cool & Act with Civility*** means keeping your head straight under pressure and setting a positive tone while negotiating. ***Stay on the Same Page*** means moving through the negotiating/problem resolution process together. Don't advance the process to the next step prematurely or before you have earned the right to advance. A heuristic problem resolution model is offered to help you and the Other stay on track. ***Engage to Persuade;*** involve the Other in the problem resolution process. If the Other buys into the problem, then there is a high likelihood that the resolution will have shared ownership, and therefore, will be more durable.

Be Cool and Act with Civility

The single most important ability a negotiator must possess is the ability to stay cool and focused under fire. Don't let them see you sweat. Once you enter the realm of emotion, things usually get out of control quickly. Your ability to think rationally and respond is severely impacted by emotions, and consequently your ability to negotiate may be compromised. In addition to dealing with the present set of circumstances, you are loading your mind with past baggage and the negative consequences of the future. You outstrip your mind's ability to think clearly and focus. Your physical being will be the first indicator that this phenomenon is occurring. If you feel yourself getting flushed, your mind racing, your pulse increasing, or feel unable to focus and think, then call a time out.

In sport, when one team has lost their edge and the other team has gained an advantage, you can see and feel it. That's when the other team calls a time out to regroup. In negotiations, just as in a sport, a time out is called to re-center and regain focus on the moment. Its aim is to disregard thoughts about the two dimensions of time that you cannot control, the past and future, and concentrate on the now. The present is the only dimension of time that we can control. We make decisions in the now that become our past and shape our future, but they are made in the present, so stay in the here and now.

The past and the future are usually used in negotiating to evoke responses from the Other party, responses that are generally intended to be negative thoughts that shift leverage. When dealing with this issue, a mantra that I have used to re-center myself is, "honor the past, acknowledge the present, and create the future." It's a perspective-adjusting device. The past *is*. There is nothing that we can do to change what has already happened. So, honor the past as it is, and move on. Judging the past is an exercise in futility, since we do it with 20/20 hindsight corrected through the lens of our point of view. The decisions of the past were made under different circumstances, using different filters and lenses that probably have changed. In short, the past is done. Move on.

The decisions and actions we take at this moment impact the future. When Julius Caesar crossed the Rubicon, when John F. Kennedy set a goal to land a man on the moon by the end of the 1960's, when Hitler invaded Poland, these acts in the moment set in motion a chain of events that created a future. Newtonian Law talks about equal and opposite reactions. This law is predictable in nature, but regrettably not so in humans. Human reaction, albeit somewhat predictable according to personality type, can elicit an array of responses to a particular situation. In any case, staying in the moment and being cool and focused will always provide a better environment for making decisions.

Staying cool and choosing civility as a behavioral code of conduct is symbiotic. They feed on each other. Being civil is not being soft. Quite the contrary, being civil allows you to stay in control of the situation, like having ice flow through your veins. There can be no anger when acting with civility because to be civil, you are required to suspend judgment and therefore emotion. P. M. Forni's "Choosing Civility" discusses twenty-five principles of considerate conduct. I have taken the liberty to further distill these principles to the essential ones that impact negotiations. They are:

Don't Panic – If you take away nothing from reading this book, please remember this one thing...stay cool. Paraphrasing Morris Massey's *"What You are is Where You Were When"*; breathe in, breathe out. Try to remember that in another hundred years there will be all new people anyway, so nothing is that big a deal. Don't allow yourself to lose your cool.

Focus on the Here and Now – Don't be somewhere else. An excellent coping strategy for maintaining one's composure and thus civility is to stay centered in the present moment. Periodically removing yourself from the situation and regrouping, practicing deep breathing and eliminating the 'noise in your head', also known as the past and future, is an excellent technique to assist you in staying in the present. The works of Eckhart Tolle and John Cabot-Zinn, two recognized experts on the topic, are rich in both technique and explanation on the subject. If this is an issue for you, check them out.

Pay Attention – In order to pay attention, you must be in the here and now. Multi-tasking and other distractions must be removed or eliminated. Paying attention requires that you master focusing. By being present in the moment, you are able to devote your energies to observation and intelligence gathering. You see things that others miss. You cannot pay attention if you are not present.

In a negotiating situation, the greatest impediment to being present is our mind working to formulate a response to an argument the Other is making. If you are formulating a response to what you perceive the Other is saying, you are not present or listening. I have struggled most of my life with finishing Other's sentences, interrupting and the like. I thought I was demonstrating that I was present and active listening, engaged in the dialogue. A technique I developed over the years was to be present by deferring my urge to respond. Instead of adding to the conversation, I relegate my role in the conversation to that of a process facilitator, a nonjudgmental neutral. This practice has helped me to stay in the moment and be present in conversations. Presence demonstrates respect; it is neutral. Being present does not commit you or alter your position.

> ## CAUTION

Relying on being quick on your feet is a poor substitute for detailed preparation and thoughtful anticipation

Acknowledge Others – To acknowledge someone is to recognize their humanity, worth and dignity. Too often power plays attempt to do the opposite. Respecting a person's presence is an elegant act; the small investment of time it takes to acknowledge another plays back many times. Simply remembering a person's name, something about what was going on in their lives the last time you met, a simple head nod in their direction, or even just direct eye contact, if it is culturally acceptable, can work wonders.

Understanding and complying with culture norms and customs are absolutely critical to the process of effectively acknowledging others. During my military years, I was stationed in Thailand. One afternoon, our crew took a taxi into town. The guy who was sitting shotgun paid the cabbie and left him a very generous tip, and then he patted him on the head. I noticed that the cabbie had become visibly upset, so I decided to stay back and asked what was wrong. (Being a gregarious sort, I tend to talk to everyone.) Unbeknownst to anyone on our crew, Thais, as do most Buddhists, believe that the temple of the body is the head. So, if some touches the head with a lower extremity, like a hand, they are in fact defiling the person in a sort of a symbolic annihilation.

Examples of failure to acknowledge are not limited to the military. As an account manager with a Fortune 250 company, I was required to make joint visits with senior management to important accounts. One of these accounts was in Toronto, Canada. During a meeting with the senior management of this important account, my Vice President and General Manager started his presentation by saying that he appreciated being invited to Toronto, the most cosmopolitan city in the United States. That was a hard act to follow. It does illustrate that we as Americans tend to extrapolate our borders, norms, values and behaviors to the rest of the world. In this case, ignorance turned a gesture that was meant to be an acknowledgement of the great city of Toronto into an insult. Innocent, you may say, but the gesture backfired. Instead of building rapport or a relationship, it perpetuated an oblivious American stereotype. If you negotiate internationally, be sure you are aware of local customs and observe them to the highest degree possible. The consequences of not observing local customs will undermine your good intent to acknowledge the Other.

Listen – "Don't try to be interesting. Be interested." There are hundreds of clichés that espouse the virtues of listening, yet we rarely observe them. If the supreme compliment is to be called a good listener, why don't we listen well? In the western world there are probably as many reasons for poor listening skills as there are people. But at the root of the problem is our need to be heard. Ironically, our need to be heard supersedes the Other's need to be heard, and we become a pack of assertive people foisting our own opinions onto everyone else.

Another reason that we interject our comments and interrupt others is that we want to show the other that we are engaged. Again, this behavior is well intended, but poorly executed. If you feel that you might forget how you want to respond to someone, do what debaters do and jot down a note. This allows you to keep your thought and not interrupt the person who is talking, thereby showing respect and acknowledging them.

Robert Bolton says, "The word listen is derived from two Anglo-Saxon words. One word is *Hlystan*, which means 'hearing.' The other word is *Hlosnian*, which means 'to wait in suspense.' Listening is a combination of hearing what the other person says and a suspenseful waiting, an intense psychological involvement with the other." Listening takes work and concentration. For most people, it is not a natural skill. It requires both suspending ones urge to persuade others and selflessness. To be a successful listener, it is essential that we suspend our judgment and simply engage with the Other.

One listening tool that I have used in negotiating is establishing eye contact with the person talking, if cultural norms allow the practice. Then I attempt to listen and hear what the other person is saying, suspending my judgment and suppressing my urge to respond. I attempt to encourage the talker by the use of non-verbal gestures, such as head nodding. Once the talker has finished, I paraphrase what I heard. This practice both checks my listening accuracy and allows me time to formulate a response.

Be Inclusive – By being inclusive, we invite others to the negotiating table as co-problem definers and co-problem resolvers. Being inclusive means acceptance of the Other's value as a person. It means not dominating the conversation and not having to make your position known. Share control and invite others to express their views and ideas without being judgmental.

Later we'll introduce a principle called Engage to Persuade. In that section, we will talk about the 'what' and the 'how' of persuasion. We live in a world that strives to be exclusive, through nationality, religion and customs. It permeates our definition of what we are defined by: where we choose to live, the schools our children attend, the organizations we join and what cars we drive. The principle of inclusiveness, however, is at the very root of persuasion theory.

Speak Kindly – Here again there are hundreds of clichés in our language and those of other countries about how kindness works and aggressiveness or nastiness doesn't. Kindness is not soft. On the contrary, speaking kindly sets you up for success.

What does it mean to speak kindly? There is more to speaking kindly than just omitting any trash talking, use of foul language, offensive jokes or comments, loud and boisterous speech, and an over abundance of hubris. By way of example, recently we met a new neighbor. The first meeting was cordial and pleasant. The second meeting with the lady of the house was impromptu at the local market. After an exchange of niceties, she related a story from her old neighborhood about one neighbor of Italian extraction "Guineaing" up the neighborhood with garish landscaping. Being ethnically of Italian lineage, I didn't show it, but I was offended by her thoughtless use of a racial slur describing Italian-Americans. Kindness in discussion stems from more than just restricting yourself to polite tone and dialogue, you must truly consider the content of your words.

Respect and Acknowledge Other's Opinions – Respect and acknowledgement are not agreement. To acknowledge someone's opinion simply means that you understand that they may have a difference of opinion, and you respect their right to have one. It validates their humanity and intellect. Too often people feel that they must defeat the other person's opinion, prove them wrong and win the argument. This does little to find middle or common ground and create a mutual reality.

When people do not respect and acknowledge Other's opinions, it sets up a win/lose dynamic where negotiation has little to no chance of producing any durable resolution. Our culture is rich in examples of 'because by definition if I'm right, then you have to be wrong' flawed logic. Issues such as women's reproductive rights, the legitimacy of Israel's right to exist, and homosexual nature versus choice arguments leave precious little room for common ground. Layering on emotion and passion pours more gasoline on the fire. Respecting and acknowledging others opinions and perspectives may not produce a resolution, but getting emotional about an issue that is unresolvable is insanity.

So, how do you respect and acknowledge someone that you believe to be an ignorant, close-minded, pompous jerk? You must detach your opinion from the person and acknowledge that they have an opinion on the matter that differs from yours. I fully recognize the difficulty in executing this behavior, but if I can do it, so can you. I attempted to develop this skill during my time volunteering as an escort at a Women's Center that provided full family planning services. First, let me say that my purpose in being an escort was not to promote the services. Like most, I would struggle with the decision if my partner had to make it. My purpose in escorting was to support gender justice and reaffirm that a woman has a right to choose what happens to her body, not a religion, a state or someone else.

Escorts at clinics such as the one at which I volunteered have one purpose: to escort patients into the center safely and minimize the harassment and bullying that Pro-Life supporters subject them to. I approached my duties from a human rights perspective; since I had no stake in the game I was pretty calm and even jovial. That is, until I became the target for the people on the other side of the argument. It's important to note that up until this point, I totally respected their opinion on the matter. However, being called a murderer and being told that god was offended by my being there promoted an equal and opposite reaction in me, one that I am embarrassed about to this day. I lashed back with ferocity, emotion and ugliness, which mirrored that of the others. I nearly became involved in a physical altercation with the protestor, who provoked my response. That night realizing that I had lost my civility and humanity by stooping to the level of those, who I thought behaved atrociously. I reread P. M. Forni's, Choosing Civility, and focused on the practice of respecting and acknowledging other's opinions.

Since that regrettable episode, I have tried not to negatively engage any people on the other side. If their behavior becomes over-the-top, I try to withdraw. If they attack, I try to smile. When they berate clients at the clinic, I focus on my purpose and if they address me I wish them a good day. I now understand that escalating the dialogue does nothing. I recognize that they have a different life view than I have. Responding negatively or in kind to the situation does nothing but guarantee that any chance of finding middle ground will be impossible. So instead, I choose to act civilly, and try to respect that we don't see things the same way.

On a somewhat lighter note, respect also means honoring others beliefs and value system. There was a saying on the Utapao Royal Thai Navy Air Base where I was stationed in South East Asia: "Everything here is stolen and it's just waiting to be taken." On trips into town, the five officers of a B-52 crew would generally travel as a unit. Although Thailand was largely safe from a war operations perspective, crime was rampant, particularly theft. Remember my friend, the Thai taxi cab driver that was unwittingly patted on the head? On a subsequent ride to Sattahip, the closest town to the base, another incident occurred. Sattahip was a collection of merchants, restaurants, bars, and brothels that provided entertainment for the personnel stationed on the base. Five of us piled into my friend's taxi, which was the size of an old Toyota Corolla with bench seats, two of us in front and three in back. I was sitting in the back seat and observed my friend pressing himself against the door, almost trying to become part of the cab. I thought it rather strange behavior. I speculated that one of the guys in the front had bad breath or body odor that was offensive to my friend. We arrived at our destination, every one piled out and I paid the cab fare.

I asked the cabbie what prompted him to position himself so uncomfortably while he was driving us to Sattahip. I was sure that his answer would be that he found something about the Electronic Warfare Officer's after-shave to be offensive. Again, I was surprised by his response and the fact that we again were unwittingly cast into the role of the Ugly American. He said that the reason he moved so close to the door was to make room for Buddha. When the two guys jumped in the front of his taxi, Buddha had no room. Out of ignorance, we symbolically annihilated this man's religious beliefs. Respect doesn't just mean person-to-person. It means all that surrounds that person as well: religion, ethnicity, family and tradition.

Rediscover Silence – All understanding begins with listening. Silence is a rare occurrence in our culture. We are constantly bombarded with messages from every form of media. Is it no wonder that when there is silence we instinctively fill it with noise. We are uncomfortable with the quiet. The core of rediscovering silence is a mindful, cognitive decision to defer comment and judgment. It is the non-judgmental practice of hearing with new ears and seeing with new eyes, which are uninfluenced by our history, our biases or our comfort zone.

Maintaining silence is hard work. Next time you're on the phone, stop talking after you finish a thought. Within nanoseconds the person on the other side will fill the gap in conversation with chatter. Silence is not in the American comfort zone. We feel that being a good communicator means lots of talking, but the opposite is actually true. Talking is feed-forward, a monologue, not interactive. Thoughtful, enlightened response requires listening to understand without judgment and formulating an appropriate response. Modern day dialogue rarely follows this formula. Instead, most dialogue is actually a concurrent monologue, independent play at its essence. Communication requires mutual expression and understanding. It is in the interstices of these two dynamics that true communication occurs.

Rediscovering silence also means being able to center us in times of crisis. Just as a newborn must learn to quiet itself when agitated, so too adults must learn to go inside and still themselves when an emotional response would be counter productive. Mastering the art of calming and centering yourself by going inside to regain focus and maintaining perspective is absolutely essential to navigating the gauntlet of a negotiation.

When we get bad news, are surprised or embarrassed, our first reaction may be to either look to the past and do a postmortem to figure out what happen and wish for a do over or project the devastating consequences of what might lie ahead as a result of what just happened. That fact of the matter is that something has already happened. Now, at this moment, you must decide what to do about it: change something, accept it, defer it or leave it. Before you are able to make that choice and the subsequent ones that may be required, you must center yourself through silence. Focus only on your breathing. Once you have regained control, then you can proceed. Re-centering cannot occur in the hyper-mediated outside world with all of its distractions. It can only be accomplished in the quiet of the inner world of a silent mind.

Respect Others Time and Space – Respect is a lost value in postmodern culture. With youth's obsession and focus on having more toys than the other guy, respect has become an artifact of time gone by. How many times have you been run over by children and their parents in grocery stores without the slightest hint of acknowledgement? How many times have you been disrespected by people not honoring their commitments on time, space, voice and delivery? How many times have people encroached on your personal space without the slightest indication that they have any respect for you? Sadly, most encroachments are not conscious. In our culture, people are often oblivious to a disrespectful action, until it happens to them.

A great microcosm for observing space encroachments is the supermarket. The law of inverses seems to apply in this realm: the cheaper the prices, the more disrespectful the behavior. Have you ever been to Wal-Mart? How many times have you been forced to alter your course of travel because a toddler walks right at you as if you were invisible? What is disturbing to me is when a teenager does the same thing while texting and doesn't have the social graces to even utter, excuse me. It's as if you don't exist, symbolic annihilation. Most disturbing of all is when the adults accompanying these children, flash a look at you as if to say, "can't you watch where you're going, you almost ran over my darling child."

Space is not limited to right-of-way issues. Space can be violated when someone penetrates your personal buffer zone, gives you an unwelcome touch and offers a kiss as a greeting when one is not warranted or expected. These are all violations of personal space, the boundaries of which have no universal definition. It is personal, and not absolute. For clues on proper encroachment, be sensitive and conscious of people's reaction to you as you approach them. To be safe, whatever distance you historically allowed as a buffer, add 50 percent more space to it.

During a visit with my then 90 year old, Italian mother, I learned that she doesn't like being kissed on the lips. She prefers the European air-kiss on the cheek method. Why? Germs. I assumed that this was a new phobia, so I asked. Her response was that she had never liked kissing on the lips and was repulsed by people casually kissing her on the lips.

I was taken aback, not because of what she said, but because all of the time I have known her I had been blind to her need for germ-free, personal space.

Respect for time is another area that is summarily abused in today's 'me first', postmodern society. Being fashionably late doesn't mean failing to show up at all. Honoring commitment of time speaks volumes about a person's respect for an Other. It is indicative of how you behave in other situations. If you cannot be trusted to be here when you said you would arrive, how can you be trusted with other more substantial commitments? "I'm always late" is not an acceptable excuse. If you know you are not going to be able to make a commitment, then don't commit to it. This is particularly frustrating to someone who is fastidiously punctual.

Be Considerate – At its essence, being considerate means respecting the humanity of another person. Respect, genuine politeness and acting with civility form the core of being considerate. Rudeness, disrespectful behavior and bullying do nothing to build a productive relationship. Remember the goal of all of this is not to defeat the person with whom you are negotiating, but to build a more durable resolution while keeping yourself from losing.

Being respectful goes well beyond politeness, which is an essential component of consideration. Respectful means demonstrating some modicum of being non-judgmental. We all have values and beliefs that we hold as truth--for us. Others perceive their values and belief to be true for them as well. Perception by definition is reality, however, your perceptions may not be accurate. Let's test the perception that organic is better for you. Yes or no? There is no universal reality of that perception. To illustrate this point, I offer organic dry cleaning as evidence. Since the 1940's the dry cleaning process used perchloroethylene, known as perc, as the cleaning agent. Like it's predecessor, carbon tetra chloride, perc is extremely hazardous and presents significant health issues to those who work with it.

There has been an industry wide movement to replace perc. There are three alternatives to it; CO_2 (carbon dioxide) cleaning, hydrocarbon, and wet cleaning. Wet cleaning uses water at regulated temperatures so that the material will not be damaged, CO_2 is expensive and requires new capital for process machinery. The study of hydrocarbons is organic chemistry that deals with molecules containing various combinations and proportions of hydrogen and carbon atoms. Hydrocarbons are the cheapest alternative by far, but are highly volatile petro-chemicals and have similar negative effects to perc. So what does organic mean when it's promoted by your local dry cleaner? More than likely it's hype, not fact. Unlike the food industry, dry cleaners definition of organic is not scientifically defined nor is it regulated. It's safe to say that the majority of the stuff that we value and believe came to us second hand, through our parents, culture, ethnicity, religion, country, educational system, friends, etc. These influences form the basis of the mélange we call our value and belief system. Layer on our cognitive preferences and the stew gets even more complex.

Some of us go through life never or rarely challenging what we have come to believe as truth. For others, experience, education or a significant emotional event can trigger a wholesale reevaluation of what we believe and hold dear. Regardless, whether or not belief systems are evolved, they exist and form the basis of one's reality. They need to be respected and acknowledged. After all, when does something become myth? Only after you stop believing it to be true.

Provide Constructive Feedback – Given the roots of the term feedback, it may well be considered an oxymoron. Feedback is a postmodern term defining the screechy noise that a sound amplifier makes from a portion of its output entering back in the form of an input. Put a microphone near a speaker to experience this phenomenon.

Today, feedback has come to mean a source of input to correct a system or behavior. Feedback can be corrective or reinforcing. It all seems totally logical. There are two problems with human feedback, particularly if it is of the corrective nature: they are receptivity and delivery. Receptivity deals with the receiver of the feedback's readiness to accept what they hear. Delivery is how the person giving the feedback presents it. Constructive feedback is input from one person to another designed to reinforce desired behavior and bring to light undesirable behavior in a positive way.

In order for feedback to work, it must be delivered in a timely fashion and the receiver must be in a receptive frame of mind. Telling is not constructive feedback. I have always found this military maxim to be true, "Praise in public, punish in private." While feedback is not intended to be punitive, the receiver may feel as if it is. To accommodate both receptivity and delivery, the following may be of great help to the providers of feedback to set themselves up for success:

- State the purpose of the discussion
- Check with the receiver for permission to proceed
- Start with any positive feedback and reinforce and encourage future behavior
- Provide the receiver with specifics of the behavior you would like to see changed
- Make suggestions as to how they might behave differently
- Express how the behavior impacted you personally
- Assure the receiver that you are there to help if they want it.

Stay on the Same Page

"The meeting of two personalities is like the contact of two chemical substances: if there is any reaction, both are transformed."

- Carl Jung

If the result of a negotiation requires durability and equity, then do not advance to the next step in the process until all stakeholders in a negotiation are in the same place at the same time. By process, I mean whatever process you are attempting to complete; answering an objection, defining terms, developing a problem statement, understanding expectations, dealing with emotions, etc. If one party is ahead or behind that will create confusion and possible miscommunication that can impact trust. The key actions are:

Develop, Syndicate and Agree on an Agenda. In my experience, this relatively simple action is not done as a routine practice for negotiations or meetings. The agenda is a roadmap for the discussions that are to take place. It starts the process of making significant agreements one small agreement at a time. Taking the initiative to draft the agenda gives you the opportunity to shape the conversation. Syndicating provides the Other with an opportunity to add their input while agreement means that it is common and shared.

CAUTION

Agenda setting, as with all other group process management techniques, must be culturally acceptable to have the desired impact

I recommend these components be included in any agenda:
- **Logistics:** Date, Time, Place
- The **Desired End Result** of the Negotiating Session – This defines both the purpose of the session and what you expect as an outcome.
- A **Table** with:

- What is to be Done, the Objective
- By Whom
- The Specific Process of How it will be Accomplished
- The Estimated Time to Complete the Objective
- **Roles and Responsibilities** for Conducting the Session
- Any **Support Materials and Resources** Required for the Session

Z Corporation Meeting Agenda

Logistics:
April 20, 2010   12:00 to 16:00
Room 135S
Z Corporation Headquarters
Lunch will be provided

Desired End Results:
Level set team's expectations and clarify concerns

What	Who	How	Time
Administrivia, Introducts and Ice Breaker	Jim	Presentation and Activity	:20
Expectations of the Day	Mike	Presentation and Q&A	:10
Introduces Speakers about Strategic Actions and Changes that will occur	Jim	Process Overview and Q&A	:10
Speakers Presentaions	Z Corporation Speakers	Presentation and Q&A	:60
Lunch	All	Post-it Note Feedback and thee analysis	:45
Report Out on Feedback	Z Corporation Speakers	Present Themes and Clarify Concerns	:60
Debrief Exercise	Jim	Summarize Feedback	:10
The Challenge Going Forward	Mike	Closing Comments, Thoughts and the Challenge to the Team	:10
Action Items, wrap-up and Close	Jim	Perspective and Exercise	:10

Roles & Responsibilities
Jim - Facilitator/Recorder
Mike - Executive Sponsor
All - Participate

Resources Required
Projector, screen, post-its, markers , flipcharts x4, masking tape and lunch

Sample Agenda

If you intend to use surprise as a tactic in the negotiating session, then you may be concerned that you will tip your hand. The practice of surprise may erode your credibility and defeats the real purpose of using an agenda. Surprise is very effective in positional, win-lose negotiations. It is also a great tactic to measure someone's reaction to new or potentially confrontational information. If you need to introduce a topic or issue that catches the Other off guard, then you can protect the element of surprise by not giving specific details and use generalizations.

If there is an agreed to agenda and the Other attempts to surprise you, then you can refer to the agenda as the contract for the meeting and defer discussion of that issue for next time. That will effectively neutralize the tactic.

Make certain that you are understood and that you understand. Words are names we use describe things and concepts. By their nature, they are not exact, although lawyers claim that they are. Without imprecision of definitions, sadly, there would be no place for lawyers. I maintain that many in the legal profession tend to exploit this ambiguity and make things more complex and subject to interpretation solely to promote their own ends. If agreements are not precise then they are subject to interpretation and legal opinion. And we all have opinions. When I utter a word or group of words it creates some mental image in your head. Hopefully, if we are communicating effectively, that something in your head matches what I intended to share with you. All too often we assume that people understand what we are saying exactly as we intended. Layer on the connotations of words, people's baggage with them and past history, it is no wonder that anyone understands what anyone else is trying to say.

Barring the mindless social repartee, which is rarely misunderstood, let's look at an example of how something that I'm trying to convey results in a misunderstanding. I was once a supervisor for a group of field sales people when the company raised prices, resulting in many upset customers who began looking for other alternatives. Many even stopped buying from the company. The business situation turned rather bleak, so I decided to charge up my team with a pep talk saying we aren't going to walk away from any more business. A straightforward simple message, wouldn't you agree?

Let's look at how each of the team members interpreted "We aren't going to walk away from any more business." One took my comment to mean that if a competitive situation arises in the future, we'll meet it. Another thought I meant they should go back to every customer who stopped buying from us and slash prices to regain their business. Still another thought I meant that we needed to sell harder and deemphasize pricing discussions; one statement, three interpretations. Who's right and who's wrong?

No one was correct and all of us were at fault. I should have clarified what I meant by that compact statement. My team should have challenged me to be more specific. Why didn't that happen? Conventional wisdom would say that the team should have just used their just common sense. Common sense leads to three different conclusions. Common sense was not the problem, common behavior was. What I wanted, but failed to articulate, was a common practice of not losing any more business based upon price. I should have been clearer, and they should have asked for clarity.

We all want to appear smart and knowledgeable, sometimes at the expense of total understanding. Unless you're clairvoyant or a super intellect, most of us don't get it the first time. There's no shame in asking for clarification.

Get consent of the Other before proceeding to the next step in the negotiating process. Since we are dealing with a problem resolving process, it is critical to reach closure and agreement of the parties on one issue or process before moving to the next. This is the essence of staying on the same page. It is incumbent on all parties to address the concerns of the Others during each step of the negotiating process before advancing to the next step. Too often negotiators attempt to drive the other party to their point of view without ample consideration and idea gestation time. This sets up a win-lose dynamic, which may lead to distrust. If the Other in the negotiation perceives that you are attempting to persuade, manipulate or intimidate them to accept your point of view, you risk leaving the more balanced and productive problem resolving space and entering the world of 'horse-trading'. At this point, people tend to become suspicious, guarded and much less cooperative. Agreements should be made one small agreement at a time, not in a big bang fashion.

A little later we will introduce a heuristic problem-solving model adapted from Interaction Associates, a consulting firm focused on change management and group problem solving, I have modified it to fit a negotiating problem resolution model. It is divided into the "Problem Space" and the "Resolution Space." It is critical that we temper our predisposition to jump to solution before fully defining and understanding the problem.

"If you cannot get agreement on the problem, you'll never agree on the solution."

- Michael Doyle and David Straus

Act as a Facilitative Negotiator. This isn't an oxymoron. In addition to understanding the people and the dynamics of negotiating, the highly skilled negotiator must be able to maintain the process of moving forward productively in a negotiation. In the negotiating arena the facilitator is not neutral, but an active participant or even a stakeholder in the negotiation. This duality of role, managing the process and the content, is what is the essence of Mindful Manipulation. The facilitative negotiator manages the negotiation process by keeping everyone on the same page. This is achieved through the use of problem resolution skills and facilitative behaviors that will be discussed later. Additionally, since the facilitative negotiator is also a stakeholder he/she must keep an eye on the content of a negotiation or the particulars of the issue to be resolved plus the use of the practices in this book.

Finally the facilitative negotiator must maintain the philosophy that strives for mutual satisfaction of needs in a pragmatic and humane way. This philosophy is captured in the practice and the principles of Mindful Manipulation. To be clear, there will be times when you will need to resort to conventional win-lose practices, either to persuade the Other to stop playing win lose or to defend yourself from exploitation.

The following is a very brief overview of the critical elements necessary to practice as a facilitative-negotiator. It is presented to expose you to the topic, not to build any skill or competencies. To master this skill set requires extensive training as a group process facilitator, heuristic and rational problem resolution techniques coupled with being a skilled negotiator.

Definitions

- Facilitator – traditionally, a person who manages the process part of a problem resolution attempt. Their responsibilities are to keep the process moving by building on agreements, honoring what has been previously agreed, suggesting tools and interventions and managing the group's output.
- Heuristic – A problem resolving process that is based on a trial and error methodology rather than a formulaic algorithm.
- Problem – A situation that requires change that is stated as a question.
- Convergent Processes – Focus, close or conclude discussions.
- Divergent Processes – Open discussions and explore.
- Process versus Content – Process is the 'how' to deal with a problem, content is the 'what' of the problem. The analogy is chewing gum. It has both process and content. The process is the chewing and the content is the gum.
- Stakeholder – Someone who is a decision maker and is affected by the outcome of a negotiation.

Facilitative Behaviors

- Avoid Process Battles – Suggest convergent or divergent processes that would further the progress of the discussion and negotiation. But if there is significant pushback, go in another direction and ask the other for an alternative process or suggest another process that might be amenable.
- Back Off – When an agreed upon process, suggestion or discussion is not going to produce the desired results, be prepared to go in a different direction
- Boomerang – A key behavior in engaging the Other to persuade is to create shared ownership. If the burden for the negotiation relies too heavily on the facilitative negotiator, transfer responsibility by boomeranging it back to the Other. It may sound like this, "I'm out of fresh ideas, how do you think that we should proceed?"
- Build in as Many Preventions as Possible – Create as many preventative actions in the design of your negotiation as is practical. Remember, preventions, like having an agenda, pay big dividends. They start the agreement process and save time and effort. Preventions are much more economical than Interventions.

- Check for Agreement – Building small agreements one step at a time is fundamental to creating a collaborative environment.
- Don't Talk Too Much – The secret to being a successful facilitative negotiator is not to be front and center in the process, but to strive to be minimally invasive. The more you talk, the more visible you are. When in doubt, shut up and be economical with your words.
- Encourage – Keep a positive environment. There will be times that your negotiating strategy demands other tactics, but do that consciously.
- Escalate Interventions as Appropriate – This should happen only when the unanticipated occurs or when there wasn't an adequate prevent established.
- Go Slow in the Beginning – It is particularly important to take extra time in the beginning of a negotiation to ensure that everyone is on the same page and small agreements can be made. Launching into an issue or dispute too quickly will invariably cause the process to slow or stall.
- Ground Rules – Establish a shared code of conduct, rules of engagement or 'how we will act' agreement very early in the process and reinforce them.
- Legitimize/Accept/Deal With/Defer – To keep others involved in the process always legitimize what they say, feel or are concerned about. To legitimize does not mean agreement, only that what has been expressed has been heard. In the process of problem resolution, issues come and go. For every issue raised the facilitative negotiator always has three options. They can accept what has been raised and move on, defer what has been said and table the issue with the consent of the Other, or deal with the issue. Dealing with an issue may impede planned progress, but if the issue is important to both parties and attempts at deferral have not been successful, you will need to deal with the issue or risk it will resurface later in the negotiation.
- Maintain/Regain Focus – Stay on track. If you become derailed return to the agenda, plan or discussion as soon as possible. Failure to do so may result in frustration and possibly a failed attempt at negotiation.
- Play Dumb – Don't be a know-it-all. Involve others by not having the answers and throwing the issue back to the Other.
- Reinforce Agreements – Use the legitimacy of the agenda, process agreements, commitments and previous other agreements to keep

progress moving forward. Recycle only if you will not be able to progress without revisiting a previous agreement. Always be prepared for the inevitability of needing to recycle.

– Use Body Language – Using your body instead of your voice is less obtrusive and invasive. It is many times a more effective way of getting to the same end. Proximity, sitting, standing, moving, facial and other body gestures are often very effective and practically imperceptible.

– Use the Group Memory – Have a prominent place (flip chart, white board, blackboard, projected technology) where the group's output is captured and visible. This technique separates the idea from the owner and makes the work being done the group's work. It also becomes the record of the meeting.

Facilitative Tools

– Advantages/Disadvantages – Create a two-column list of the advantages or disadvantages of a particular topic. Stick with one column until exploring it further seems to be counterproductive. All input should be captured without evaluation. You can use other facilitator tools to perform data cleansing. Use the Group Memory.

– Ask Basic Questions (Reporter Questions) – Ask What, Who, When, Where, How, How much, How Many, etc. to analyze or explore an issue, problem or situation. Use the Group Memory.

– Ask the Expert – To avoid speculation agree to bring in a consultant, expert or other knowledgeable person to offer opinions on technical, legal or more challenging questions outside the participant's scope of expertise.

– Best, Worst Most Likely – For perspective, evaluate a situation by creating a list of what are the best case, the worst case and the most likely scenarios that can occur. It brings balance to a discussion. Some people are intrinsically negative, others by nature are more positive. Use the Group Memory.

– Both AND – Create agreements and buy-in by combining two ideas into one. Ownership becomes shared and syndicated.

– Brainstorm – Originally a Madison Avenue advertising exercise, this technique is about generating a list of ideas around a particular topic. Quantity, not quality, is the goal of this process. Qualification, the discussion about and criticism of ideas, is deferred until after the brainstorm has ended. The facilitator should encourage the group to set a 'reach and stretch' goal of a certain number of ideas. Historically, production of ideas comes in two distinct waves. First, to arrive are the obvious ideas. Then a mental second wind usually happens when less obvious, more creative ideas tend to flow. Be careful not to cut off a brainstorm prematurely. Also, brainstorms are intended to be a free flow of uncensored ideas. It is particularly important in a negotiation to set clear ground rules as to commitment and accountability prior to the exercise. Use the Group Memory.

- Build up and eliminate – These are master strategies that work in opposite ways. One attempts to add more to the process the other attempts to reduce the variables to a manageable set.
- Categorize –Put ideas, problems, resolutions or issues into buckets. Use the Group Memory.
- Checker Board – Create a multi-dimensional matrix to evaluate a particular issue, idea or solution against a variety of criteria. It is applicable to problem resolution evaluation and problem analysis.
- Create a Picture – Create a visualization of the issue, problem or resolution. Invite others to contribute. Use the Group Memory.
- Cut-it-up and move it around – This is a great exercise to play with possibilities by creating alternative configurations of future states of processes. Use the Group Memory.
- Diagram – Classic flow-charting is an excellent example of this technique. Can be used for both 'as is' and 'to be' states. Can be created at varying levels of granularity. Use the Group Memory.
- Work Forward/Work Backward – Another set of master strategies deigned to apply a consistent frame of reference to a situation, problem or issue. Usually applied to anticipate potential problems with a resolution. Working backward helps understand how the problem occurred.
- Is/Is Not – An artifact of the rational root cause analysis problem solving school, Is/Is Not attempts to discover the changes and difference in a situation that cause a problem. This is accomplished by comparing an object with a problem to a very similar or identical object that does not have the defect. Then the reporter questions are applied to both objects to identify any differences. Use the Group Memory.
- Lasso – A simple circle around something in the Group Memory that the group has hit on help form the basis of agreement.
- Legitimize -- To keep others involved in the process always legitimize what they say, feel or are concerned about. To legitimize

does not mean agreement, it simply acknowledges that an idea has been heard.

- Multiple votes – Allow people to vote for multiple items in order to get buy-in and have a voice. Using the Group Memory, generate a list of ideas, issues, etc. To reduce the list to a manageable number assign each person multiple votes so that at least one of the ideas they voted for survives. Collapse similar ideas into one and multiple voting in concert with one another. Here's a way to calculate the appropriate number of votes that each person gets. Number of Votes = Number of options divided by the number of stakeholders plus one vote.
- Negative Voting -- Use the Group Memory to determine what obvious things, if any, can be removed from a list.
- Piggy backing – This is a technique that builds onto someone's comment or idea. It avoids hijacking ideas and pride of ownership issues.
- Plus – Delta – This is a variant of what I like about/ I don't like about is the plus/delta or plus/minus. It is a great feedback tool to determine if you're on track or if there are things that haven't surfaced yet but need to be addressed. The way it works is to create two columns or pages on the Group Memory. One side is for the pluses the other for the minus or delta (delta is a symbol for change). Since man is the inventor of the negative, always start with the plus side (people are critical and tend to want to change things). Ask: "What worked?" Brainstorm a list of the positives. When exhausted, move to the minus/Delta side. Ask: "What didn't work?" Ask the participants to state what didn't work as a problem, not as a solution. Allow a fixed amount of time for each column to be developed.
- Post-it exercises – This technique can be applied to a variety of other exercises. Using Post-it notes as the medium to communicate adds both a visual aspect and anonymity to the process. It is also a great intervention to neutralize people who tend to dominate a session. Simply have people write their thoughts on a Post-it. One thought per Post-it, then place the Post-its in the appropriate place on the Group Memory.
- Prioritize – On the Group Memory, categorize a list of items into general buckets (categories) such as High, Medium and Low, to perform triage on a list. Create general categorizes to make decisions on when to act, what's important or what to defer.

- Rank Order – On the Group Memory, create a list of alternatives in ascending order of importance, severity, consequence, preference, etc. Use the Group Memory.
- State as a Question – This is particularly useful in problem definition. By stating the problem as a question you subconsciously start looking to resolve it. It states the problem in a future state. Start every problem with the words. How To.
- Straw Votes – Use a non-binding show of hands to get a sense of the importance of an issue.
- What Others Have Done – This is an informal benchmarking to replicate resolutions that others have implemented. It saves reinventing the wheel. Use the Group Memory.

Mastery of these skills and behaviors coupled with strong problem resolving skills is the secret sauce to successfully and mindfully manipulating a durable resolution of an issue and executing a sustainable agreement. If you make people feel as if they have won, or at least that they have not lost, they truly have won. If people feel part of the resolution, they tend to live with, own and support it. Mindful manipulation strives to reach consensus in a negotiation through intimate involvement and creating a real sense of winning.

Use a Visual, Heuristic Problem Resolution Model. There are six phases of this model. It is important to stay on the same page by closing and agreeing to advance before entering the next phase. Our Western culture has historically rewarded those of us who get the right answer quickly. This approach is counterintuitive. It calls for defining the need or problem before creating solutions to resolve it. Advertising presents solutions to problems that may not exist. We are spring loaded to the solution mode. My advice? Don't go there.

WARNING

Negotiating is a problem resolving process. Conventional wisdom asserts that everything is negotiable, but that's not true. Don't try to negotiate problems that are not negotiable. It is a tremendous waste of time and energy

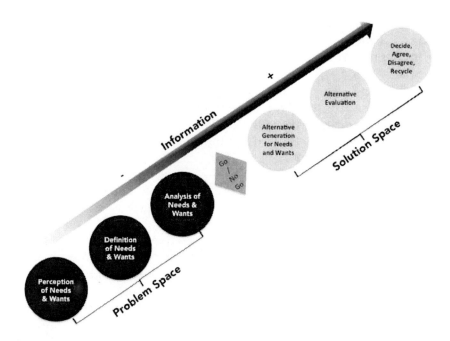

Adapted from Interaction Associates, Inc.'s "Interaction Problem Solving Model"

Here are the phases of this negotiating problem resolution model:

- **Perception of Needs and Wants** -- Opening positions, perceptions, feelings and expectations about what is required, past history, situational review.
- **Definition of Needs and Wants** – Separating what is needed from what may be desired. A definition of the problem or negotiating issue that is to be resolved.
- **Analysis of Needs and Wants** – Discussion to determine the needs (must haves) and wants (nice to have) and their relative priority.
- **Go/No-Go Decision Point** – Is the problem resolvable by negotiation and is it worth resolving?
- **Alternative Generation for Needs and Wants** – Contingent on the relationship between the parties, free to limited exchange of ideas to resolve the issues occurs in this phase. At the extremes, ideas may either be brainstormed collectively or the demarcation of positions drawn.

- *Alternative Evaluation* – Although typically not conducted in a public forum, this evaluation phase may include compromise, the Give and Take process. It may include what is traditionally called hard bargaining.
- *Decision Making to Agree, Disagree, Defer, or Recycle* – The crisis phase of a negotiation may be characterized by use of demands and tactics. Ultimately results in agreement, compromise, deadlock or reversion to a precedent phase. This is where most traditional negotiations start, totally short-circuiting the problem resolving process.
- *Operationalize the Action Steps* – Have a concrete plan. Ensure every stakeholder understands who will do what when.

Deal with Issues and Objections. During any phase of the resolution process, objections, also known as complaints, will surface. As in all problem-resolving interactions, you always have three response options. You can ignore the objection, defer it to be addressed later, or deal with it. It has been my experience when objections are raised that you usually have to deal with it or face becoming disconnected from the Other. A great technique to assess if the issue being raised is real or not is to ask the Other: "Are you serious?" Be careful to use a non-threatening tone of voice and non-verbal gestures. Surprisingly, if the objection is gratuitous they will back off quickly. Ignoring is another way of testing to see if the objection is real. You must be masterful at this technique, because it can easily backfire if poorly executed.

For example, our current home has hardwood floors and required the purchase of numerous area rugs when we first bought it. That's where I met Joe the Rag Merchant. There are many other rug dealers in our area, but Joe was extremely knowledgeable about rugs. He provided excellent guidance on value and what to buy based upon intended use. He is also a great storyteller, who brings life to rugs. He painted a picture of a rug being made in some exotic land by skilled craftsmen one knot at a time, blending the exquisitely dyed skills and wools into a one-of-a-kind masterpiece. Some of our selections were expensive hand knotted rugs and others were the more reasonably priced machine-made variety. When it came time to negotiate, Joe ignored any overtures to discuss price. He simply continued to write up an invoice with the price marked on the tag and took the conversation in a completely different direction. He talked about his new grandchild, the youth development program that he hosts on the upper level of his store, and anything else but price. His technique caused me to forget that I raised the price issue at all. In retrospect Joe practiced all of the skills and techniques that we have discussed. Unless you are Joe, who has his craft mastered, be very careful of ignoring objections.

Issues that must be addressed to stay on the same page come in four flavors. They are Misunderstandings, Doubt, Real Problems and Perceived Shortcomings. Let's discuss how to properly and effectively respond using an, if/then response scenario. If the person with whom you are dealing is raising an issue or objecting because they **misunderstand** what you are saying, then you must **clarify** so that the person receiving your message understands what you intend. If a **real problem** is being raised, such as the wrong price on an invoice, late delivery on previous orders, a defective product received or poor service experienced, then the appropriate response is to **show action** to remediate the situation. Too often I have personally experienced totally wrong responses to this issue. Offering an apology or an excuse falls far short of addressing the issue. Action is required.

If the Other is expressing **doubt, skepticism** or **disbelief** of what you are offering, then **proof or evidence** is required to remove that barrier to progress. Lastly, if the Other is raising an issue that they **perceive as a shortcoming**, then ensure that there is not a misunderstanding. If not, then **sing the company song** that will be discussed later in the book.

Think about it. Ignoring or deferring the address of any of these issues will grind progress to a full stop. These are showstoppers. If not addressed appropriately, they can severely impact the results of the discussion and the problem resolution process.

Let's take each of the issues and discuss how to offer an appropriate response. If the Other does not understand what you are attempting to communicate, then you are experiencing a Misunderstanding. The action that needs to take place is to clarify what you were trying to say. This can be frustrating, because the issue might be that there is a bona fide misunderstanding or that the Other is playing dumb. To clarify a misunderstanding, you need to assess if the Other really doesn't understand or is simply using the tactic of playing dumb to gain additional information. Attempt to restate, not repeat, what you previously offered without sharing additional information. Take the responsibility for the miscommunication and rephrase the statement to more clearly communicate to the Other. If the misunderstanding is not clarified in three or four attempts, ask the Other, "what seems to be at the root of the disconnect?" Once you think that you have adequately clarified the issue, then check with the Other to confirm that you have indeed cleared the misunderstanding before proceeding to the next step.

Unlike misunderstandings, Real Problems are not resolved by explaining. You need to act to resolve the issues. Real problems may take the form of performance issues or capability deficiencies. As an example, a manufacturer that has plans to grow beyond its existing service footprint may not consider distributors that do not have service capabilities in the new expansion territory. Even though your distribution company might have served the manufacturer well, your lack of capability in that geography presents a real problem for the manufacturer. To resolve the issue, you might have to develop a plan to grow your capability service to that new geography. Performance issues such as product/service quality, timeliness and accuracy of documentation must be resolved before going to the next step to stay in sync with the Other.

A classic objection faced by sellers is the often-heard phrase, "your price is too high." Again, we face the quintessential question, are these ploys simply to get you to lower your price or are there real problems. The easy way out for a seller is to treat the objection as a real problem and drop their price--but does that action really resolve the issue? We need to peel back the onion to get to the core or root of the objection. Price may only be the symptom or a tactic designed to test if there is any fat in the seller's offer. The real problem may be that our product/service is over designed for the applications. That's a fit or offering issue, not a price issue. Free advice: always get to the heart of the matter before making a concession.

Doubt is skepticism and is rather straightforward. If someone doubts the accuracy or validity of what you have said or claim, then you need to show proof or evidence that your statement or claim is valid. Be careful not to offer too much or submit a proof that does not resonate with the Other. Before offering evidence, have the Other commit to defining what proof or evidence would satisfy his/her doubt.

The last type of issue and the most difficult to deal with that we may encounter is that of a perceived shortcoming. Perception is between someone's ears. If someone believes something to be true, by definition it is true. Arguing whether something is true may not result in the inability to move the conversation forward. If you cannot address the misconception by clarifying, then use 'the Company Song.' In a nutshell, the Company Song is a series of messages that relays the same message in a different way. The message will always be consistent, but the words may be different. When faced with an Other that sees your offering as having a perceived shortcoming, first attempt to see if you can clarify the issue to carefully have the Other realize their perception may not be accurate. Failing that strategy, step back and present the Company Song as a way to minimize the impact of that erroneous perception. Remember first determine the nature of the objection or issue being raised by the Other. Next, confirm with the Other what you are hearing and the nature of what they are saying, Call it what it is, a misunderstanding, doubt. Then offer the appropriate response to what is being raised, and check to see if your response has resolved the issue.

As a heuristic problem resolution model, this method is based on trial and error, recycling and iteration. It is not linear and may not proceed sequentially. It can be a frustrating experience for most linear people, who tend to focus on results rather than process. Staying on the same page means that you must keep one eye on the process and the Other on the desired end result. Facilitative skills are key to advancing the process and staying in sync. Negotiating skills are essential to testing and ensuring that information sharing is not to your disadvantage. The key difference between traditional problem solving and negotiating is that full disclosure is rarely a matter of course. The beginning of a negotiating process can easily be characterized by a lack of information and guarded behavior, unless there is a long, positive history and earned trust. As the process progresses, information will either flow or not depending on how trust and rapport are cultivated. By moving to a subsequent phase of the process prematurely, we actually erode trust and rapport and replace it with suspicion and doubt.

Getting consent before proceeding allows you to be able to stay on the same page and move through the negotiating process at the same pace, thus earning your right to advance to the next step. Humans, particularly those of the Western variety, tend to think that once you move to the next step, there is no looking back. Collaborating with the Other and progressing at the same pace requires both parties to be in the same place at the same time. Negotiation is a process of discovery. New information is constantly coming into the public arena. When one party in the negotiation learns something new, it may cause confusion in their mind and require clarification, proof, action or context. In any event, until resolved, the negotiation will not progress. In fact the parties will have to regress to an earlier stage to deal with the new information.

Engage to Persuade

" The easiest way to sell a man a new suit is to have him try it on and see how good he looks in it."

- Ms. Bessie Spradling

Ms. Bessie Spradling was a very unassuming sales person. We were co-workers at a men's store in the city where I attended college. She was not only a good salesperson; she was outstanding. Bessie consistently outsold everyone. Her philosophy was to let the customer sell himself; you just create the opportunity for him to buy. Though the philosophy doesn't *always* work, the point is that the more you get people involved in the decision, the more ownership they have and the easier it is to close on an agreement. Some problem resolving tools to help with the process of engaging to persuade are:

Objectify and Depersonalize the Issue. Never make the person into a problem. Objectify and depersonalize it by making the problem a thing separate from the person attempting to resolve it. This technique allows the parties to work collaboratively on it, rather than point fingers, make accusations or deal with the emotional baggage.

CAUTION

It's easier to make the Other the problem than to agree on the problem in objective terms. We are preconditioned to the assign blame to people

Agree on the Problem. After making the problem an 'it', give it a name to which all parties can agree. A problem is a three dimensional object. As you turn the object, you get a different perspective or view of what it looks like. One party's view is two dimensional and limited. The totality of the picture lies in the collective view.

WARNING

Perception by definition is a reality, however, that reality may not be accurate

By encouraging a sincere, collaborative discussion on defining the problem, a more complete view of the problem is developed and a face-saving exit is opened for those who had an inaccurate perception of the problem.

NOTE

Start with a straw model or rough draft of a problem statement to kick start the process, be careful not to try to use it to manipulate the situation. It is imperative that a spirit of openness to modifying the straw model be sincere. If it is not, credibility and trust may be lost for the duration of the negotiation

Play with Ideas: Encourage Exploration of Needs, Options and Consequences. Persuasion results from effectively involving people, not talking them into something, dazzling them with your brilliance or baffling them with inaccuracies, lies and misrepresentations. People tend to believe more in what they say themselves than what others may tell them. A sense of choice and progress tends to motivate most people to engage in a problem resolution dialogue.

Advances in learning technology for both children and adults point out that play can be catalytic in helping people understand concepts, retain knowledge and foster buy-in. So when you throw an idea into the discussion and someone picks it up and starts playing with it and changing it to fit within their thought process, you have a choice. You can either become upset that someone is co-opting your great idea and not recognizing your brilliance and insightfulness, or you can relish the fact that someone else thinks your idea is good and is playing with it to make it their own. The essence of persuading is involving others in the process. A classic example is the customer liking the way they look in the suit that you asked them to try on.

There is an element of selflessness required in persuading someone. We all appreciate being recognized to varying degrees. When another takes the idea that you have planted and runs with it, you may lose ownership and credit for it, but if you were attempting to persuade you have succeeded.

CAUTION

When people play with your ideas they will tend to change them. Be careful not to get upset at losing control of your creation. Remember, it is the objective to make your idea our idea

Persuasion is a continuum. It ranges from Apathy to Commitment. It defines the level of alignment with the Other and the behavioral cues indicative of that state. If you pay attention, the Other will emote concrete indicators of the issues that are preventing them from commitment. In fact, most people will not be either immediately or totally persuaded to buy what you're selling. What generally happens is someone takes issue with or opposes your idea or suggestion. They're not playing with it, so is that bad? Opposition, provided you can discover further what is at the root of what they are opposing, can be positive. People may oppose what you say for one of four reasons; they have a misunderstanding of your statement, they don't believe what you are purporting, there is something truly incorrect or flawed in what you said, or they perceive a drawback to what you offering. Once you are able to define and validate the basis of their opposition, you can address the issue straight away. Don't view opposition as a negative situation, but an opportunity to advance the process of persuasion, if you can successfully deal with their objections.

Let's walk through the continuum and some verbal cues that will assist in helping identify the Other's level of alignment with your proposition. We'll approach the continuum from a hierarchical perspective from high to low, Commitment to Apathy. Each of the levels will have some behavior indicators associated with it. Once you identify the exhibited level of alignment, you should attempt to raise it to the next level. Think of these phases of alignment as gates that you must get the Other to pass through on the way to gaining Commitment to an idea, course of action or an agreement. This may be a slow process, but advancing without it tends to backfire. Remember to stay on the same page.

When the Other is **Committed,** their word choices can sound like "When can we start?" "Absolutely, we agree" and "Let's do it!" Tone of voice, rate of speech and general body language tend to be highly energized. **Play** is the level just below commitment. It may sound like, "What if we ...", "Can we try ...", "What if we change this ...". This is the beginning of transferring ownership from one party to the collective. Be careful not to react negatively when the Other plays with your idea or proposal. Pride of ownership may derail your efforts to gain commitment. I once had a supervisor who made a habit of playing with my ideas before he committed to doing anything. He would figuratively try on the ideas I proposed before buying them. Initially, I would get upset when he did this. I felt that he was stealing my ideas, but in reality he was just becoming comfortable with them. By playing with them, he made my ideas his own. Once I realized that his playing was a good thing, I looked for the cue to tell me that he was sold. In reality, I accomplished what I had intended; to create a champion for my ideas. Ego is a funny thing. Keep it in check and your eye on the goal.

The next level down is interest. The cues that indicate **Interest** are: "Tell me more"; "How does that...?"; Can it do...?" Prior to getting to interest, you must pass through **Analysis**. This phase is critically important in that to reach this point, the Other has made a Go/No-Go decision to take action. During the evaluation phase, the Other may use phrase such as "I'm listening"; "What do you have?"; "How do you compare to...?" In this phase, you should expect to see skepticism and drawbacks raised. The lesser phases show a decrease in commitment, starting with **Challenge** (I don't believe that; I disagree; It's expensive), and moving to **Complaint** (Your service sucks; I'm not pleased with...), **Avoidance** (Call me next time; I'll get back to you), **Aggression** (Never call again; You're a liar; See you in court), and **Apathy** (It's not my job; I only work here; I have no power). Opposition through apathy exhibits negative emotions, especially when it comes to gaining commitment, because the Other responds in a passive manner and doesn't give you much indication of what to do to get them to the next level.

The first step in gaining commitment is to determine where the Other is on the continuum. Do not assume that you know; test it by asking questions and listening for their responses, watching their behaviors and paying attention to their non-verbal cues.

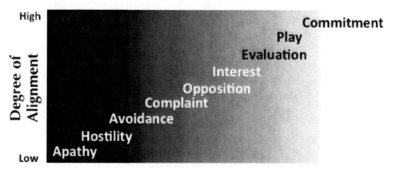

Emotion Exhibited

Align to the Continuum. The following chart attempts to tie the emotions that are exhibited with the verbal cues that are being offered by the Other. The more accurate you are in identifying the Other's commitment level the smoother the process will flow. Sometimes personalities will generate false signals; someone being polite with a low degree of interest may emote signals that are interpreted as more positive. Someone who is more direct may be more interested than his or her emotions indicate.

Emotion Exhibited	Verbal Cues
Commitment	When can we start; I agree; Let's do it
Play	What if...; Can we try...; What if we change...
Interest	Tell me more; Who else has...; How does it...
Analysis	I'm listening; What do you have

Challenge	I don't believe that; I disagree; It's too expensive
Complaint	Your service sucks; I'm displeased with...
Avoidance	Call me again next time; I'll get back to you
Aggression	Never call me again; You're a liar; See you in court
Apathy	It's not my job; I only work here; I have no power

Consider the Problem in Context. Context provides meaning to facts. Most facts that are taken out of context can be manipulated into half-truths. Facts are the currency of arguments. Arguments are used in debate to make a case. They rely primarily on one type of approach; you are either in favor of or against alternatives. The more facile and convincing a presenter is in manipulating facts, the more successful he or she will be in persuading the Other. The purpose of this section is defensive in nature; simply remember to consider the context when facts are presented to you.

Facts offer proof or give validity to an argument. Proof or evidence can also come in several forms with varying levels of confidence associated with the form. The least credible and lowest form of evidence is anecdotal. It is episodic, non-statistically based, but irrefutable. The efficacy of evidence can be determined by the protocol, rigor and breath of the event that produced the resultant conclusion. In any case always ask: "What is different about the context of the proof now versus when it was generated?" Evidence can always be manipulated to suit the position of the Other. It is context that can provide a reality check on the validity and sustainability of the fact. Facts are only true in the context in which they were discovered. If the context, that is the circumstances surrounding the fact, remains constant, as it was when the fact was discovered, consider it a fact. However, if the context appreciably changes from the time of discovery to the time the fact is called into an argument, consider the fact suspect. This practice will ensure that both parties stay on the same page from an information point of view.

Summary – Ends and Means

Since negotiating is a problem resolving process we need clear principles of engagement. They constitute the how of negotiating. The Rules of Engagement are:
- Be Cool and Act with Civility. Stay focused and calm during negotiations. The Other frequently uses ploys such as anger, force and other emotional plays.. Be firm, but always treat the Other with respect, dignity and care.
- Stay on the Same Page. Make sure that you understand and that you are understood. Get the Other's consent to move the agenda forward. Use a visual, heuristic problem resolution model in the negotiation.
- Engage to Persuade. Decouple the problem from the person. Make the problem an "it." Ensure that you agree on the real problem before attempting to resolve it. Get the Other to play with ideas to gain emotional buy-in.

Try This:

Try to get to a problem definition using the principles of engagement; Be Cool and Act with Civility, Stay on the Same Page and Engage to Persuade. Go no further than getting closure on a problem definition. Attempt to be nonjudgmental in your preferences and opinions. Pick a topic that you are very passionate about. Find someone that you know that doesn't share your passion or may have a contrary point of view.

Evaluate the conversation using these questions:

- What was the hardest behavior to practice?
- Why do you think it was so difficult?
- Had you not practiced the principles of engagement, what do you think would have happened?

Chapter Four: Not Everything Is Negotiable

"Very little good has ever been done by the absolute shall."

- Anonymous Clergyman

This is particularly true when we apply it to how political ideology can be used to highjack an entire branch of government and grind it to a full stop. I offer the 111th, 112th and 113th US Congresses and how they have failed to act in the country's best interests and instead have become embroiled in a battle of wills pandering to special interests instead of the people who elected them.

Case Study: The 111th, 112th and 113th US Congress

The Story: In the three years following passage of "The Affordable Healthcare Act" these congresses have done little to nothing of substance. Harry Truman would have given this band of do-nothing-legislatures hell.

Why the Negotiations Failed: These two legislative bodies have been characterized as ineffective, the most polarized since the reconstruction, in the pocket of the Political Action Committees (PAC) and failing to serve the best interest of the American people. In addition to continuously seeking campaign funding from PACs to fuel the re-election bids, they are extremely divided along party lines. This polarization is driven by rigid adherence to political ideology and moralization instead of focusing on pragmatism and doing what's best for the country. One party wants to revert to a distorted, idealist version of the way America was and the other wants to take America to a place it has never been before. There seems to be no common ground.

In short, you cannot negotiate morals (abortion, same sex marriage, drug legalization) or dogma (immigration, imperialistic policies, worldwide militarism). This is the conundrum that is entangling the legislature. The members of Congress need to step back and free themselves from the yoke of PACs, dogma and religion-based morality to search for the common bonds that Americans share. This will allow for progress and a return to the negotiating table in earnest. Collaborative, enlightened negotiating and effective problem resolving cannot be achieved until the important issues facing the country are redefined.

"Dogma is the enemy of human freedom"

- Saul D. Alinsky

Contrary to what conventional wisdom espouses, not everything is negotiable. This section is designed to help you understand if negotiating is an appropriate intervention to resolve the problem.

I have personally seen people attempt to negotiate things that are not negotiable. Sadly, it is a tremendous waste of time. At a minimum there must be something of significance to negotiate, a modicum of common ground to build an agreement on, reasonably cool and controlled heads and a problem type that is in the negotiating arena. We'll discuss which problem types fit into the arena later in this section. You may be surprised at the number of problem types that are out of the negotiating bounds. Yet many people try in vain to accomplish the impossible.

My definition of negotiating states that we are attempting to resolve a problem. That implies understanding the issue or problem and dealing with it, not deferring or ignoring it. Compromise can be a type of deferral tactic in that it delays the eventuality of dealing with the core of the problem. It allows you to reach a temporary short-lived equilibrium, but nothing more. You can negotiate a compromise, but that is a much less durable resolution. The Principles and the Practices are applicable to reaching compromise, but recognize that it is a less desirable state. In some cases, however, compromise might be the best that is achievable at the time.

So what's in and out of the realm of negotiation? Let's start with simple situations. You cannot negotiate with yourself, that process is called rationalization; in extreme cases those who attempt to self-negotiate may require psychotherapy. You cannot negotiate if you are already in agreement; resolution is achieved by getting the parties involved to recognize that they are saying the same thing and are, in fact, in agreement. Sometimes, however, parties in agreement can talk over each other and fail to realize their similar ideas.

CAUTION

If you don't recognize that you are violent agreement with the Other, it usually results in a disagreement

Negotiation is not applicable to situations that are governed by Groupthink or the Abilene Paradox. According to Dr. Jerry B. Harvey, the Abilene Paradox describes a situation in which a group of people collectively decides on a course of action that is counter to the preferences of any of the individuals in the group. It involves a common breakdown of group communication in which each member mistakenly believes that their own preferences are counter to the groups and, therefore, does not raise objections. A common phrase relating to the Abilene Paradox is a desire not to "rock the boat."

Groupthink, researched by Irving Janis, is a psychological phenomenon that occurs within groups of people. It happens when the desire for harmony in a decision-making group overrides a realistic appraisal of alternatives. Group members try to minimize conflict and reach a consensus decision without critical evaluation of alternative ideas or viewpoints. Factors such as group cohesiveness, structural faults and situational context play into the likelihood of whether or not Groupthink will impact the decision-making process.

The Abilene Paradox is a form of Groupthink. It is supported by social psychology theories of social conformity and social influence, which suggest that human beings are often averse to acting contrary to the trend of the group. Likewise, it has been recognized by psychologists that indirect cues and hidden motives often lie behind statements and acts, frequently because social disincentives discourage individuals from openly voicing their feelings or pursuing their desires.

The Abilene Paradox is related to the concept of Groupthink in that both theories appear to explain the observed behavior of groups in social contexts. The crux of the theory is that groups have just as many problems managing their agreements as they do their disagreements. This observation rings true among many researchers in the social sciences and tends to reinforce other theories of individual and group behavior.

CAUTION

Negotiation is different than traditional problem resolving because full disclosure rarely happens as a matter of course

I offer a special thanks to Dr. Jerry L. Talley for allowing the use of his problem categorization typology that follows. His work provides an excellent framework to describe where negotiation is and is not appropriate. This provides a great guide for determining if problem types are negotiable.

As a starting point, use an acid or litmus test to determine if there is a singular, definitive correct solution to a problem. If there is, the solution cannot be negotiated. If there is not, the problem can never be permanently solved. It may only be resolved and may be grist for the negotiating mill, if there is common ground and it fits the following typology. One word of caution, a problem may have common ground, it may fit one of the in-bound categories and may be worth resolving, but heightened emotions that are not controlled can sabotage the negotiating process. As we examine the eight different problem types, we will determine if the resolution is negotiable or out of the negotiation bounds.

WARNING

There are some problems that you just can't resolve, so don't waste your time trying. Maintain the status quo may be the best you can do

<u>OUT OF PLAY</u>: Problems that Usually Are Not Negotiated

Problems Which Are Puzzles have objective solutions, and typically have known and reliable methods for a correct answer. In some instances, there is only one correct answer, but please note that in most cases there can be multiple correct answers to solve the problem. Puzzle problems are technical, mechanical, financial or mathematical in nature. The most pressing need is for expertise. Once found, the solution will be obvious to any appropriate observer. The problem can be carved up into pieces and addressed separately, and solutions can then be applied from elsewhere.

Issues: We are so comfortable with puzzle problems that we often overuse the category. The linear, rational process for puzzle problem resolving can be seductively attractive precisely when the emotional, people-issues are dominant, which often means that other problem types are probably more appropriate.

The main challenges of puzzles are ensuring that the problem resolvers have a stable definition of the problem, the requisite skills and a sound group process.

OUT OF PLAY: These types of problems are resolvable but usually not by negotiation

Problems That Are Too Rich are almost the exact opposite of puzzles. While we are often certain there is at least one answer, the resolution is not objective. In fact, we are typically facing a wide array of possible choices. The situation calls for a visionary or artistic effort, not a technical one. Once found, the decision will not be obvious; it may remain controversial well into implementation. Rather than expertise, the most pressing need here is for judgment, intuition, innovation and sometimes courage.

CAUTION

There is a very fine line between vision and hallucination

Issues: The visionary leap that is often the core of a Too Rich problem does not blend well with negotiation. Once someone has an insight about a new future, it needs to be compelling for an audience (workers, investors, potential customers, etc.) but that same audience is usually unable to find that focus on their own. The space for negotiation is around implementation of the vision, but not the generation of it. A process that does fit (and could be a form of negotiation) is mutual exploration. Members of a community, for example, may need to come together around a vision for their town in the future (*What do you want to see in Los Angeles 2050?*). The purpose of interaction, however, is not compromise and eventual convergence; the purpose is exploration of possibilities and getting beyond the obvious.

These problems require attention to an eventual audience (employees, investors, customers, directors, regulators, etc.) but also looking beyond what that audience might be able to articulate. They should be inspired by the final outcome, but also surprised by it. The other major concern is how to leverage a group, when the essential activity is typically private. A group composition of a vision statement is usually a bland compromise; an individual vision statement has the potential for being bold and innovative.

OUT OF PLAY: Typically not resolvable by negotiations. Once the vision is defined, the implementation of the resolution may be negotiated.

Problems that are Complexities emerge when enough actors behaving independently form an almost organic entity: a marketplace of buyers and sellers, employees in a company, companies in a market segment, all the supply chains feeding into a single company. All of these phenomena exhibit order and structure well outside the intentions of anyone ostensibly in charge. The organization of such systems is emergent, an unpredictable property spawned by the relationships among the players.

Issues: Complex systems are fundamentally unknowable. We can capture trends and patterns, but they are mostly heuristic, and never exhaustive. We can nudge a system, but we cannot totally control it or drive a specific solution. A complex system will answer back, and often with a message we did not expect.

The difficulty in observing systems is that we are *in* the system, not outside of it. Our observations and growing knowledge change the system, so it is no longer what we thought it was. Attempts at fixing a problem also change the system. It is an ever-shifting target.

OUT OF PLAY: Not resolvable by negotiations. The current relationship between K Street Lobbyist and elected politicians in Washington is an example. The system will not be changed through negotiations in congress, but by external grass root demands to change the system or action by the judiciary.

Problems with a Moral Impasse: At this point I need to define and differentiate morality, ethics and law. Morals are a set of deeply held, widely shared and relatively stable values within a particular community. Ethics are more philosophical involving the study of values, and the justification for ethical actions. These philosophies can then be applied to specific situations by practitioners such as in the practice of medicine, scientific discovery, conduct of commerce, treatment of combatants and weapons of war, to name a few. The law is a compilation of rights and responsibilities established by specific governments that are used to maintain social order, resolve disputes, and distribute wealth according to people's needs.

Conflicts like the abortion debate, the Israeli-Palestinian conflict and the Bosnian-Serb conflict represent a problem with moral impasse. Antagonists not only avoid compromise, but they are against any interaction. Their goal is annihilation of the other side, not accommodation of their point of view. In these problems, there is no common authority or common ground that can compel the sides to come together.

"The truth is rarely pure and never simple."

- Oscar Wilde

In the Protestant-Catholic wars in Ireland, there was a greater authority: mothers. Their strident argument that a dying child does not care whether the bullet is Catholic or Protestant eventually forced the sides to admit that the cost of their conflict was way too high; a compromise was essential. Today, in the Middle East, the tolerance of loss of life means there is no basic human value that demands an exploration of common interests. Sadly, there is nothing to lose or it has not exceeded the threshold of unacceptable pain.

Issues: Negotiation would be impossible unless you're willing to risk violence.

OUT OF PLAY: Since problems of this type have no common ground, they are not in the domain of negotiated results.

Problems with Politics: The distinguishing feature here is that problems are usurped to support an ideological agenda and long-standing alliances. There is no real concern for the problem except in how it can be twisted or used to fight another purpose. The response of Congress to health care reform was a classic case; there was little interest in what works (we have 50 states with different health care delivery systems, but no one ever looked at our own laboratory to find the system with the best health outcomes). What we *did* see was rhetoric about 'creeping socialism' or 'social Darwinism' that made it clear any preference for a solution was based on its ideological value, not the resolution of the actual problem.

Issues: Beliefs overtake logic in this case. Reason gives way to an ideologically driven agenda. Bipartisan politics gives way to dogmatic power play. Negotiation would only fuel the ideological nature of these debates. What we need instead is to point to the ideological conflict and honestly admit that no one is concerned with solving the problem on its own merits.

OUT OF PLAY: Regrettably, the situation must regress to a lose-lose before any progress is made to get to compromise.

IN PLAY: Problems that Can Be Negotiated

Problems With Uncertainties are dominated by the unknown or unknowable variation in key variables. Typically, resolutions vary significantly depending on some uncertain future development. The solution has to be contingent on future events, making for multiple possible solutions rather than one best solution. The problem resolving effort has to be drawn out into the future so we can watch unfolding events and modify the solution as needed. The problem resolving team cannot disperse, they have to remain engaged to oversee the adjustment of solutions as circumstances reveal themselves.

Issues: There is a need for shared agreement here, but not around how the future will be, only around what futures we should be considering. The agreement needed is on a set of scenarios that deserve exploration and tracking. The actual future will reveal itself, and will not be constrained by any agreement among the parties involved.

For example, we should not negotiate around the number of children entering our school system in the next decade; we need to agree on the range of possibilities (same as now, noticeably more, noticeably less) and then work together on our response in each scenario. By their very nature, these problems require making assumptions about an unknowable future; the process is fragile and easily attacked, but it is also essential. The worst possible choice is assuming there is only one possible future. Writing compelling scenarios is the essential kernel of this problem type, and it is a rare skill. The pressure to settle on the most likely scenario will be intense, and it will challenge the leader to keep the group attentive to multiple futures.

Be careful not to confuse uncertainty in the observer with uncertainty in the world. Just because we are confused does not mean the world is random. Sometimes we just need to do our homework.

IN PLAY: Typically resolvable by negotiations. Long-term agreements with remedies for specific scenarios are common in business. Prenuptial agreements would fit into this category.

Problems That Are Disputes are the classic conflicts of multiple stakeholders with colliding interests. While cooperation may be difficult in these scenarios, it is also essential, since no one can proceed without the tacit permission of the others (although that power is usually expressed through a veto rather than positive support). The driving need is for a safe and equitable forum where parties can surface their interests and explore options for the most satisfying outcome for all parties concerned.

Issues: In other problem types, it is appropriate to seek a solution; in this problem type, we strive for a safe forum where the participants can find their own solution. The neutral facilitator becomes more critical than the subject matter expert. Without the safe forum for negotiation, the players will be tempted to pursue political solutions.

Once the appropriate forum and norms are established, it is usually possible to bring all the players to the table and explore the interests behind their opening bargaining positions. If they can find a joint solution, they still have to create a structure for enforcing compliance among possibly reluctant parties.

IN PLAY: A safe, trusting forum is required to be most effective. Time spent establishing trust is paramount to resolving the problem by negotiations.

Problems That Are Dilemmas come from our simultaneous commitment to incompatible goals. Our effort to maximize one goal undermines our success at the other. Faced with an apparent conflict of interest, the representatives of each side tend to become even more ardent advocates, which only provokes an equal escalation on the other side. Dilemmas are never really resolved, only managed to a degree of effectiveness. The ongoing nature of dilemmas makes a process for finding solutions more valuable than any particular solution.

Issues: It requires a mind shift to see one dilemma instead of two goals, but until we make the perceptual shift, it is extremely hard to envision the synergy required for managing a dilemma. Without that insight, people only work for a compromise, which will leave both sides unsatisfied. Here both Dr. Talley and I would make the strongest possible claim that a win-win negotiation is not achievable. If there are two perspectives, then the participants have not yet understood that they are in a dilemma; they are still attached to one goal, without realizing that it is intimately interconnected with another (seemingly incompatible) goal.

Negotiation here would lead only to a compromise, which is not the innovative, synergistic outcome we want for a dilemma. If some people are fighting for quality (in health care, education, public services, etc.) while others are fighting for fiscal constraint (lower head count, constraints on equipment, limiting eligibility, etc.), then the outcome will be a negotiated blend of the two, when what we really want is both. In a dilemma, the real negotiation is not around the solution, but around understanding the nature of the problem and finding a new set of relationships that allows for radical cooperation and innovation. The solution, however elusive, is less valuable than the process we use for finding it. The solution in a dilemma is always provisional, temporary, and subject to revision, but the process for finding a solution will need to be repeated.

Since there is no permanent resolution, the process for exploring options and for learning from experience becomes more important than the actual solution. Ongoing management requires a relationship among people who used to be antagonistic to each other; a sense of respect and mutual regard is essential.

IN PLAY: Albeit not optimal, dilemmas can be resolved by positional negotiations, where a temporary compromise might be achievable. Game theory may also come into play in dealing with dilemmas. At best, a win-lose result can be achieved. Compromises tend to result in systems that are built to backfire, creating more problems than they resolve. Priority should instead be placed on the process and relationships behind the resolution process.

In Summary – Not Everything Is Negotiable

Contrary to widely accepted myth and conventional wisdom, not every situation can be resolved through a negotiating process. The table below is a quick reference to aid in determining if negotiating is practical and appropriate. Is it any surprise that others warn about discussing religion and politics? Facts carry little weight in the face of belief, faith and ideology.

Problem Type	Negotiable	Not Negotiable
Dilemmas	X	
Complexities		X
Disputes	X	
A Moral Impasse		X
Puzzles		X
Too Rich		X
Politics		X
Uncertainties	X	

Try This:

Using the table above, List examples from your own life for each category of problem. How did you attempt to resolve the problem? If you inappropriately chose negotiation as the methodology of resolution, what where the results?

Part III: The Practices

The Practices are a distillation of the best of conventional negotiation theories that are still relevant today. The remainder of this book is design to be used as a resource manual. I suggest that you review the contents prior to entering a negotiation for anything of substance. There are detailed explanations of rituals and rites of the traditional negotiation dance. These are the survival skills necessary to effectively negotiate. Though they attempt to optimize your negotiating leverage and place you in a position of strength, they are presented to provide a defense if the Other attempts to exploit you.

WARNING

YOU ARE ENTERING THE DOMAIN OF WIN-LOSE
What follows will provide you with defensive tactics. Over reliance on them as a will be thrust into a positional negotiation resulting in suboptimal results

You must have an intimate awareness of these practices and be facile in performing the requisite behaviors in order to take negotiating to the next level. These skills are the table stakes of negotiating. Without command of them, you can be extremely vulnerable in a negotiation with an Other that has mastered the practices. Couple the following practices and behaviors with the principles of *Mindful Manipulation* and you will be ready to take a giant leap forward in your ability to create durable resolutions to negotiable problems.

Chapter Five: Best Practices Before Negotiations

Ask: Is the Juice Worth the Squeeze?

"Don't fight a battle if you don't gain anything by winning."

- Field Marshall Erwin Rommel

Before entering the field of combat, a skilled military leader always assesses the situation by asking these questions. Can I win? Is the battle worth it? Should I fight now, or would it be better to until wait another day? What are the best, most likely and worst possible outcomes? Negotiators must also understand what's at stake, if we can win and, most importantly, if the negotiation battle is worthwhile.

WARNING

Most battles are not worth fighting, so too with negotiations

Negotiations are not free. They consume resources, time and emotional energy. Sometimes submission may be the most expeditious, but also the most effective tactic. I love the opening quotation, "Is the juice worth the squeeze?" It is the quintessential question to determine if negotiating now, later or at all is appropriate. Measure the terrain, assess your Other, and determine what is to be gained or lost as you pick your battles. The intent is to avoid the "lots of churn with no butter syndrome."

The following graphic is designed to help you evaluate if you should invest time and effort into negotiation. Make realistic estimates of the likely Results Achievable relative to the Effort Required to secure them, then decide if you should negotiate or not.

Aim High

"You miss 100% of the shots you don't take"

- Wayne Gretzky

True or false: people who aim high generally achieve more than those who don't. It is true; those who expect more usually get more. Life proves that. In my experience, expectations are directly proportional to negotiated outcomes. If little is what you expect, little is what you get. The converse is true as well. Let me provide a real example of how this plays out in life.

WARNING

The higher that you aim, the greater the possibility of deadlock

Over the years, I have been engaged by large corporations to train their sales teams. In one particular simulation I use the buyer has major supply problems and consequently has absolutely no bargaining power or leverage. The buyer is at the mercy of the seller. The seller, of course, does not know this unless the buyer mistakenly tells him or her, which would not be smart. The sellers are told that they must settle for a minimum price and volume to qualify for a sales incentive and keep their position, which is far below what the buyer is willing to pay. Guess where the vast majority of the negotiations settle? That's right, at or near the minimum price and volume to make their sales incentive. I then adjusted the price threshold for the incentive in the simulation. The sellers then closed for a higher price to reach the new incentive. You generally get what you ask for and that's all. This applies to management expectations as well.

Clearly aiming high has a lot of upside, but how about potential downsides? There are at least two. One is the risk of pushing too far, and the other is frustration. If you push too far, you are asking the Other to adapt too much. If you exceed this point, then credibility and motives come into play. Frustration is a result of attempting to deal with someone who appears to be unreasonable and unbending. Both can result in eventual deadlock. Later, we'll talk about discounting your own leverage, but as in all of nature, there exists an opposite force holding on to our assumptions in the face of reality. Sometimes we set goals that are outside the realm of reality and believe the assumptions that we have unconsciously imbedded in the goal without testing them.

Always Have a Fallback Position

One of the best ways to reduce pressure is to establish and create a fallback position, or a Plan B. Negotiations are all about how to handle situations. If you believe you have a situation that can only be resolved one way, you have no fallback; no other option and you abdicate any leverage you might have had in the situation.

WARNING

Without an actual or perceived fallback position, you are powerless in a negotiation and at the mercy of the Other

Plan A is clearly your first choice. It's the one resolution to the situation that would work the best, but more often than not, a plan doesn't work out the way we had hoped. That's where Plan B, C, D and E come in. They give you options. They relieve the pressure you feel when you have to have to deal with a sole source. Remember to always establish at least one fallback. You don't have to use it; it just has to be there. Creating a fallback position may be more an illusion than reality. You should make the Other think that it is a viable alternative and you intend to use it if necessary. Having a fallback says that you have real options and you will decide on the best-balanced resolution. Think of these options as competition. If you are a buyer, whom will you choose to supply you? If you are a seller, whom will you choose to supply? Fallbacks may be other competitors, make versus buy or a completely new disruptive technology.

There are fallbacks other than having to buy or sell. One fallback that you always have is choosing not to agree, a deferral, an intermittent 'deadlock' or pause in the action. This pause in the negotiation serves as an excellent fallback--it can restore your sense of power and may keep you from sweating it out. In a negotiation the only place that they have to be real is in the mind of the Other. Flexibility will always increase leverage in a negotiation. It is derived from clearly separating your needs from your wants. This is something most people get very confused about. We will discuss the difference next.

WARNING

The information that you give away when you are in the selling mode generally comes back to bite you when you're in the negotiating mode

The ultimate fallback position can be litigation, particularly in a litigious society like the United States. You might say that going to litigation is extreme, which is true, but if you have no other options, it may be your only fallback. Use the legal route discretely, because; it is extremely expensive and time consuming, and someone always wins and someone always loses. There are some who believe that entering the legal realm is actually a lose-lose proposition, but again the threat of uncertainty of winning may actually drive the win-win. How many times have people gone to court initially then settled the matter out of court? The vast majority of the legal system would overload and grind to a halt without these out-of-court settlements.

Assess Leverage

"Power concedes nothing without a demand. It never did and it never will."

- Frederick Douglass

It is always better to work from a position of strength. Generally, we have more power than we think we do. We tend to focus on our shortcomings and amplify the strengths of the Other. It is a natural human phenomenon, part of our human condition. The secret to overcoming this problem is to do an objective reality check. Get the emotion, the baggage, the negative self-talk and ego out of the process. Stick to the facts and assess the relative power balance in a negotiation. One caveat about this activity; be prepared to reassess. Negotiation is a process of discovery. We rarely have perfect knowledge and, if we are receptive, we learn more as we journey through the process.

CAUTION

We generally have more leverage in a negotiation than we think. We tend to focus on our limitations and the Others strengths

So what are these sources of leverage in negotiations? There are many more than you think. We will explore the short version, rather than an exhaustive list of sources of leverage in a negotiation. Here's a brief list with explanations:

Affiliations – It's not what you know; it's whom you know. Connections, networks and relationships are formidable currency in the negotiating process. A properly placed phone call by a high ranking associate, or a mention by someone with clout can shift the balance of negotiating power and provide leverage to the party exploiting the affiliation. Having the inside track is always a great advantage.

Creativity – Creativity as it is applied to negotiating involves literally kicking old ideas in the pants. It does not have to be revolutionary, but it certainly cannot be the SSDD (Same Stuff Different Day). A unique or novel approach to the 'how to resolve the business' issue is usually a game changer. Creativity is a differentiator that offers leverage in a negotiation. Its uniqueness makes it a 'game changer' and the creative party a sole source. One risk associated with creativity is that it usually presents an untried and unproven solution, so risk taking may be required. Don't forget the old IT adage that no one was ever fired for buying IBM. This is particularly appropriate if the party that you're dealing with is relatively conservative.

Emotion – The discussion here is not about using emotional behavior as a tactic, but understanding and controlling your own emotions in the negotiation process. Kimberlyn Leary, Julianna Pillemer and Michael Wheeler wrote "Negotiating with Emotion" in the January-February 2013 issue of Harvard Business Review. They outlined six steps to help get in touch and control your emotions during a negotiation.

–   Rather than suppressing emotion, the following mental exercise help you get in touch with your emotions, anticipate issues, address them and direct them in a positive way:
–   Imagine that you have successfully completed this negotiation, how do you feel?
–   Why is feeling this way important?
–   What can you do prior to the negotiation to put yourself in the best mental state to realize the desired state that you imagined?
–   What might throw you off-balance during a negotiation?
–   What can you do if something throws you off to regain your balance?
–   How do you really want to feel when you're finished negotiating?
–   Controlling your emotions in a negotiation is critical. The party that has mastered this practice has a distinctive advantage.

Knowledge – The more you know about a topic, generally, the better you will do in a negotiation. Be careful not to confuse data with knowledge. Data are facts, figures and any information that is not contextually bound. In other words, it does not pass the 'so what' or 'how does apply in this situation' test. Data overload as a tactic used in a negotiation is designed to inundate the receiver to confuse, confound and obfuscate the issue at hand. Information that is knowledge always is contextually bound and related directly to the issue to be resolved. Generally speaking the more you know the better you are positioned.

Market Conditions – The effects of market elasticity and supply and demand always affect negotiations. In a market driven economy, leverage for the seller usually increases in a short market and decreases in a long one. The reverse is true for the buying side. Recognize if you are in a buyer's market or a seller's market. Also, remember they change in polarity.

Money – Purchasing power or leverage is unlimited if you are not constrained. Money can be both an asset and a liability; an asset in that if you want something you can buy it, a liability because the more money you have, the more you tend to spend. Sometimes you will pay too much for goods and services simply because you can out-bid or out-pay someone that has lesser monetary leverage.

Negotiating Experience – Generally speaking, a more experienced negotiator will prevail. But as with any skill or competency, complacency and repetitiveness tend to lead to mistakes. So be alert. A great example is the 30-year veteran airline pilot who forgot only once to properly configure the leading edge slats and trailing flaps for proper takeoff configuration. This lapse of memory and failure to adhere to procedures cost everyone on board their lives. Usually the consequences of mistakes by experienced negotiators are not as dramatic as the crash of an airliner, but they can have some devastating results. Don't get sloppy and don't believe your own press. In this case, if you believe your own propaganda, you are in deep trouble.

Options – Also known as fallbacks. Always have options. A lack of options puts a negotiator at the mercy of the person with whom they are negotiating. Leverage is greatly diminished, if not eliminated, if you do not have options. The creation of a fallback position is absolutely essential for preservation of legitimate leverage in a negotiation. Fallback positions do not have to be in-kind options. Ask, how else can I satisfy my *need*? In the case of union strike negotiations, a temporary lose-lose resolution is clearly a fallback in lieu of reaching agreement and creating a contract. Deadlock, or failure to agree or resolve an issue, is always a fallback position at the negotiators disposal. And litigation is a final option.

Other's Perceived Strengths – A great place to look for leverage in a negotiation is what we perceive as the strengths of the person with whom we are negotiating. An overdeveloped strength can actually wind up pointing to vulnerability. Take the case of any country that has tried to wage warfare in Afghanistan. The recent problems encountered by Russia and now the U.S. point to the fact that conventional metrics determining military strength are not appropriate when fighting in Afghanistan. Both the U.S. and Russia were structurally and militarily muscle bound. The conventional tactics and measures of strength are no longer valid.

Or take the case of computing technology start-up Microsoft toppling the formidable industry leader IBM. IBM was the leader in office automation and mainframe computing. Enter a disruptive technology, the PC, which changed the marketplace. IBM tried for years to play in the new space and attempted to dominate it, but exited with the sale of the PC computers to Lenovo in the PRC in 2004. IBM remains a dominant force among software providers ranking second behind Microsoft in 2013, but ahead of giants like SAP and Oracle.

Physical Presence – Some people just suck all of the oxygen out of the room. Physical stature, size, gender, culture, age and aesthetics can also impact a negotiation. Dressing up or down can change the tone of the negotiation, either to formalize it or downplay it. As a minor example, even the color of clothing can have an impact, black versus bright multi-colors. Proximity and use of your body can affect the dynamics of a negotiation. Provocative women's clothing can both demean a woman's credibility in a negotiation and simultaneously distract a male Other. Understanding body language, both its application and interpretation, can be a tremendous asset in negotiations. Make sure that you are not unconsciously sending signals or doing things that erode your power base. Consciously pay attention to how YOU affect the negotiating dynamic. Be aware of YOUR behavior and tensions that YOU may create.

Privilege – This is a critical element to consider when dealing with religion, gender identity, cultural and ethnic practices and values, social status, wealth accumulation, etc. Privilege is a form of leverage that is assumed and usually taken for granted as an entitlement or gained by being part of a majority, such as gender, ethnicity, sexual preference, health, sound mind, etc. It is not as important to assess your sources of leverage in this realm, but rather analyze where the Other does not enjoy the same privileges. Being in a majority is always a great advantage in a negotiation. Be conscious of your assumptions that everyone shares the same leverage. Be careful that you do not create relationship problems by making inane assumptions and comments about the Other's privilege.

Another form of privilege in business is being recognized as the industry leader. IBM had been recognized as the industry leader in the technology space for decades. Hence, the saying that "No one ever got fired for choosing IBM." Technology has become so segmented that IBM's leadership has diminished in computing hardware or is non-existent in Software as a Service (SaaS) applications. Still, IBM's reputation and leadership remains strong in the technology sector.

Problem Resolving/Facilitation Skills – Most great negotiations are about problem resolution versus positional brinkmanship. If you are able to focus the discussions and keep on course, you will more likely get to the end. Again, it is important to recognize that resolutions are not permanent. So the better a person is at resolving and facilitating resolutions, the more likely you are to have a resolution. Further, the more thorough and thoughtful the process of resolution is, the more durable and longer lasting the resolution will be.

Just a point of clarity, our culture has associated facilitation skills with softness. They are not. Remember a good facilitator can also be a great manipulator. They can effectively play problem solving jujitsu with the Other and manipulate them to the facilitators desired end. Beware!

Proof/Evidence/Legitimacy – This form of leverage is extremely powerful. For something to possess legitimacy it must be applied consistently, perceived as fair and accepted by those who it affects. You should always expect the Other to demonstrate skepticism during a negotiation. Use evidence anytime that you need to provide third party validity to your claims. Proof, evidence and legitimacy all come in many forms: anecdotal, technical data, research, experts, testimonials, trials, documents, price lists, survey results, awards, and the list goes on. The purpose of using this form of leverage is to move perceptions from claims to facts. Be particularly aware of using anecdotal evidence. It is usually derived from a singular experience, but is irrefutable. When confronted with this form of evidence you can always challenge the applicability of it to the current situation.

Rank or Station – Sometimes referred to as authority, generally speaking the higher the authority the easier it is to negotiate. If you are the decision maker, then you can decide. That's why when you are negotiating you should never be afraid to take on a higher authority. They generally are not into the details and minutia of the situation and more likely to want to close. It's the nature of leadership. There are downsides to authority as well, ego being one of the greatest liabilities.

One of my first corporate negotiations where I experienced how higher authority works was when two top leaders of huge chemical corporations met at an industry event at the Waldorf Astoria in Manhattan. We minions had worked on a deal for several months and we were negotiating at the sub-penny per pound level. Remember, at the volumes we were promised, pennies add up and fall to the bottom line directly. A meeting was scheduled between our poorly informed new CEO and the other company's equally ill-prepared president at this event. In a matter of two minutes they cut the deal with the following exchange; "What's it going to take to wrap this up?" The response by the Other executive was quick. Our CEO said, "Then we have a deal."

Months of tedious, precise and detailed work concluded with a simple, "Then we have a deal." Those five words gave millions of dollars away over the life of the agreement. Why and how did this happen? Ego and total authority are the twin culprits. When the president of the Other Company made his demand, in his mind our CEO had no way out, or did he? Yes he had ways out. He could have said he needed to take it to the board of directors. But he didn't. He made the deal because he could, and that's ego.

Risk Taking – This one is really straightforward; the higher tolerance that you have for risk, the more options you have and therefore the more leverage you command. The converse is true as well. The lower your risk threshold, the fewer your options and therefore the less leverage you have. The secret for the risk taker in a negotiation is to know when to fold. That attribute differentiates a professional from an amateur in both gambling and negotiations. We are always placing bets. Some people are predisposed to seek gain while others gravitate to avoiding risk.

Kahneman and Tversky uncovered an interesting spin on risk taking in their research investigating apparent anomalies and contradictions in human behavior. When offered a choice presented one way, the subjects of the experiment might display risk-aversion, but when offered essentially the same choice in a different way, they might display risk-seeking behavior. Their work demonstrated that people's attitudes toward risks concerning gains might be quite different from their attitudes toward risks concerning losses. This was exemplified by an experiment by Richard Thaler where students were told to assume they had just won $30 and were offered a coin-flip where they would win or lose $9. Surprisingly, 70 percent of the students opted for the coin-flip. When another group of students were offered $30 or a coin-flip in which they got either $21 or $39, a much smaller proportion, 43 percent, opted for the coin-flip. The same consequences were offered, but framed differently.

Some of the problems of interpreting human behavior in the face of risk have to do with the problem of people making decisions on the basis of subjective assessments of probabilities, which may be quite different from the objective, or true probabilities. Events of small probability that have never occurred before may be assessed as having a probability of zero in decision-making, but small probabilities add up when chances are taken repeatedly. Most people discount a risk with a small probability of occurrence to that of zero probability. What happens to the probability of avoiding a small risk event when the probability is increased, say doubled or even tripled? The likelihood of occurrence is now two or three times greater, but because the risk is seemingly small, it's still considered to be zero. The implication on negotiations here is to watch how risk is framed and how you frame risk when it is presented.

Viewing risk taking and risk avoidance through the lens of Atkinson's Theory of Achievement Motivation provide another perspective on risk taking. The theory posits that most people are motivated to achieve or take on a task when there is a challenge that offers a 50/50 probability of success. These people are primarily motivated by achievement. However, there is also another group that will take on tasks, projects and the like at the extremes of the probability curve. They are motivated by zero percent or 100 percent probability of failure. Why? This group is motivated to avoid, not to achieve. At zero percent chance of failure, success is assured and there is no risk. At 100 percent chance of failure, there is no risk because the task was impossible to achieve.

Strength or Power – This source of leverage is usually relegated to the realm of physical power or strength. Military power is a subset of this source. In times past, the size and technology of a country's military determined who was more powerful. If an Other was much more powerful than you, you either hoped that the Other stayed away or the Other vanquished you. In the sporting arena strength or power is usually a function of size, talent and depth. That is the physical superiority of one team versus the other, the skill level or ability of the team members relative to the other team, and the breadth and distribution of talent of one team over the other.

A lesson in military or combative strategy can be learned from combatants with inferior military power. In Vietnam, the NVA and Viet Cong changed the game from traditional battlefield tactics to guerilla warfare. They used a new type of warfare that rendered the Other's traditional power seriously compromised. Another example is when forces, independent of a country, dealt a devastating blow to the most heavily armed and powerful military in the world by highjacking commercial airliners and flying them into buildings.

Time – The greatest ally or enemy in a negotiation is time. We'll discuss more about time tactics later in the resources section of this book. Time is the great equalizer. The longer a negotiation drags out, the more information winds up in the public forum, equaling the leverage. One critically important note here is that you should always establish a deadline in your negotiations. Deadlines can always be renegotiated, but if there is no deadline, a great incentive to reach conclusion or close is absent.

```
CAUTION
```

**Quick negotiations usually have the extreme outcomes.
Good for one party, bad for the Other**

Along with establishing a deadline, always ask when is the right time to negotiate. When will I have the greatest leverage? Something that usually comes into play in a negotiation is referred to as the regret principle. It states that the value of what is received is always higher before it has been delivered. Practically speaking, you are generally in a better space to negotiate before you commit than after. Buyer's remorse is another artifact of the same sentiment.

Trust -- At the heart of any negotiation is trust. Relationship selling is built on this principle. Like having a good credit rating, if you have the trust of someone, protect it. If you have not yet earned the trust of someone, be prepared to work to earn it. If someone does not have your trust, make him or her earn it, fully. Never give trust gratuitously; make people work for the trust that you bestow on them. Sometimes trust can serve to blur the lines of true loyalties.

The Unexpected or Surprise – Surprise works because it is not predictable or anticipated and temporarily sets the Other back. It creates confusion, doubt and uncertainty. The liability associated with the unexpected only works until it is anticipated and defended against by the Other. To take advantage of the unexpected in negotiating, be consistent but not predictable. A countermeasure to the unexpected is to anticipate from the Other's point of view or perspective. That requires understanding the Other. Counterintuitive actions usually surprise people.

Value – Dr. Bradley Gale popularized Value Analysis in the 1990's. Gale states that you can plot the price-performance relationship for competitive products or service offerings and calculate a 'fair value line' that projects the theoretical performance requisite for any price. The slope of the line is indicative of the degree of commodification of the offerings in the category. The flatter the line, the more commodity-like the offering. I'd like to take his work a step further and apply the concept of value to negotiations.

NOTE

Value only exists if the perceived benefits outweigh the perceived cost. Perceived Value is anything that the Other thinks has worth. Perceived Cost is anything that the Other believes detracts or is required to achieve the perceived benefit.

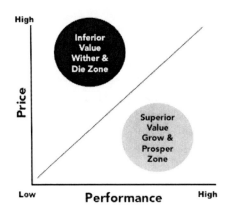

If an offering is above the Fair Value Line, it is called an inferior value. Either the performance needs to be increased, the price reduced or a combination of both to reach the fair value line. If the offering is below the line, then it is called a superior value. Depending on these relationships, the negotiator may be able to manipulate the price performance relationship to his or her advantage. This graphic is the basis of value selling. Most people can calculate the incremental value of their offering, but usually fail to extract it in a negotiation. Why? We tend to separate the selling and negotiating processes. We tend to apply different practices to each activity.

I once delivered Value Selling training globally to a major multinational corporation. During the course, we painstakingly calculated value to the tenth of a cent per unit, but when it came time to negotiate the participants made concessions in dollars freely and gratuitously. What happened? I think that most people decouple the selling process from the negotiating process. Instead of a continuum, they treat them as two separate and discrete phases. They are not. Selling deals with 'if' you will do business, and negotiating deals with 'how'. They are inextricable and happen simultaneously. If you have a superior value, you should be able to increase price but not reach the fair value line and still maintain superior value.

What do procurement people try to do with the price-performance relationship? They try to commoditize your offering and create the illusion that the slope of the fair value line is horizontal, which would mean that there is no adjustment to price regardless of performance. That's their job, and it's how they are measured. Why do they refer to your product or service category as a commodity and their role as a commodity manager? It's to lower your expectations and resistance. It's a not too subtle form of psychological warfare.

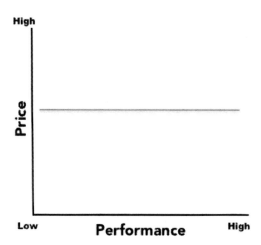

```
┌─────────────────────────────┐
│            NOTE             │
└─────────────────────────────┘
```

True commodities are rare. Look at all aspects of your offering and find something that differentiates it

As with all sources of leverage, they usually must be recognized by the Other to be actionable. In other words, we tend to allow or legitimize the Other's leverage. By our acknowledgement of the Other's leverage, we bestow that leverage on them. This is not intended to encourage delusional behavior and pretend that leverage doesn't exist, but in many cases, negotiating leverage or power resides in the mind of the person with whom we are negotiating. Said differently, my negotiating leverage is in your head and yours in mine.

Do a Reality Check

Prior to entering a negotiation, do a reality check on your perception of your assets and liabilities in this situation. Always do the same from the Other's perspective. Assessing and determining the impact on the Other's leverage balance may provide you with additional sources of leverage. Recognize that leverage is not absolute and highly dynamic. Always be ready to capitalize or to exploit your sources of leverage and to mitigate the effects of your deficits.

Put your negotiations in context by considering all the sources of leverage discussed earlier. A strong knowledge of the situation, personal skills, authority and responsibility, brand identity, time, technology, price and performance can all contribute to a stronger understanding of every negotiation. Follow this simple matrix to categorize what you know, don't know and are worried or confident about for a pending negotiation.

This tool is an adaptation of Porter's Five Forces that is intended for strategy development. I have modified it to be a team effort using Post-it notes to evaluate a negotiating situation. Blocks A, B & C can help you organize and address the forces at work in a particular negotiation. Block D asks, relative to marketplace, where this negotiation is framed in terms of buyer and seller leverage, the likelihood of an interrupting disruptive technology, the threat of substitution or being displaced by a competitive offering and the likelihood of a new supplier or competitor entering the market. These are all outside forces that can have a great influence on your negotiation, and as such they are important to keep in mind.

The Reality Check is intended to present a balanced perspective of the landscape that defines the negotiation. It works on the assumption that both sides possess both leverage and limitations. The graphical representation creates a powerful picture of reality. It is a dynamic tool and as new information is gathered, the graphic can be updated to provide the latest picture.

Reality Check

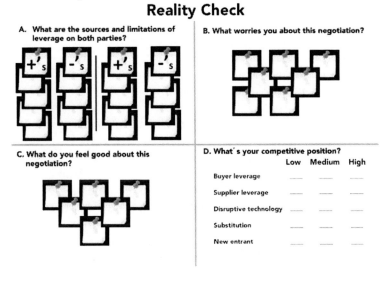

CAUTION

We tend to focus on the Other's leverage and our own limitations. Remember that there is always pressure and leverage on both sides of the equation. They are rarely in balance or totally one-sided

Hope for the Best, but Plan for the Worst

"In preparing for battle I have always found that plans are useless, but planning is indispensable"

- General Dwight D. Eisenhower

CAUTION

Avoid <u>thinking</u> something will never occur! Things always change

So is hoping for the best results a bad practice? Yes, if you do not anticipate and plan for the worst outcome as well. This practice is easier said than done. How do you hope for the best, but plan and anticipate the worst? You almost have to become an optimistic pessimist. Isn't that a contradiction in terms, an oxymoron? I call this optimist/pessimist duality a pragmatist. You should optimistically set hopes and goals, but then apply a good dose of pessimism through a fairly rigorous reality check and look at the forces at play on the negotiation. Porter's Five Forces coupled with the job aid called the "Planner" in Resource I of this book will provide a solid foundation to assess the viability of your target or goal for the negotiation. Once your goal or target for the negotiation is established, then we need to do a comprehensive 'what if'. Assess your target regarding the potential problems that may occur, the likelihood of occurrence and the impact on the result if it occurs. Then create mitigating actions should the problems occur.

CAUTION

Spend your time appropriately by creating actions for highly probable situations that can have the highest impact on your goal or target. Those of lower probability or consequence may be considered acceptable risks

Use the Planner

CAUTION

It's a lot easier to ride the horse when you're facing the direction that it's going

The Planner is a comprehensive guide for executing a negotiation. You will find it in the Resource Section of this book. Use your judgment to determine the extent of the planning investment that you want to make. The two key criteria should be the stakes at risk and the familiarity with the terrain. By terrain, I mean the people, their culture, gender, generation, and cognitive preferences involved in the negotiation. Feel free to duplicate the Planner as many times as you want in order to plan for a negotiation. Much of what's contained in the Planner has been and will be discussed already. The Planner is relatively self-explanatory, so I will not belabor the need for planning further. But I would like to reemphasize the part of the planning process that historically is skipped: people.

Referring to Principle I – **People Are Different**, we have explored several factors that influence negotiating style and skills. They are cross-cultural, cross-generational and gender considerations in addition to our individual hard wiring and cognitive preferences. If not dealt with properly or if the negotiator is unconscious of these forces, the factor and differences can have a detrimental effect on the outcome and success of a negotiation. However, if appropriately managed, these factors can have a tremendous positive effect on the process. In a nutshell, it is critically important to understand both the music and the movement of the culture, generation, gender and cognitive preferences of the Other with who you are about to negotiate. If you do not, instead of dancing to music, you will be generating a lot of noise. Depending upon the importance of the negotiation, appropriate time and effort should be allocated to the understanding of these factors.

This mélange of culture, capability, skill, knowledge, experience, ethnicity, religion, creed, tribe, sexuality and beliefs causes human being to be relatively unique, like snowflakes. The closer these collective attributes are, the higher the similarity of the people involved; the more variation, the more dissimilar. This is all true save the fact that the more we can understand and appreciate our mutual differences, the more we can discover common ground and build more durable resolutions. Please note that race was omitted from the list of differences. Race is an arbitrary artifact created by people attempting to collectivize themselves and others into somewhat all-inclusive groups for exploitation. Scientist will tell you that there is no delineation of race beyond human. I offer Hitler's Nazi Germany as testimony of the manipulation of race. We use this misconstrued concept of race as a short-hand to assign attributes to a collective, thus creating an easy to understand stereotype that, in reality, may not exist.

Chapter Six: Best Practices During Negotiations

Ask for More

Always ask for more than what you are willing to take. Leave yourself room to negotiate. Room gives you latitude to maneuver. It allows the Other to realize their expectations and feel as if they have also won. It provides space so that you can test and determine reality. Lets approach the idea of 'asking for more' by examining where the big mistakes are made in negotiating.

Another reason to ask for more is that people generally discount your requests. The way the principle works in opinion research is like this, I ask you to modestly change your opinion about a topic. Most people would adjust their opinion somewhat, but rarely do they accept the entire shift. There is an innate discount factor applied. Researchers say that the greater the request for shift, the more willingly people accept change. This holds true until the demand is viewed as outrageous, manipulative or ridiculous. Once that point is breeched, then credibility is out the window. So again, set your sights on being near but not exceeding the absurd or the ridiculous. The trick is that you're dealing with people, and people have differing views of where that point resides. Spend time anticipating where the point of the absurdity in an opening offer might be for the person with whom you will be negotiating.

Where do people screw up in a negotiation? There is no one place or one reason, but in my experience I have observed four extremely sensitive times where mistakes often occur. They happen when we are setting our own expectations for the outcome of a negotiation, when we make our initial offers to buy and sell, when we make mistakes during the course of the dialogue by saying something without thinking and, finally, at the end when internal and external pressures to close get very heavy and hard bargaining takes place.

WARNING

Be careful what you ask for, you just might get it

Expectation Setting – As previously discussed, our expectations are largely driven by our perceptions. Expectations are highly susceptible to the "Pygmalion Effect", that is they tend to become a self-fulfilling prophecy. To most of us, our perceptions are a combination of facts, beliefs, biases, intuition, experiences, and gut feelings. Expectation setting in a negotiation should not be approached in a cavalier, fly-by-the-seat-of-your-pants way. To short circuit this opportunity to screw up, always:
- Determine what your expectations are. What are the best, worst and mostly likely outcomes, and why? Plan your fallback position.
- Project what you think the expectations of the Other party might be. What are the best, worst and mostly likely outcomes for them, and why do you think that's the case? What do you anticipate the Other's fallback to be?
- Plan the questions you will ask as a test to confirm or refute these assumed expectations.

Opening Offers – Be painfully aware that your initial offer defines the top or bottom of the negotiating space. Be deliberate and leave room to negotiate. Why? Because most rational people expect a degree of give and take in the dance that is negotiating. Also, you really do not know where the Other party's expectations reside. Be prepared to give a rationale for your opening offers and legitimize the offer with evidence whenever possible. Make the Other work to get a concession from the opener. Never make a gratuitous concession; it confuses people.

The consequences of having an opening offer that leaves you room to negotiate but exceeds the Other party's expectations of the desired outcome can be devastating to you in the results of a negotiation. Be careful; like first impressions, you only get one chance to make an opening offer. If it's wrong, you are propelled into the damage control mode.

Mistakes or Screw Ups – A glib comment, an information leak, an errant document, the Other party's conversation with a 'non-negotiator' in your organization, a miscalculation, a wrong assumption and a whole host of other unanticipated occurrences can have a huge effect on a negotiated outcome. In the best case, they will put you on the defensive. The remedy is prevention. Planning and control is key. Control access to information, your organization and higher authority.

Heavy Pressure/Hard Bargaining – The unwarranted drive for closure can lead to huge mistakes in a negotiation. Referring back to the cognitive preferences section, this trait may be typically exemplified by those who are MBTI J's (Judgmental). Their propensity to get things completed makes them vulnerable to being exploited when heavy pressure is applied. Making massive concessions or divulging proprietary information is usually done at the very end of a negotiation when the heat of the battle replaces the calm and cool. Here's some free advice: if you are near the end and things are becoming confused for you or happening too rapidly, call a time out and regroup. I attended a seminar on negotiating led by Dr. Karrass many years ago. He related a story about a bachelor friend, who when in the crisis phase of a personal negotiation, always said that needed to check with his wife before committing. No one ever asked if he was married. It is a way to regroup and recalibrate. Plan your 'outs' in advance.

Avoid The Law of Holes

"No man has a good enough memory to be a successful liar."

– Abraham Lincoln

I am not attempting to be a moralist in this section, but rather a pragmatist and a provocateur. Lying is part of the burden of being human that most of us carry. Some shoulder more than others. I'm not going to argue the right or wrong of the practice, but simply ask you to consider the consequences of lying or always telling the truth. As Winston Churchill once said, "In wartime, truth is so precious that she should always be attended by a bodyguard of lies." Some of us treat every situation as a battle, while others do not.

History does not support the fact that Honest Abe was always totally honest. He must have dipped into the lie cookie jar a time or two. As an example, the great emancipator was striving for equality for blacks. But Lincoln did not believe that free blacks or former slaves could successfully be assimilated into American white society. His first preference was to relocate the former slaves to colonies in South America. As it turned out, the Emancipation Proclamation was a political and power tactic that he used in the U. S. Civil War aimed directly at the Confederacy. Lying is sometimes politically and practically expedient. I contend that without lies, politicians would usually wind up abysmal failures.

As proof, I offer Jimmy Carter, the 39th President of the U. S., who was arguably the most truthful and honest man to serve as president in modern history. He brokered peace in the Middle East and characterized the energy crisis we are currently dealing with as a problem that required action. He made the following pronouncement that he honored throughout his presidency and probably his life, "I'll never tell a lie. I'll never make a misleading statement. I'll never betray the confidence that any of you had in me. And I'll never avoid a controversial issue." He was smart, honest, direct and a nice guy. But domestically, he was a bust as a president.

"The victor will never be asked if he told the truth."

- Adolf Hitler

Sometimes it takes a tough guy or gal to get things done. This is true in life as well as politics. Total honesty can be as fatal a flaw as having no credibility. I have a friend who categorizes people by percentage of believability in what they say. If he viewed you as totally credible he would refer to you as a '100-percenter', no credibility was a 'zero-percenter'. During my association with him he never awarded either extreme score, but he clearly had people in different places on the scale. Everyone who can is doing it or has done it. It's a matter of degree. You should always assess the consequences of telling or not telling a lie. If you do consciously choose to tell one avoid getting caught in it, and if you do get caught go into damage control mode to minimize the negative impact and ensure that it does not become the cause of your undoing.

"The great enemy of the truth is very often not the lie, deliberate, contrived and dishonest, but the myth, persistent, persuasive and unrealistic."

- John F. Kennedy
-

Always observe the First Law of Holes. That is, if you find yourself in one, caused by being exposed in a lie, stop digging. The best way to observe this simple practice is to avoid starting to dig a hole. The hole is a metaphor for saying something that paints you into a corner. If we are to avoid these holes, then we need to understand what causes them. The simplest practice is to keep communications with the Other clear and concise. Failing that, there are many holes that we can fall into; getting caught in an outright lie, over exaggeration, over promising, stupid comments, going off into stream of consciousness monologue, talking too much and, my personal favorite, jamming the airwaves. Let's take a look at each of these pitfalls and develop interventions to keep the hole from becoming a black hole, which is a region of space where gravity prevents anything, including light, from escaping. After a black hole has formed, it can continue to grow by absorbing mass from its surroundings. In other words, being in a black hole literally sucks.

This is the best advice for getting out of any of the aforementioned holes:
- *Getting caught in an outright lie* is probably the worst-case scenario. If this happens to you, apologize, admit that you may have misspoke, and attempt to move on. As Ricky Riccardo immortally said, "When you're splainin, your losin." Change the topic, go in a different direction and move on.
- *Over exaggeration* – admit that you might have misspoken and move on.
- *Over promising* – admit that you might have misspoken and move on.
- *Stupid comments* – apologize for being glib or not thoughtful and move on.
- *Going off into stream of consciousness monologue* – avoid the stream of consciousness diatribe at all costs. You are paying for the shovel that eventually will bury you.
- *Jamming the airwaves* – shut up!!

How to Stop Digging When You Find Yourself In One

When you have been outted, for God sake, stop digging. You are no longer in recovery mode, but dealing with damage control. Realize that the chances of you digging yourself out by talking are slim to non-existent. Recognize that continued digging will only worsen the situation. Apologize, admit you may have misspoken or have been misunderstood, change the subject using verbal jujitsu or just shut up.

WARNING

When you find yourself in a hole, stop digging. If you don't, it may be indicative of an impending disaster

Don't Rush

No matter how much urgency there may be for you to close a deal, never portray that urgency to the Other. Time is your greatest ally in a negotiation, but it can also be your biggest enemy. It generates one of the highest sources of leverage in a negotiation. Time is the great equalizer. The longer a negotiation drags out, the more information winds up in the public forum. The greater the urgency, the less information is exchanged. The rush for closure results in fast or quick negotiations. However, the longer a negotiation drags on, the less likely an agreement will be reached.

The key characteristic of these fast negotiations is the extremes of the outcome. As part of my negotiating curriculum I have conducted hundreds of negotiation simulations over the years. One fact that continues to be evident in these simulations is that extreme outcomes are a product of one of the participants rushing to closure. If you are not the party with the greatest knowledge, don't rush. Rushing also signals urgency. Urgency signals a need to resolve regardless of cost. This behavior is usually symptomatic of the Other feeling pressure to close and that their needs or problems are without any other resolution options.

*"**Never interrupt your enemy when he is making a mistake**."*

- Napoleon Bonaparte

The preceding quote provides solid guidance on quick negotiations. However, even if the Other is making a devastating mistake in the negotiation, closing too eagerly or too quickly may send a signal that warns them that something is amiss. Quick acceptance of an offer mistakenly may make the Other think that they screwed up. The best practice in the face of receiving an offer that you cannot refuse is not to jump at it, stretch it out, let the Other gain a small concession from you, or ask for more, not a lot, but a little more.

*"**Positive thinking will let you do everything better than negative thinking will**."*

- Zig Ziglar

It's not the situation that causes stress; it's people's reaction to the situation. People have different tolerances and reactions to situations. Reactions to stress can manifest themselves in urgency, panic or withdrawal. If this sense of urgency is obvious to the Other in a negotiation, it can kill your bargaining power. Negotiating under duress can be suicidal. If you feel like you must make the deal urgently without options, then you render yourself powerless. Unless you can control yourself and not disclose what is really driving you to negotiate now, you put yourself at the mercy of the Other. You may know that there is pressure for you to deal, but you don't have to share that with anyone else. Never let them see you sweat, simply means keep the pressures that are driving you to yourself. Remain calm, cool and collected in the face of adverse circumstances.

WARNING

Telegraphing, displaying or communicating your stressors in a negotiation will place you at a significant disadvantage and may led to catastrophic results

Set yourself up for success by mentally preparing as if you are entering the field of battle. Anticipate questions that the Other might ask to try to reveal needs, urgencies or anxieties that you might have to answer. Plan and rehearse your responses. If you don't have someone to practice the responses with, prepare mentally. It is better to have thought through your responses than making stuff up as you go. It's important to make your responses brief and succinct. Don't offer too much information, because it will signal that there is more to the story to be uncovered and encourage further probing. Be especially aware of the use of silence by the Other.

Try to control the field of play. If you cannot, minimize the impact of pressures on you to negotiate. It's important to note that pressures are likely to be discovered in a non-negotiating forum; over lunch, in emails, at social gatherings or on the golf course. If these pressures are discovered they shift the balance of power to the Other person. The earlier that they are discovered the more power can be exploited.

On the other side of the coin, always try to understand what is making the Other sweat. What pressures are driving the Other to be negotiating at this moment? There is always a reason why the Other is talking with you at a particular time. Always ask yourself, what pain are they feeling or what is keeping them from reaching a goal? Pain is a situation that people want to change, mitigate or eliminate completely. Real pain always has a cost associated with it, either monetary, emotional, gain or relationship. Think of pain as dissatisfaction with the present situation. The more pain, the more sweat. Once you quantify and qualify the pain, you can calculate the leverage or bargaining power you have in the negotiation. If the total cost of pain exceeds a threshold greater than the cost required to remediate it, then the Other will generally take action. If it does not exceed that threshold, then nothing will happen.

Whenever possible, negotiate proactively rather than reactively. This strategy affords you time, and time can always be used as leverage. On the flip side, it's always more advantageous to negotiate with someone who has pressure on them, as that pressure is a form of pain. Pressure drives closure. Without pressure, negotiations could last forever. Diplomatic negotiations have taught us tremendous lessons about this important element of negotiation. The Vietnam peace talks and the never-ending Palestinian/Israeli discussions are two examples of heavily one-sided pressure. In the case of Vietnam, the pressures throughout the United States to end the war were played out in the media. National evening news generally started off with the daily American body count. The frustration with the war spread from college campuses to the streets. On the then North Vietnamese side, there was no pressure or urgency to end the war, despite casualties that were at least two orders of magnitude greater than the Americans.

Remember, "Never Let Them See You Sweat." Don't share the pressures that are driving you. Remain calm, cool and collected in the face of adverse circumstances. Never show the chinks in your armor. Bring the conversation back to the commercial realm, always remember that the buyer has to buy and the seller has to sell. There is always pressure on both sides; it's a matter of degree. Don't tip off yours.

Sometimes negotiation can be a form of combat. There are survivors, and there are casualties. We refer to the casualties as losers and the survivors as winners. The casualties, however, may be walking wounded in that they might not realize that they've been compromised, like returning soldiers with PTSD (Post Traumatic Stress Disorder). Their wounds are discovered well after the actual combat. So too in negotiations, many participants in the process come to find or believe they got screwed well after the deal was done. This builds resentment, distrust, animosity and often retribution.

Test

**Trust nothing and no one in a negotiation.
Test everyone and everything, most of all,
your own assumptions and expectations**

I once had a friend who, when making any new acquaintance with a potential of being more than that, would test the new acquaintance's ability to keep confidences. She would share a piece of relatively trivial but interesting information about herself with the new person and ask him or her to keep it in confidence. Sometimes the information was true, other times it was fabricated. If the information came back to her, she knew that the new acquaintance was not trustworthy and would treat them as such. If the shared information did not enter the public forum, she began to trust the person and the relationship had potential.

What my friend did was to test before trusting. We tend to either implicitly trust or be suspicious. If you trust implicitly, then more often than not you are setting yourself up for disappointment and betrayal. Don't blame the perpetrator; blame yourself because you are the one who blindly trusted. The Confidence Game is built on a foundation of trust. Don't allow yourself to be the victim. Accept little to nothing at face value. Test the integrity, information, claims and intent of people with whom you deal. Pay particular attention to those with whom you have little to no experience. Though being suspicious of everything and everyone has its issues as well, including becoming paranoid, it is the only way to be sure of a person's trustworthiness. Most of all don't trust your own perceptions, expectations and assumptions. Apply the same rigor to them as you would with a new acquaintance.

Separating Fact from Myth: In The Absence of Facts, People Invent Them. What's the difference between a fact and a myth? A fact is something that you believe has proof backing it up. A myth is something that you no longer believe to be true. People have great difficulty separating what they believe from certifiable facts. Further, much of who we are is grounded in belief supported by what we think and not what we know. So is it any wonder that people draw upon their belief systems and extrapolate facts? Is this lying? Is it dishonest?

Some people lie, others don't. When someone converts what he or she thinks into a fact and that fact is not true, it is perceived as a lie to the person who receives the information. Dishonesty is a matter of intent. If I am purposely trying to deceive you, then I'm being dishonest. How about if I make a mistake that causes someone to have the wrong information? Again, intent is the measure. Intent is not something that is readily apparent or easily measureable to the Other. Since intent is not transparent then any information offered that is not true can be considered a lie by the Other.

CAUTION

Regardless of the intent, if information that is offered is not factual, the effect is the same. It erodes trust and integrity

Shut Up

"It's very important in life to know when to shut up. You should not be afraid of silence."

- Alex Trebek

This is sage advice from the long time host of TV's Jeopardy, Alex Trebek. Sales people tend to think that their job is to convince and persuade by talking. Most sales professionals have been traditionally selected because of good social skills and a 'salesy' personality. But when you are talking, you are not listening. When you are talking you are giving information, not getting it.

WARNING

When in doubt - shut up

This problem is exacerbated by the fact that we tend to think that selling and negotiating are separate and discrete activities. Most sales processes have several phases to them. One of those phases is usually called negotiating or hard bargaining. It is as if we miraculously transition from selling to negotiating, when in reality it just doesn't happen that way. Again, selling determines if you are going to do business, and negotiating determines how the business will be done. They happen simultaneously and are inextricably connected.

Most communications experts state that to engage in truly meaningful dialogue, the conversation should be balanced. Most negotiations are not intended to engage in meaningful dialogue. These negotiations are about give and take, or trade offs. If you are giving, the Other is taking. The negotiator must be able to discern and validate the strategy of the Other and act accordingly. If the game is positional, then you're playing win-lose. Create a vacuum of silence and be comfortable with it. This is a practice and it will pay dividends quickly.

It has been said that it is far better to be interested than interesting. Yet most of us gravitate to being interesting. How does someone become interesting, by being charming, charismatic, dynamic and entertaining? All of these descriptors share at least one common attribute: being persuasive, selling yourself. Salespeople generally think of themselves as people-people. They are usually likeable, have good personalities and can carry a conversation. These attributes predispose them to talk a lot, giving away potentially critical information and intelligence. Be very careful.

What's Your Hard Wiring: Fight, Flight or Freeze
Regrettably, whether innate or learned, we all have a default response to things that catch us by surprise like being caught in a lie, half-truth or misstatement. Because of our reptilian brain, we tend either to resort to fight, flight or freeze. In the heat of the battle we must control our natural response to unexpected stimuli and replace the knee jerk reaction with a cool, calm, thoughtful, measured and effective response.

1. *If your base response is fight,* to dig your heals in and start swinging, your tendency is to talk your way out of a situation. Sometimes this leads to going on the attack. This was my dad's default. Dumb strategy! Unless you're dealing with someone with a sub par IQ, recognize that you've been busted. Apologize, clarify and move on.
2. *If your base response is flight*, and you do not engage but run away, then running away will not help. You will only play into the fact that whatever you did was smarmy. Trust has been breached, so suck it up and apologize, clarify and move on.
3. *If your base response is to freeze*, the deer in headlights syndrome, get control of yourself. Although he didn't intentionally

lie, Uncle Nick defaulted to this behavior when he got caught by one of his exaggerations. Your inability to respond due to your frozen state will ultimately paint you as culpable. Thaw out and apologize, clarify and move on.

Suck it up, think rationally, deal with your natural responses and mitigate the damage caused by falling in the hole. Apologize for any confusion that you might have caused, clarify your position and move on.

Get Commitments

What's your reaction to this statement; "People don't appreciate what they don't work for." Most people I have spoken with agree with the statement. So what are the implications to the negotiating process? The bedrock of the issue is commitment. In negotiation, mutual commitment is absolutely essential. Unilateral commitment is a death spiral. If selling determines 'if' you're going to do business and negotiating determines 'how' we will do business, when should you start building commitments?

WARNING

If you're making unilateral commitments, the deal is either dead or you are in a very weak position

Time after time, I have witnessed that salespeople are inclined to push, not pull. What tends to happen is that in the selling mode salespeople take on the responsibility for all commitments without reciprocity from the Other party. I'll send you X; I'll follow up; I'll do X; etc., with little to no commitment from the Other. Like sales, negotiated agreements don't happen in a step-function fashion. They are built incrementally, step-by-step. If small, mutual commitments are not solicited along the process, then the likelihood of reaching agreement in a Big Bang way is just hoping for the best.

Commitment throughout the selling and negotiating processes should be mutual, specific and increase as the process develops. If it is not, it should serve as an indicator that the deals may be in jeopardy. Ironically, many people fear asking for a commitment because of fear of rejection, which would signal the deal is in jeopardy, or fear of damaging the relationship. The factors of gain and relationship play out here.

Discovering the Pain

Buying and selling always involves motivating someone to change. Why should people change anything? Is it because it is fashionable, and the thing to do? No! There are two conditions necessary for change to occur. There must be either an intolerable dissatisfaction with the present situation that has exceeded a threshold (pain), or a need for something different to reach a goal or achieve a particular end. In both cases, the value garnered by the change must exceed the real and emotional costs of making the change. You must satisfy the conditions; the benefit of the change must exceed the cost of changing or the discovery of the pain that keeps them from reaching their objective must be transformed into a business issue with monetary consequences to make change happen.

Perception plays into the equation because benefits are anything that is perceived to have value and costs are anything that is perceived to detract from the value of the change. The lens that must be used is the perspective of the person you are dealing with, the Other, not yours. Discovering pain is not a trivial task. If trust and rapport between parties is relatively high and the stakes of the game are relatively low, then the discovery process can be easier. The converse is also true. Expect that the pain, benefits and cost will not be obvious, but obfuscated. The key to unearthing the real pain, impediments to goal recognition, perceived benefits and costs are through skillful questioning techniques and a sound questioning strategy.

Triangulate to Validate

Triangulation is a navigation term that uses multiple sources to determine where you are, to establish a fix on location. Applying that concept to the process of negotiation can triangulate where we are in the process. The following is intended to provide some additional insights into how to gain and test the validity of the information about the Other.

One way of triangulating is what I call the lawyer approach. Ask the same question multiple ways to see if there is any deviation in the answer. If there is a change, the lawyer dives deeper and surfaces the issue, and backs someone into a corner to make his or her point. This approach can yield some great information, but be careful. Continually asking the Other the same question multiple ways can seem like an interrogation, which may produce some information gain but might damage the relationship and erode trust. In business, good questioning technique is an art form. Unlike in the courtroom, in negotiations the Other is not obliged to answer every question. Negotiators' questions are not usually binary or close ended to make a point. In negotiations you should always validate your information. Asking multiple versions of the same question is a viable option, but use it sparingly and not in an obvious way. So what are some other options to gain or test information to determine its validity and worth?

Penetrating an organization by finding non-negotiators who are willing to share information and advocates who further your position are two excellent sources of triangulation. Procurement professions tend to limit access to their organizations to prevent this triangulation activity from occurring. They purposely limit the access to persons who might unwittingly divulge or corroborate information that can erode their leverage and weaken their negotiating position. Great sources of information and validation in the Other's organization are; technology, operations, administrative, sales and marketing. The time to foster relationships with these functions and people is *before* a negotiation. Sales have long been taught to penetrate an organization in depth. When procurement discourages or forbids this practice, the best policy is to ask for forgiveness, not permission.

Competitors, user groups, trade associations and the Internet are potentially rich sources of information about the Other. These sources are usually full of rumors and speculation, but there is always bit a truth in rumors. The grapevine in most organizations is still viewed by employees as the most reliable source of information. There are always leaks in organizations; find the source and you've hit the jackpot.

A final word of caution; playing dumb is a good strategy if you're an actor playing a detective on television. Taken to an extreme, it can greatly diminish ones credibility and value as a negotiator. There is a fine line between practicing humility by deferring to the Other and playing dumb.

Ask Great Questions: They're Powerful

WARNING

Carefully planned, thoughtful and efficient questioning can provide rich information, while building trust and rapport. Random, hostile and ineffective questioning usually kills a deal

During a class on reviewing the fundamentals of selling, there is an exercise requiring the participants to gather information. The questioner is assigned the duty of asking only open-ended questions. If he or she asks an open-ended question, then the respondent answers with strategic information. If closed questions are used, then the respondent must only answer yes or no. For example, all of us have had this or a similar experience where the person on the other end of the phone will ask, "Can you spell that?" For me this usually is about my last name. Most people would spell their name. What the person on the other end has just done was to ask a closed question. The appropriate answer to their question is either yes or no. Because I view this type of interaction as sport my answer is usually "yes." If I'm in a really snippy mood, I might respond with T-H-A-T.

A skilled negotiator needs to be mindful of what questions are asked, and provide only the information requested. Back to the exercise--this course was a review of selling fundamentals with an assignment of getting information by using open-ended questions. I personally observed a very experienced sales person ask 13 closed questions in a row and not recognize it. Why did this happen? The answer lies in the phone conversation example. The vast majority of people would spell their name when asked, "Can you spell that?" Thereby providing much more information than was actually requested. The power of the question is incredible, both from a asking and answering perspective. Great lawyers and reporters build their reputations and track records based on their command of questioning technique. Most people totally undervalue the power of the question.

Another critically important skill is to ask questions in a way that does not upset the Other, but invites them to divulge information. Let me illustrate. I have been a loyal Apple user forever. I had one of the first Mac cubes. I toted around a 16 pound Mac-luggable, and currently have a few MacBook Pros, iPads, iPhones and iMacs and a Mac Pro. One of my Magic Mice, which is a Bluetooth wireless mouse, stopped working. I brought it to the Apple Store to have it checked out. I explained the problem to a Genius and he looked at me and asked, "you know that they need batteries?" After I recomposed myself and put the spring back into my neck, I said, "Really, I thought that they were solar powered." That exchange caused me to question my loyalty to Apple. I'm sure that the Geniuses get lots of dumb questions and descriptions of problems, but his question really upset me. If he were what he claims to be, he might have asked the question like this; "How fresh are the batteries?" He would have found out that I wasn't born yesterday and I knew the device used two AA alkaline batteries to power it and were at 100 percent power. Before you ask a question, make sure that it's not going to trigger a negative response by the Other. That is, unless you intentionally want to trigger one. The secret is in the practice of the fundamentals, so let's quickly review:

WARNING

How you ask the question is more important than what you ask

Open-ended questions allow for a wide range of responses. Their purpose is to excavate information that is not known or unclear to the questioner. They're good for openers and exploration. The technique can also be use to triangulate or confirm information. They start with:
- Why?
- What?
- How?
- When?
- Tell me more...
- Oh?

Closed-ended questions limit a range of potential responses. They are used to confirm and obtain specific, factual/tactical information. They sound like:
- Who?
- How many?
- How much?
- Which?
- Where?
- "Is, Can, Will ... ?" All leading to yes/no answers

WARNING

Be careful not to ask too many closed ended questions. It will come across as an interrogation

Test and summarize with closed-ended clarifications:
- "So, your position is..."
- "Let me see if I understand your position..."
- "What I hear you saying is..."

Conditional questions are great because they automatically put a string or condition associated with a potential, but uncommitted concession. They sound like:

- "What would your position be if we could...?"
- "If we offered *this*, could you offer *that*?"
- "If you were to offer *this*, what would you need in return?"
- "Under what conditions could you accept *this*?"

Provocative questions generally yield a superior quality of information. They generate higher value information than a simple open-ended question because they involve the person being questioned and draw on their personal perspective. It legitimizes them as a person and causes them to reflect on the answer. They also provide context for the question since they are being asked to analyze, speculate or express a personal point of view. Here are a few examples:

"What are the alternative solutions that you see to
   this particular issue?"– ***Analysis***

"What do you think would happen if we are unable to
   agree to *this*?" – ***Speculation***

" Why do you think *this* is important to your company?"
   Personal Opinion

Answer a Question with a Question. A great tactic to turn the tables is to answer a question with a question. This questioning tactic should be used strategically and sparingly, since it can be viewed as gamesmanship and a way of avoiding. When you answer a question with a question, it usually catches the Other off guard so that the response may yield critical information. As an example, let's flip a provocative question by answering it with a question.

Question:
"What do you think would happen if we are unable to agree to *this*?"

Response:
"Why is that important?"

or
"Why do you ask?"

Four Powerful Questions – I have found that these questions, when asked appropriately at a strategic moment in the negotiation, cut directly to the heart of the matter. They stay in the problem space and focus on needs. As in all probing, plan your questions to get the maximum bang.

- "What do you see as the <u>problem or issue</u>?"
- "What exactly do you <u>need</u> me to do?"
- "<u>Why</u> (is that important)?"
- "How exactly does that <u>work</u>?" Or, "What would that <u>look</u> like?"

A Questioning Strategy – This answers the question, what are you trying to achieve? Are you trying to build rapport and trust, explore pain, needs and impediments, explore consequences and payoffs or explore options? Or are you simply on a fishing expedition? Your questions should be designed to follow that strategy. Without a question strategy, your questions will seem random, unfocused and could be irritating.

If relationship and gain are the currencies of negotiation, then information is the fuel that powers it. As a general principle, the party with the most information has the most power. A questioning strategy deals with ways of getting more and better quality information. It also allows the practitioner to give and use that information both strategically and tactically.

Rules for Answering Questions – Observe these rules when being asked questions:
- Someone can ask any question of you that they want, but you are not obligated to answer it. Countermeasures that you can use are to feign ignorance; say that something is proprietary or that you don't have the authority to divulge that information.
- In a high stakes, positional negotiation, be very conscious of the speed, tone and the manner that you answer any question. The best practice is to be very deliberate and thoughtful when

answering any question, no matter how trivial, and respond in a flat, slow, non-emotional tone.

Get Information

If you don't ask for it, you won't get it

"The truth is so precious that a bodyguard of lie must surround it"

-- Winston Churchill

What Information -- As highlighted earlier, contrary to definitions of the phases by most popular sales processes, like Sandler, Miller Heiman, et al, selling and negotiating are not two separate activities or phases of doing business. They are on a seamless continuum and are inextricably linked. If something happens in one of the phases of the selling process, it affects it and carries over to the subsequent phase. When we are selling we are in the mode of persuading, which most sales people consider synonymous with convincing by telling. The graphic below can be used to start the process of understanding and using information from a strategic perspective. Always assess what information is known and unknown by each party.

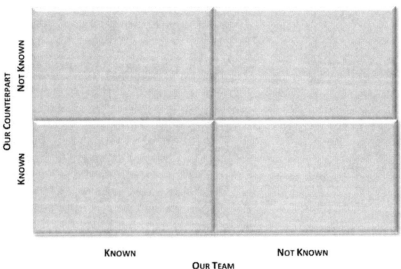

In both selling and negotiating, there is always give and take of information. The question is, which information do you give and which information do you keep from the Other, while gaining information from them? The following are some definitions that will assist in categorizing information as to its strategic importance.

Definitions:

Confidential – Information that is not shared under any circumstances.

Sensitive – Information that can be shared with extreme caution and under duress in return for valuable information from the Other.

Advancing – Information that can be shared to advance the relationship in return for information from the Other, if needed.

Conversation – Information that can be shared readily, which has no bearing on the negotiation.

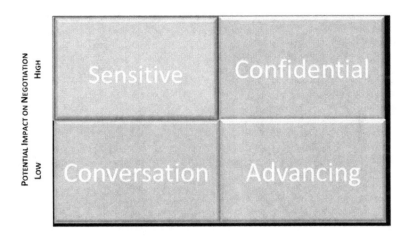

High/Medium   Low/No
Degree of Latitude to Share Information

Once you assess the strategic value of your information, think of it as intellectual capital. Then put yourself in the Other's place and assess their intelligence by categorizing the information that they possess. The secret of information trading in a negotiation is to get higher value information in return for information with lower value to you. If you are dealing with a skilled negotiator, expect the same information trading strategy from them. Again, mastery of questioning skills will separate winners from losers in this practice.

Watch Carefully

"Beware of the naked man who offers you his shirt."

-- Navjot Singh Sidhu

Listen to the music, but always watch the dance. By analogy, the music and lyrics are symbolic of what's communicated in a negotiation. The dance is the expression of behavior. More often than not, the music and lyrics don't sync with the behavior or the dance. Words can be rehearsed and measured, but some reactions can be involuntary. If they are not in sync, which should you believe?

Based upon Malcolm Gladwell's book *Blink*, the answer may lie in what follows. John Gottman is a psychologist at the University of Washington. His research deals with how behavior, both oral and physical, is predictive of marital health. Gottman has been running the same experiment since 1980. After rigorously analyzing a 15-minute conversation, he and his staff are able to predict with 95% accuracy which couples will be together 15 years later.

Couples come to Gottman's laboratory and are hooked into a sophisticated sensing system that measures all sorts of voluntary and involuntary body responses. They are videotaped with particular attention to the facial area. Then they are asked to talk about anything that is a point of contention in their marriage for 15 minutes.

The data and video are analyzed, coded and scored. In negotiations, we don't wire or videotape the Others to gather data about their emotions during the negotiation. What Gottman's work proves is that the majority of signals we send telegraph our true feelings. These messages are both voluntary and involuntary. Things we can and cannot control.

Gottman and his team used a repeatable, tested algorithm to code and score words and behaviors. The police, CIA, FBI and other law enforcement agencies have techniques as well. Regrettably, we as negotiators are not armed with these capabilities. Wouldn't it be great if we could determine if someone were lying simply through observation? What we *can* do in a negotiation is to be very observant of verbal and non-verbal communications. If there is a 'disconnect' between the words and the body language, it is an invitation to test why there is one.

The Resource section of this book will deal with tactics and countermeasures that are frequently used in the negotiating arena. Tactics are words that are intended to elicit a desired response. Our work as negotiators is to understand the motive, strategy or why the tactic or behavior is being employed. What is going on behind the apparent words and gestures? Why are they saying and doing these things? What are they hoping to achieve? Behind every effective tactic there is a strategic reason for its use. Once we understand the reason, we can respond appropriately.

Send A Coherent Opening Message

Your opening offers set the floor and the ceiling of the negotiation. Be extremely careful what you commit to and ask for in the beginning of the negotiation. If you have a list price or any other form of legitimacy, use that as your opening offer. If your offering is a superior value, always ask for significantly more than where you expect to settle.

WARNING

Your opening offers set the floor and the ceiling of the negotiation. Be extremely careful what you say in the early stages. Like a first impression, there aren't any Mulligans or do-overs

Starting high or low should not be gratuitous or approached in a cavalier fashion. Crafting a message that explains or provides rationale is an absolute imperative to maintaining your credibility and building your case. Later on, we'll discuss The Company Song. Repeating that message multiple times in a variety of ways must support the message you craft. The big question is what do you want the Other to hear, understand and internalize. That message needs to be positioned early and repeated frequently and consistently.

Recognize Tactics and Respond Appropriately

"Sometimes a cigar is just a cigar."

- Sigmund Freud

Tactics and countermeasures make up the music that energizes the dance of negotiation. No work on negotiations would be complete without a brief discussion of three categories of tactics and their paired counter-measures. The tactic is designed to create a particular response, and the counter-measure is designed to neutralize the effects of the tactic. The categories we will discuss are; time, pressure, illusion and authority. They are Illusion tactics – used to disguise and to confuse the situation. They tend to create illusions and false reality.

$$\boxed{\text{NOTE}}$$

Sometimes a statement or question is just a statement or question, but most of the time it is intended to elicit a particular response or tactical maneuver

Tactics and countermeasures are largely in the domain of horse trading, bargaining, and give and take. However, all competent negotiators must have a strong command of them to be able to recognize them when used and respond to and neutralize or minimize their impact. It's the language of traditional negotiation. You must be fluent in that language.

Time Tactics – *Time is a particularly formidable form of pressure. Because of our conditioning and preoccupation with time, its use as a tactic is seldom challenged and generally accepted as fact. Remember, you should challenge any time related artifact if it is forcing you to make decisions that would influence the results of the negotiation.*

Time tactics prey on those who exhibit a sense of urgency. Not too long ago, our new Boxer puppy suddenly developed a growth on one of her front paws. As concerned puppy parents we ignored the advice *of our day care proprietress to just leave it alone, and took her to our longtime veterinarian. We were informed that it would be $500 to extricate the growth and we needed to act fast, but we decided to get a second veterinarian's opinion. What we learned was shocking. The second vet deemed the situation to be a veterinary emergency, meaning that if the vet did not act quickly enough the situation would resolve itself and the opportunity for revenue lost. Suffice it to say we are no longer with the former vet. This exemplifies what I refer to as the "Call Girl or Urgency Principle," which says that the perceived value of the service is higher before it's delivered than after.*

Deadline (Parkinson's Law) – Deadline is both a tactic and a counter-measure. It is used as a tactic to create an uncertain end to negotiations. It is designed to force closure and create potential risk. If negotiations are not concluded by a certain arbitrary date, there will be consequences. In my experience, most deadlines are self-imposed and usually negotiable.

Deadlines can be used as a counter-measure in dealing with a phenomenon called "Parkinson's Law." It states that people will expand activity and collection to fill the available space allotted. In other words; one engineer, one project, one lifetime. Without deadlines, activities would continue in perpetuity.

Countermeasure: The rule of thumb concerning deadlines is that you should always establish them, but never treat them as sacrosanct. Occasionally, deadlines are absolute. It is always better to understand that reality early in the negotiation and prior to bumping against it. It's far easier to renegotiate a deadline earlier in the process than trying to do it in the heat of the battle.

Deadlock should always be considered as a viable option, particularly if there are no other alternatives. Deadlock must always be considered as the ultimate fallback position. When all else fails, reach a position of deadlock or non-agreement. If you have no alternatives and you are not willing to deadlock, then you are literally powerless in a negotiation.

Walking away from negotiations is a soft form of deadlock. Sales people try to prevent people from walking away because they know that a certain percentage will not return and the sale will be lost. Walking out of a negotiation can be thought of as a temporary deadlock, but the deal may be dead. Take Dr. Karrass' bachelor friend who in the heat of a negotiation always says that he needs to discuss the issue with his wife. Isn't that a gentle, non-relationship damaging way of walking out?

Countermeasure: The only way to break a deadlock is to change something. You are deadlocked on the totality of the agreement. By changing one attribute of the deal, you change it entirely. It may not be enough to break the deadlock, but it might cause reengagement with the Other.

Sweat Equity is, in short, making people work for what they get. It subscribes to and exploits the premise that people do not appreciate what they have not invested in or worked to achieve. Sweat equity means not conceding anything unless someone has worked for the concession.

An example of sweat equity is having someone put skin in the game. Skin could be in the form of tangible investment or work. Give nothing gratuitously, be it agreement, concession or offers. You must make the Other work for absolutely every piece of turf they get from you.

This concept of sweat equity was made real to me recently during a political drive to increase voter registrations. Working the streets at a local music festival, I was surprised and sometimes shocked at people's response to being asked if they were registered and if not, would they like to spend five minutes to do so. Remember that we are talking about a right and privilege that was denied to women and a vast portion of minorities in this country until fairly recently. "Naw, I don't do that," "Why waste my time?" and other more colorful expressions were encountered more often that I had hoped. The right to vote is granted without having to do anything to earn it, so many have devalued this privilege.

Countermeasure: When someone makes you work and asks for a commitment, put a string on it. Ask for something in return.

Quick Negotiations A few generalizations about quickies: first, the person with the better quality information will always come out on top. Second, quickie negotiations always result in an absolute winner and an absolute loser, unless both parties are absolutely clueless. Advice: If someone makes an offer you cannot refuse, ask for more. Why? Because if you accept that initial offer too fast, you will send a message that the offer was a mistake.

Remember that you are always negotiating perceptions and expectations. A quick response to a frivolous offer sends a huge signal that someone made a big mistake. If you win big-time, keep it to yourself. Usually in quickie negotiations, one of the parties gets screwed. It may not be apparent immediately, but it will surface at some point in time. If repeat negotiations between the parties is warranted, then it's incumbent on both parties to ensure the no one gets the short end of the stick.

Countermeasure: When you have the urge to say yes to a quick deal, stall for a bit and see what happens.

Bids, Request for Proposals, Request for Quotations, and Auctions are areas of lots of confusion. Aside from legal differences, there are fundamental structural differences in each of these terms, yet we tend to jumble these terms together into one meaning. The result is that we are possibly trading our negotiating leverage by responding in potentially inappropriate ways. This often results in making unilateral concessions and unwittingly, figuratively pulling down our pants. So let's look at each of these terms and their tactical value.

Bids – This is necessary when you are required to submit a bid to find out the ground principles. Is this truly a bid where the lowest bid on a specified product or deliverable wins, or is it a bid that triggers the finalists in a negotiating process? Both are possible, but there's a world of difference between the two. Let's walk through an example. Say that you're a contractor who has been asked to bid on a project. You put in your bid thinking that this is a prelude to a negotiation. As a good negotiator, you add a little fat into the bid, so that you can make a concession and appear to be easy to work with. Much to your dismay, you find that the bid was awarded to someone at a price higher than your bottom line. As an example of the converse, say you assume that the bid is a one shot deal. You sharpen your pencil and offer your bottom line, only to find out that you are now competing with three other competitors and none of your bids are acceptable. You're screwed. Your options are to take a tough stance and not budge or cave in and lower you price. Both options have their associated risks.

Request for Quotation (RFQ) – In my experience, an RFQ is a prelude to further negotiations. Sometimes it is treated as a bid process, other times it is not. My advice to the negotiator experiencing this process is to clarify the principles of engagement before you participate in the process. This may be an over simplification, but I have seen many companies upset because they were operating on an incorrect set of assumptions concerning the principles governing the process. Advice: always clarify the principles to which you are committing. If possible, get them in writing.

Request for Proposals (RFP) – An RFP differs from an RFQ in that there is more latitude to be creative in a proposal versus a bid. Bids are generally apples to apples comparison. Proposals may resemble an orange to bananas comparison. Proposals may present difficulties to the requestor since they occasionally turn into a difficult evaluation process, because the proposals may be game changing. This can be challenging particularly when you may have to compare and decide among proposals as similar as a lime, an ear of corn and a chicken. Proposals almost always have a secondary negotiating process associated with them.

Auctions – Have you ever been to an auction or, worse yet, paid too much for something that you really didn't want or need? Auctions put time on steroids. By creating a sense of urgency, they force people to decide quickly and sometimes emotionally to a situation. In many cases you are not negotiating with one party, but multiple parties. The auctioneer is not really participating, but simply facilitating the process to its desired end: getting as much as possible for the item.

In recent years, reverse auctions have come into vogue. The game here is to buy something for as little as possible. The process is usually facilitated by the use of technology; webinars followed by hub centered bidding. It has been somewhat effective for more commoditized products and services, but has failed miserably in the more specialized product and differentiated services arena.

Stalling is used as a tactic to gain information, advantage or create frustration in your counterpart's camp. Say your team is aware that the Other has committed to a deadline with their management on delivering a major sale to your company. Stalling can be used to gain additional concessions, particularly as the deadline approaches. It is important to realize that you always want to assure the Other that the deal remains right around the corner, that all you need is "more information" or "a little sweetener concession." This tactic can nibble away any fat in a deal or secure information that would not be attainable any other way. It may or may not be useful in the current negotiation, but may serve as great capital in subsequent negotiations. Experienced negotiators understand that business-to-business negotiations are rarely once and done. Compounding the matter is the career mobility of today's businessperson. You may negotiate with someone when they were working for Company X and you were with Company Y, but a year later, both of you could find yourselves negotiating representing two different business concerns. Knowledge transcends the situation. A more important currency is the knowledge about who you are in negotiation with.

Stalling can also be used to reveal differences in perspective, test resolve and identify weaknesses in the organization with whom you are negotiating. A classic example of how stalling worked to an advantage was the Vietnam Peace Talks conducted in Paris. They dragged on ad nauseam for years. Americans, being Americans, displayed a lack of patience and became frustrated with the peace process, ultimately labeling it a failure. Was it actually a peace process or was it a negotiating ploy of stalling used by the North Vietnamese to drive a wedge in the American collective to divide factions and test their will to support and to continue the war? Either way, it worked. Vietnamization was declared by then President Nixon to encourage the South Vietnamese to take responsibility for the war with the communist North. It failed miserably and the U.S., as the French did earlier, left Southeast Asia in glorious defeat.

A more contemporary example seems to have unfolded in the hall of the U.S. Congress. Blatant bipartisanism has ground the wheels of change and progress to a screeching halt. The ultimate political stall tactic, the filibuster (a form of deadlock), has been used to kill politically volatile legislation.

Countermeasure: Set a deadline and hold to it, or walk away.

Refusing either to engage negotiation in a meaningful way or to make any offer or counteroffer can be an effective tactic as well. The purpose of refusing is the same stalling, to reveal differences in perspective, test resolve and identify weaknesses in the organization with whom you are negotiating. Refusing is a tougher and a much more in your face tactic. It sets up an adversarial dynamic that could quickly escalate to the realm of the emotional or a battle of wills.

Countermeasure: Set a deadline and hold to it, or walk away.

Pressure Tactics – *These are non-time related tactics that keep the ball in the Other's court without you having to make concessions or give meaningful information.*

Take-it-or-leave-it is a tactic that works far better than it should. Why do people use this tactic, and why does it work so well? This tactic, if it is used, should be used sparingly. It sends a strong signal that the end has been reached. By design, it is intended to conclude negotiations.

What happens if someone repeatedly presents different offers and counter-proposals with a take-it-or-leave-it suffix? Their credibility is breached. Generally speaking, take-it-or-leave-it should only be used when you have reached the end stage, where the implied consequence of not taking it is deadlock. Regrettably, people overuse this tactic and dilute its impact.

Other ways of expressing the same intent are "that's as far as I can go," "we're nearing the end of the road" or "this is the very best I can do."

Again, the purpose of this tactic is to end the give and take of the negotiating process. It is designed to make a binary decision on a set of conditions that define the offer. So if you hear a take-it-or-leave-it, you actually have three options. One, you can take it. Two, you can leave it. And three, you can change something in the offering and re-engage the process of negotiating. Once you change any aspect of the offer, its totality has been changed and it is subject to negotiation. It is here where understanding the differences between needs, wants, must haves and nice to haves is critical. If needs and must haves are not truly satisfied by an offer, then the tactic may be effective in signaling that the end is near.

Countermeasure: Leave it, if you can, but never bite if you think it's a bluff.

"Fait accompli" in French literally means, "the deed is done." This tactic is designed to terminate negotiating, not to encourage it. This tactic is overused and abused in the Western world. MSRP, Manufacturer's Suggested Retail Price, is a classic fait accompli. Agreeing to the terms and conditions of a software download or any other standard boilerplate is in reality a fait accompli. There are literally thousands of examples of this tactic employed in everyday life. Question anything that is printed. The fait accompli is designed to stave off negotiating through formality and documents. Get in the habit of challenging something on a formal agreement. You will be surprised to learn that not everything is cast in concrete.

Ways to test a fait accompli are to propose changes to the wording of a legal document or to offer something less than the listed price on an item in a store. Usually you get the line, "I'm not authorized to change pricing" or "Sorry, I can't do that." There are policies in most retail establishments to discourage negotiating that do not empower floor level people to adjust pricing. If you want to test the validity of the price, do not be afraid to ask, "Who can I talk to that can adjust the price?" This will be covered in more depth during our discussion of Authority Tactics.

The fait accompli is powerful because it adds aura of legitimacy. We are predisposed to take heed of something that is printed, particularly double-spaced and in Santo font. Santo font is named after a colleague that had the ability to cram more information on a single page than anyone I have ever met. The technique he employed was to use infinitesimally small font sizes, hence Santo font. As a general principle, whenever possible, put things in writing and present it as if it were a done deal. Do not leave space for editing since prompting change goes counter to what you are trying to accomplish.

Countermeasure: Challenge the legitimacy of the fait accompli by picking it apart and asking for line item breakouts.

"You've got to do better than that" is a tactic that shouldn't work as well as it does. It is designed to test the situation to determine if there is fat or a pad in an offer that can be removed. Most people feel that there needs to be some movement, no matter how small, as a sign of good faith and fair play when you negotiate. To accommodate this need, people add fat and pads to their initial offers expecting that give and take will occur.

One of the universally agreed-upon tenets of negotiating is to leave room to negotiate. It's tough to negotiate if you already have delivered your final offer when the process was initiated. You literally paint yourself in a corner with no options other than to make undesirable concessions or to become the tough guy negotiator and continually repeat the same offer.

A great response or countermeasure to the 'You've got to do better...' tactic is to ask, "How much better?" or "Exactly what do you need me to do?" The object of these questions is to have your counterpart make an offer without you making any commitment. If you use "You've got to do better than...," your counterpart responds with, "How much better?" a good response would be, "What is the best that you can do?" "You have to do substantially better," "You're not in the realm of reality yet" or, "Are you joking?" The secret is to ask questions, not provide information. The strategy behind this tactic is a 'fishing expedition.' Do not provide information until you are certain where the conversation is headed and all issues are properly vetted.

Countermeasure: Ask how much better you have to do, put a string on any concession you make.

Bullying and Intimidating are very aggressive behaviors that should be personally contained, but for some reason they're not. Bullying in negotiation is a vestige of a foregone era where the practice was pervasive in the negotiating arena. This was particularly true in labor negotiations. Bullying in the early days resulted in violence and involves more than one incident of aggressive intimidating behavior. This repeated pattern usually involves a bully with more power or the convincing appearance of more power. According to Lutgen-Sandvik, bullying can include acts that are intimidating, humiliating and isolating and can be verbal or physical, blatant or subtle, active or passive.

The underlying message is that the bully will keep engaging in unwanted, negative behavior, which you are powerless to stop. This sense of powerlessness grows and the target of the aggressive behavior begins to feel bad about himself or herself, as well as frightened of the bully. Bullies tend to be highly confrontational people who seem to enjoy being in conflict. Bullying is part of their life-long pattern of thinking, feeling and behaving. This began before they took this job. Bullies are trying to overcome a sense of weakness or fear in themselves, although they are usually not aware of this. They are unconsciously driven to find and attack what I call their targets of blame, because this helps them briefly feel less anxious and helpless by hurting others.

A bully's target can be anyone. It's not personal. It's about the bully, not about the target. These bullies are stuck trying to prove to themselves and others that they are superior beings. They tend to be really afraid of being seen as inferior, but this fear is not conscious and they will become very defensive if you suggest that they are worried about being seen as inferior. They show frequent disdain and disrespect towards those closest to them. This is mostly verbal, but they may engage in humiliating jokes, tricks or maneuvers to make you look bad and to make them look good. They have a lot of all-or-nothing thinking and tend to jump to conclusions. "You're with me or you're against me."

Some bullies go beyond just wanting to appear superior. They enjoy hurting other people. They fear being dominated, so they try to find someone, somewhere, who they can dominate. As long as they are harming someone else, they feel less vulnerable. You may feel that you are being manipulated or in danger, as bullies tend to have a short fuse and can easily fly into a rage. Be skeptical of strange schemes. They are con artists.

Bullies may be highly suspicious of others and may believe that you are taking advantage of them, when you don't even know them personally. Most bullies feel that they are victims. They think that you are a danger to them, and so they believe they are justified in attacking you. While it may seem that they are enjoying bullying others, it is not true enjoyment. They enjoy the momentary feeling of being in power. Most people don't need to have power over someone else in a negative way, but for most bullies, that is the only satisfaction in a daily struggle of feeling that they are everyone else's victims. Remember, this feeling is not conscious and you will make it worse if you suggest this to them.

Countermeasure: So what can you do if you are caught in a negotiation with a bully? Unlike in schools and companies, there aren't any anti-bullying programs or formal methods of recourse available in the realm of negotiating. But there are some lessons that can be drawn from these more formal processes. Here are some suggestions:

- Recognize that the problem is not you. Don't take bullying personally.

- Bring the behavior and its impact on the negotiation to the attention of the person who is bullying you.

  Let me give you an example. Years ago I managed a sales team that had a number of major accounts in the automotive business sector, one that is renowned for a bullying management style especially in dealing with suppliers. On one occasion, I was called in to be the heavy in a pricing negotiation. We had sent a notification of our intent and an agenda to set the stage.

The meeting started with a volley of personal attacks, punctuated with profanity, insults and name calling by their senior leader. A few minutes into the diatribe, the leader paused and I stood. In the calmest voice I could muster, I said something to the effect of, "I recognize that you are upset, but I will not subject our team to this disrespectful behavior and personal attacks." I offered two options; he could continue in the same vein, which would force us to leave, or he could conduct himself in a respectful business manner and we would stay to listen to what he had to say.

What happened next was unbelievable. It was as if I had stuck a pin into a giant balloon and all of the hot air rushed out. I watched as the leader physically shrank into his chair and took on a softer, more conciliatory and respectful tone. In the end we still raised the price and lost the business, but this was our strategy; raise the price and lose very bad business.

- Escalate the issue to your management.

- Escalate the issue to the counterpart's management. This is an escalation that should be carefully considered. Once you pull this trigger, you have passed the point of no return to normalcy with your counterpart.

- If there is no course of appeal and you really want to do business with this organization, you may just have to suck it up and remember you're not the one that is sick.

Hardball and Brinkmanship, two similar negotiation tactics that are often put in place in particularly positional and competitive negotiations. Playing hardball refers to employing an uncompromising and ruthless methodology, in which you are unwilling to budge in a negotiation. Brinkmanship involves pushing events and important parts of the negotiation to the limit, or onto the brink of disaster, in order to press for a certain outcome.

These tactics are frequently seen in politics and military strategy. In theory, brinkmanship works by pushing the Other to back down in order to prevent disaster. In order to be effective, the party practicing brinkmanship must create the impression that they are willing to let things explode and use extreme methods rather than back down. This was seen in the Cold War, where the threat of nuclear force was escalated as an influencing factor.

The danger here is that your negotiation can quite literally spiral out of control. Hardball inevitably has a negative impact on your relationship with the Other, which can sabotage current and future negotiations. It also allows for very little wiggle room, leaving you with only two options: agree or reach deadlock. In brinkmanship, you can only play the game of negotiation chicken for so long. A slippery slope can develop in which your threats will continue to escalate, increasing the chances of things getting out of control. In the Cuban Missile Crisis, John F. Kennedy and Nikita Krushchev issued warnings about nuclear force with increasing severity, but never validated their threats. By its very nature, brinkmanship operates by creating a pressure situation so intense that the only options are for one person to back down, or for both parties to experience defeat.

Countermeasure: Dealing effectively with this tactic requires you to call the Other's bluff, just as Kennedy called Khrushchev's bluff during the Cuban Missile Crisis in the 1960's. Both sides were purporting to go to nukes, but when the US intercepted the Soviet Navy, the Russians blinked.

Escalation as a pressure tactic works on the principle that those with higher authority are more likely to make concessions than their subordinates. This is usually true because those with higher authority are generally not as close to the details as the people on the line. Another reason it works is that those with more power generally like to be the good guy.

Countermeasure: Have a clear escalation policy that everyone in your organization understands. Build firewall to prevent people subverting the organization by escalating.

Illusion Tactics – *Like a magician, these tactics are used to create misdirection. They disguise the intent through actions that send a different signal. These tactics are designed to generate a response that plays into the strategy.*

Fiat is a command or act of will that creates something without further effort, an authoritative determination, an authoritative or arbitrary order. Those who are in power often use this tactic. If left unchallenged the dictate will stand as an agreement. It goes something like this, "based upon your performance you will receive no raise in wages this year," or "We are not accepting any price increases at this time."

Countermeasure: Challenge the legitimacy of the statement. Remember from the section on Power in the form of Proof/Evidence/Legitimacy*:* For something to possess legitimacy it must be applied consistently, perceived as fair and accepted by those who it affects. If any of these criteria are not met, challenge the legitimacy of the dictate or Fiat.

Technology increasingly technology is being used tactically to foil Others' attempts at negotiating. The strategy is to have technology; Enterprise Resource Planning Systems (EPS), Point of Sale Systems, Interactive Voice Recognition systems (IVRs), websites, etc. act as an intermediary without human interaction or to limit the ability of people working in the system to be able to change the decision making algorithms built into the systems. View technology as a tactic created solely to discourage negotiation and deviation from the standard rule set.

Countermeasure: Escalate; ask to speak to someone with authority. If their answer is not satisfactory, go higher. Ask who has the authority to make changes. Don't waste your time arguing with someone who is powerless. Control your emotions. The person that you are dealing with at the beginning usually has no power and is a pawn in the game, so be nice to them. If you get stuck in a phone menu and are prompted to press a number, hit "0" repeatedly or if you are dealing with a voice recognition system, say "representative" repeatedly.

Bad faith is a concept in negotiation theory where parties pretend to reason to reach settlement, but have no intention of doing so. For example, one political party may pretend to negotiate, with no intention to compromise, for political effect.

Countermeasure: If you can, avoid those who have a reputation for practicing negotiations in bad faith. In the course of discussions if you learn that someone is bargaining in bad faith, terminate the discussions immediately. You cannot win and you are wasting your time.

'*Split the difference*' is an overly simplistic tactic that shouldn't work as well as it does. It's a nice tactic in that it shows willingness to compromise in a reasonable fashion. It attempts to show both good will and good faith bargaining. So what's the problem with such a nice gesture? Nothing, if you intended to make a unilateral compromise of half the remaining difference.

Advice to those making offers or counter-offers: never ever offer to split the difference. Not unless you have exceeded your expectations or are trying to conclude a negotiation and you want the Other to feel as if they have also won. If you are on the receiving end of a split-the-difference, don't accept it automatically. The question you should always ask is, "How much more of the difference do I want in order to conclude negotiations?"

There are several risks associated with split-the-difference. One is that if you don't accept the tactic, you may be viewed as not playing fairly. Another is that these types of offers happen so fast that compromises are made without a full understanding of what was offered and accepted. Finally, split-the-difference is, in a way, a 'mini' quickie negotiation. As you recall, quickie negotiations usually result in one side feeling like they gave too much away.

Be careful with this very nice tactic; it isn't all that it seems to be. Always remember to ask yourself how much more of the difference you want. Feeler types are prone to offering and accepting the split-the-difference. They will invariably trade gain for relationship, keeping things nice and in balance. This tactic is intended to wrap up a negotiation in a nice way. On the surface it seems to be a fair and equitable way of concluding a deal, because each party is making a concession to go halfway. But when this offer to split the difference was made, did both parties actually concede? No, only the one proposing to split the difference has made a concession. Ironically, most people jump at the offer.

Countermeasure: If you hear the words, "Let's split the difference," first recognize it as a concession, and then discipline yourself not to accept it. After you have yourself under control, ask yourself, "How much more of the difference do I want?" Say, "I cannot do that."

No sometimes means yes and sometimes means no. A professional negotiator is trained to say no to the first offer, even if the offer exceeds his or her wildest expectations. Why? Because if they bite on the first offer, it may very well send a signal to the other party that a major mistake was made in presenting that offer. "No" can be a simple test to see if there is more available. Stay away from the trap of making repeated offers to someone who just says "No" or "That's not good enough." It's a death spiral. All that is accomplished is a one sided attempt at resolution. If someone says "No" repeatedly, stop making further offers. They are pushing you for a better offer. In other negotiations, however, when someone says no, it means no.

Countermeasure: How can you tell? Find out what the problem with the offer is, then attempt to engage in mutual problem resolution.

Unresponsiveness is a variant of the "No" tactic. Someone who acts as if they are unresponsive may actually be using the tactic of saying no without actually saying no. Their unresponsiveness may invite further concessions or information flow without them acknowledging anything.

This tactic is not harsh in that there is no direct confrontation. The use of silence may be nothing but an attempt to garner a sense of where the other party is relative to the negotiation by pretending not to engage. In essence, this tactic is intended to have the other party lay out their position prior to engaging in dialogue.

Countermeasure: There are several ways to counter this tactic; one is to overtly confront it by asking for a response, another is simply to disengage. The risk of this tactic is that if the unresponsiveness of the other party was sending a real signal that the initial discussions were not in the realm of reality, it could set up a negative dynamic and derail the negotiations.

Lying as a tactic is not smart. The problem with lying is not the lie, but maintenance of it. Don't do it, because if you get caught in one, your credibility will be suspect from that point on. Effective probing and testing usually will surface lies as told by the Other.

If you get trapped in a dilemma where answering truthfully will put you at a disadvantage, you have multiple ways of avoiding the lie. You can ignore the question completely and talk through it. Another way to avoid lying is to declare the question not relevant or state that the answer would divulge proprietary information, so you cannot respond. Limiting your authority can be an effective countermeasure here. Stating that you cannot answer for certain or that you do not have the privilege of that information can work. Pleading ignorance is another deferral technique that can work occasionally as well. Use it sparingly.

"Me, I'm dishonest, and you can always trust a dishonest man to be dishonest. Honestly, it's the honest ones you have to watch out for."

- Johnny Depp

Silence is a variant of being unresponsive, but more situational. It is a particularly effective tactic when used on the telephone. Our societal norms predispose us to fill any pauses in conversation with chatter. It's a corollary of Parkinson's Law, which states that we will fill time allotted with activity. We will fill voids in conversations with words. They may be meaningful words or not, but you can bet that if there is silence for more than a few seconds, someone will jump in and start to talk. Try it next time you are on the phone; just stop talking. I guarantee that the person on the other end of the line will start to squirm and wonder what's going on.

Silence is a powerful tactic because it defies social convention and common practice. Have you ever been in a one-way conversation where you might as well be invisible? I had an extended family member, who shall remain nameless, who has the ability to have a conversation where the other person is an observer rather than a participant. You don't have to say a word; just her catching your eye will initiate a monologue that is reminiscent of being at Disney Park's

Mr. Toad's Wild Ride. It is a most frustrating experience because she forces you into silence. Make no mistake, she is in charge of talking and you don't bother interrupting her. If you do, she will either ask a rhetorical question and go on with her soliloquy or continue spewing words onto whoever is present to reflect the sound of her voice back to her.

If you know someone like this, they can be excellent teachers from two perspectives. One, they force you into silent submission. Forget about getting a word in, "it ain't gonna happen." Two, they will demonstrate how, with very little probing, you can get a world of information; some good and a lot of junk.

Marriage counselors have an exercise they recommend to help get couples taking again. It goes like this. One of the participants has to talk for thirty minutes without interruption. The other listens and does not interrupt. Having experienced the exercise first hand, I came away with two new insights. As the speaker, you can't control what comes out of your mouth when you are required to talk extemporaneously for thirty minutes. And as the listener, I spent the bulk of my psychic energy trying not to interrupt rather than listening.

Countermeasure: I have long espoused the power of the question as the critical delineator of a good negotiator. I have come to the conclusion that great negotiators have command of both formulating truly provocative questions and listening skills that engage silence as a perfected practice. To appear truly engaged in a conversation and remain silent is a tremendous, formidable skill. It encompasses the use of non-verbal communication, which is body language, to send messages of encouragement and engagement to the other. It is Zen-like. At its core, the ability to be silent requires discipline and focus. For it to become natural requires practice and perfection of the art.

Data is pervasive, but largely irrelevant. Data is almost always shaped to validate or prove a point that someone is trying to make. Rarely do the facts speak for themselves. The facts are manipulated, exaggerated and edited to support the assertion that is being made. Remember that an assertion is a statement made without the benefit of support from facts. Data is created to support the assertions and elevate them to fact status.

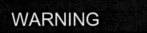

View all data presented in a negotiation with deep suspicion. Question it!

Let's examine how data might be presented as facts. What claims can you make with the following graphical representation? Do you think there is volatility and unpredictability?

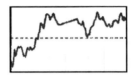

On the surface, that may be the conclusion that you come to, but as we look at the same data within its context, we see a markedly different picture. In the next graphic we see that there is some volatility, but it is not significant. It appears to be a good day for all indices traded. It was a good day for the Dow Industrials, and even a better day for the NASDAQ.

DJIA	16,389.62	221.58	1.37%
NASDAQ	4,355.24	77.94	1.82%
S&P 500	1,872.53	26.80	1.45%
FTSE 100	6,823.77	115.42	1.72%
NIKKEI 225	14,718.71	69.25	0.47%

Let's look at some other ways that data can be manipulated to make a point. How about market share? Which of the two graphics represents true dominance in a market?

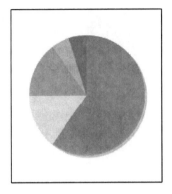 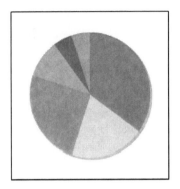

The competitor in red displayed in the first graphic seems to have a much more dominant market share than the red competitor in the second. But what is the graphic really telling us? Nothing. It does not tell us the size of the market, what the market is, the growth rate or the rate of decline of the market, just to name a few missing details.

Visualization is the preferred method of delivering information. Compound this preference for visuals with the pervasiveness of PowerPoint presentations and you have a fertile method to make half-truths, misrepresentation and myths into facts. In his essay, "The Cognitive Style of PowerPoint," Edward Tufte states that, "in particular, the popular PowerPoint templates (ready-made designs) usually weaken verbal and spatial reasoning, and almost always corrupt statistical analysis." Our dependence on visualization of data can easily be exploited by terminological inexactitude, which is the practice of bending the truth.

Countermeasures: Here are some guidelines to follow when dealing with data in a negotiation:

- Never accept data presented at face value.
- Drill down and understand the context in which the data was collected, analyzed and presented.
- Always have data of your own to support your case.
- View all data with a suspicious eye.
- Bring your own data.

Good Guy - Bad Guy is a tactic that, like most, is designed to distort reality. Also referred to as good cop, bad cop, it plays on the juxtaposition of the archetypes of good and evil. Watch any interrogation scene in a television police drama. The mean, forceful cop comes in and berates the suspect. After the requisite amount of time, the bad cop leaves and the nice, friendly cop offers water to the person being interrogated. The sudden change in approach usually leads the novice criminal to spill their guts to the good cop. In business, we also have good guys and bad guys. Salespeople should always maintain a semblance of being the good guy. Who are some bad guys that the salesperson can invoke?

Here's a partial list; legal, the government, their boss, the economy, the Environmental, Health and Safety Group, accounting, operations, policies, etc., the list goes on. If you need a bad guy, use them. If you are being presented with a real or illusory bad guy, then understand that, just like the police drama, the good guy and the bad guy are on the same side, and it's not your side.

Countermeasure: Realize that the good guy and the bad guy have the same motives. Bring your own bad guy.

The Bogie, also known as a **Red Herring** or a **Smoke Screen** is a target, sometimes real, sometimes not. As a tactic, bogies are used to test the Others and create a distraction. They force choice. Used in conjunction with other tactics, like **Sweat Equity,** they can be formidable in depleting the Other's ability and desire to chase an elusory target.

One way that I can describe a bogie is an antiquated weapon system I encountered while an Air Force aviator many years ago. The ADM-20 'Quail' was an air-launched decoy missile carried by the B-52 strategic bomber. Designed to approximate the radar and infrared images to that of the B-52 and to fly at the same speed and altitude, the Quail was used during an actual bombing attack to confuse an enemy's defensive radar network. With both Quails and B-52s penetrating the enemy's air space, it would be difficult for air defenses to distinguish one from the other on their radar or heat seeking detection equipment.

It's clear why the Air Force would use bogies to protect the B-52, but why would someone use a bogie in a negotiation? Actually, negotiators use bogies for the very same reason the Air Force does. That is to protect the primary asset. The bogies used in negotiation are protecting the information asset, which if known to the Other, could have a negative impact on the negotiated outcomes or can be used to test resolve.

Countermeasures: Aren't bogies really lies? Well, it depends on how they are presented. Some are, in fact, outright lies. Others are couched in a way to lead the other to draw conclusions and fill in blanks on their own. In any case, deception and sleight of hand are in play. The risk in using this tactic is that once discovered, there can be a breach of credibility. This is particularly harmful for someone who engages in repeat negotiations with the same people or is involved in a relationship-oriented sale.

How do these bogies sound? They come in many forms, but the most prevalent are presented as competitive offers or advice. If you suspect that a competitive situation is really a bogie, ask to see a written proposal. If the person is claiming to have a competitive offer, write a declaration explaining the specifics of the offer. Make sure volume, time and terms are spelled out as well as the competitor's identity. If challenged as to why you need this documentation, a good response might be that, "I certainly trust you, but there are people in my organization who require this sort of document to substantiate a competitive situation." You could also say that the law requires formal documentation to comply with the Robinson-Patman Act. In other words, use higher authority or a bad guy to maintain your good guy role.

Bait and Switch is unethical and usually illegal. However, it's used pervasively, such as in sales that advertise deep discounts while supplies last. When you get to the store and the advertised model is sold out, you are upsold on a better model. Upselling is not illegal or unethical, but deliberately promising something at a dramatic savings to lure or bait the buyer into purchasing another higher value/margin offering is. If you find yourself in what you perceive as a bait and switch situation, leave. Usually people are ill prepared to deal with the tactic effectively.

Countermeasures: If you find yourself caught in an illegal exchange, escalate to a higher authority. If not, walk away.

The Nibble is designed to extract a little more from the negotiation. It's usually disguised as soft and not substantive. It works because it doesn't materially impact the overall negotiation. It is hard to refuse because saying no may kill the deal, and it allows the other party to appear cooperative and capitulate something of little to no importance in the grander scheme of the negotiations. For example, in years gone by, salespeople traded payment terms without a second thought. That was until the financial people started holding sales accountable for DSO (Days Sales Outstanding), which is a measure of working capital required to finance longer terms of sale.

Nibbles are requests to throw something small into the deal in order to close it. Whether it's asking for free alterations for the two suits you just bought, an upgrade to the floor mats in your new car or getting an extended warrantee thrown in, they are all nibbles and come at a cost. It's like the late Senator from Illinois, Everett Dirksen once said, "A billion here, a billion there, and pretty soon you're talking real money." If you can't get a dinner, get a sandwich. Nibbles are a great way to overcome your fear of asking for things in a negotiation. The stakes are low and the worst thing someone can say to you is no.

There are ways of discouraging nibbles as well. Every business and negotiator should anticipate the nibble and have either system firewalls to prevent them or training on how to respond. A great way of testing a nibbler's resolve is to respond with "Are you kidding?' This comes at the risk of embarrassing the nibbler, but can reveal their true intent. Another great way to discourage nibbling is to say that you "Do not have the authority to do that" or "it's not our policy." Overnight courier service, FedEx, is a frequent nibble. One way to discourage this nibble is to use the following, "I would be happy to overnight the package, what's your FedEx/UPS account number?" ten to one odds you'll get a response like, "Just send it standard delivery."

Firewalls are a far better way of not only discouraging the nibbler but also neutralizing the tactic completely. Firewalls are built into your IT systems and limit the transaction authority through either an approval process or workflow to complete a nibble transaction. Prior to the advent of these systems, airline gate agents were able to upgrade travelers at will. So, if you were nice to the gate agent and there was a seat available in first class, they could upgrade you easily if they wanted. Airlines still upgrade passengers if they cannot sell the seats, but the airline, not the gate agent determines who gets the upgrade by programming the decision criteria and authority into the system.

Countermeasure: If you don't have firewalls, build them, especially if you can't have policies, procedures and training to dissuade the nibble. Put a string on any nibble someone attempts.

Funny Money disguises the real value of money. It's not always about price or cost. Whether through the use of chips in a casino, monthly lease payments to drive away in that Audi R8, realtor fees or points to buy down interest percentage at closing, or terms and conditions of sale, they are all reshaping money. If you are on the buying side, always think in terms of the real money that is being hidden by the mask. If you are on the selling side, find ways to disguise the money by reshaping it to be more attractive and less obvious.

CAUTION

Think through all of the terms and conditions that constitute an agreement. Quantify the real financial impact on the deal

Why do you think financial planners are happy to take one percent or less annually to manage your portfolio? The percentage is payable whether your wealth increases or decreases. The 1 percent or less is targeted below the threshold of pain with the implied promise that they will be able to manage your wealth in a positive direction, regardless of market conditions and definitely better than you would be able to yourself. Oh really? Ever hear of the monkey and the dartboard experiments? In 1988, the *Wall Street Journal* began a contest that was inspired by Burton Malkiel's book, "A Random Walk Down Wall Street." The Princeton Professor theorized that "a blindfolded monkey throwing darts at a newspaper's financial pages could select a portfolio that would do just as well as one carefully selected by experts." This has turned into a long-term contest that has yielded inconclusive results. The principles for measuring performance have shifted over the years, as has the equities performance. The jury is still out.

Countermeasure: Always think through what the actual financial implication is in real money.

Broken Record comes from a concept that may need some explanation for the post Boomer generations. Prior to magnetic tape, compact discs and MP3s, music was recorded on vinyl media called records. One major drawback of records is that they were easily damaged and would infinitely repeat a track. This repeating process was referred to as a broken record. Compact discs can exhibit the same phenomenon.

Broken Record as a tactic is to repeat the same message time after time. Repeated messages reinforce what has already been said. After a while, hearing the same message tends to influence the believability of the message and the resolve of the person saying it. The broken record can initiate some bad triggers. If used improperly, it can come across as scolding or demeaning, like scolding a child:

"I told you to do your homework."
"But ... blah, blah, blah."
"I told you to do your homework!"
"That's not fair."
"I told you to do your homework!"
"My friends parents' don't ..."
"I told you to do your homework!"

Countermeasure: Create a unifying company song message of your own. Craft three or four short, clear messages that all say basically the same thing. Repeat them often and whenever the opportunity arises.

The Dog's Breakfast is a tactic that has many other names, but it intends to confuse and disguise the real issues by creating a bunch of non-issues. The goal here is to separate fact from fiction. A conversation with someone employing this tactic may resemble one that you would have with an adolescent that suffers from ADHD.

Countermeasure: Stay focused and play the Broken Record or Sing the Company Song.

"What if I ... ?" This tactic is nothing more than a shopping expedition. One party is posing hypothetical situations without any commitment. If the Other responds with a course of action, they have made an unwitting concession. The intent of the tactic is to attempt to get insight into cost structure, price points or see where the Other's interest starts to peak.

Countermeasure: When you hear, "what if?" recognize that what follows is a non-concession. This tactic is used to get information and concession without making one on your end. The counter to the "what-if" is to ask for something in return, a sort of reverse what if. If you respond to the "what if," then put a string on what you make as a counter-offer.

Putting Strings on Concessions, strings are great. They're like a yo-yo because you can put something out there and pull it back without changing your position. They are conditional concessions. They go like this: "If you do X, then I'll do Y." If someone doesn't take you up on the offer, there is no obligation on your behalf.

Be careful not to make this a tit-for-tat trade off. The offer and the demand, or the string, do not have to be equal in value. Ideally, you want to trade something with little to no value to you for something of significantly higher value. It may not always be possible to accomplish, but as the Rolling Stones so eloquently immortalized, "you can't always get what you want, but if you try, you just might get what you need."

Strings are an absolutely wonderful way of avoiding unilateral concessions, because there are always conditions attached to your offer. Kids use strings all of the time. "I'll go to bed, if X" or "I'll clean my room, if Y"

Countermeasure: When responding, put a string on your own concessions.

"Illusory" Contracts are agreements that give the illusion of being legally binding, when in reality, they are not. To be an enforceable legal contract, an agreement must contain four critical ingredients; manifestation of mutual assent, consideration, legality of object, and capacity of parties. Since all contracts, personal and commercial, are central to the conduct of business and are intended to summarize the totality of an agreement, a discussion of what constitutes a legal and binding agreement and what does not is an important one. It does not fall into the context of this book, but telling them apart is why God created commercial lawyers. An understanding of how contracts work will give insight to the negotiator on discerning tactics from reality.

Countermeasure: Always get good legal counsel on contractual issues.

Asking for Price Ranges is a seemingly innocent request when trying to budget or plan for expenses. Here's a situation, you are selling a developmental product that is going into another developmental product. Your customer's volumes and your costs have not been established. The buyer asks you how much your product will cost him. You respond by saying that the costs are not fully developed and volume commitments are not established. She says, "just for planning purposes give me a range."

To be cooperative you give a range of possible cost from $150 to $275 per unit. Lots of wiggle room, right? Not really. When you give a range the buyer immediately focuses on the lowest price. You have now unwittingly established an expectation in the mind of the buyer. How about answering the request with something like: "in the low to mid $200." Even though you probably covered the price issue, depending on the actual volume commitment, you might be labeled a sandbagger or a gouger.

The problem is that you are responding to a request with only part of the information you need to be accurate. Price ranges are a no win proposition for sellers.

Countermeasures: Put a string on your price; ask for a volume commitment in return. If you are forced to provide a price, default to the highest price anticipated. If it's too high you run the risk of killing the deal or inviting competition. It's always better to under promise and over deliver. Another way to handle a request for price ranges is to say I'm not allowed to do that.

Terminological Inexactitude is a phrase coined by Winston Churchill during WWII in describing President Roosevelt's deliberate process of being vague. The Thesaurus defines vague as, not precisely limited, determined, or distinguished; "an undefined term"; "undefined authority." By being vague or inexact leaves room for maneuvering, but doesn't confine the one being vague, inexact or ambiguous. As a tactic it is very effective if not overused. It allows the Other to determine what you mean without you having to define it in exact terms. The words that are generally used when practicing this tactic are ambiguous directional opposites like higher or lower, better or worse, sooner or later, more or less and the like. If the Other interprets something that is not in your favor, you can simply say, "That's not what I meant," or you didn't understand what I said." The worst-case scenario is that you will need to better define what you intended.

Countermeasures: Ask, "What exactly do you mean?" or "What exactly are you saying?"

Authority Tactics– *Authority tactics give you the power to decide or approve. The following are levels of authority as they apply to negotiations. The level of authority should be considered in light of the following discussion.*

**You cannot sell to someone who has
no authority to buy**

Full Authority is the ultimate power in a negotiation. It allows for swift decision-making and gives the ability to command respect and admiration. It can be a seductive ego trip. Having full authority must always be good, right?

If you have full authority, you are literally on the spot. There is no backing out or waffling on issues. You are the ultimate decision maker. I raise again Dr. Karrass's story about his bachelor friend who would always say that he had to check with his wife. No one ever called him on the fact that he did not have a wife. The point of this anecdote is that people generally expect other people not to have full or ultimate authority.

To take the discussion a step further, there are many ways that those with total authority can avoid the perils of having no way out. You can say you have to confer with trusted advisors or a board of directors, consult with legal counsel, evaluate the financial implications, sleep on it or take time to mull it over in your mind. No one can effectively argue against these actions, because they are prudent, logical and what most people would do in a high-stakes environment.

Ironically, the people who are most likely to make large concessions are people at the top of the organization. They are not overly familiar with the intimate details of an issue, but their ego drives them to get things done. That's why taking on higher authority is generally a good strategy for someone to resolve an issue quickly. It avoids protective firewalls put in place by organizations and goes directly to the decision maker.

Countermeasure: The question someone in a position of authority should always ask prior to engaging in a negotiation is, "What authority *don't* I want?" In other words, what limits should I put on myself before being drawn into decisions in the heat of the battle?

No Authority on the surface appears self-defeating. Why would anyone deal with someone with no authority? It's because there are no other options. For example, there is virtually no authority built into legitimate Internet transactions. Why do you think that most customer service personnel have little to no authority to deviate from the script? Because, having no authority is intended to discourage negotiation. The primary customer interface in retail also follows the same strategy.

If you cannot negotiate with someone, what good are they in a negotiation? They can build a personal bond and act as the relationship people. The can escalate your case to a higher authority. Just as an aside, upset someone with no authority on the telephone and be prepared to be on hold for a long, long time as your call is forwarded to the next level for attention. Many companies track interactions with customers and record their interactions. They may formally and informally classify customers in their CRM systems as PIA's, crocks and other less flattering terms.

Remember that having no authority does not mean that you have no power. Anyone who has had dealings with civil servants, postal workers, IRS people and other bureaucrats knows that if you piss them off, there will be reprisals. Their power lies in the fact that they are there to administer the policy and process to the letter. They know ways around it, but if you try to run them over, you will find that they know every painful and time-consuming step in the process that is saved for especially negative clients.

Countermeasure: Demand to speak to someone with the authority to do what you need.

Limited Authority is really Undefined Authority or Discretionary Authority. It is desirable because you can pick and choose which decisions are in your capability. The best way to describe it is "Soft Authority"; it's situational, undefined to the other party and not hard and firm. If you have a high degree of authority to decide, then you can choose to exercise that level by making the decision or postponing by claiming that you do not have the ability to make that decision. The operative question that you should ask prior to any negotiation is, "how much authority do I want to exercise in this negotiation?" It will keep you safe and out of trouble.

Having limited authority is the best of both worlds in that you can execute if it is advantageous, or defer if the situation may present adverse consequences.

Countermeasure: Limited authority is slippery because the true limits of authority are not defined in advance; they are discovered during the negotiation. To mitigate the effects of this tactic, attempt to define what authority the Other has at the beginning of the discussions. Be careful. If you are also a practitioner of this tactic, the Other will probably require you to divulge as well, thus neutralizing your ability to use limited authority effectively.

Create Advocacy

Creating advocacy is developing a relationship with one or more of the Other's team who will support your case when you are not present. Other key roles of the advocate are to get information about the Other's situation and test options off-the-record. The advocate may be your voice in the Other's organization, but make no mistake, the advocate works for the Other.

The characteristics of a good advocate may include; respected by the Other's organization, balanced, logical and persuasive.

There is no greater example of advocacy than the modern day political lobbyists. They do the bidding of a collective special interest group and multiply their individual power exponentially. These advocates plead the case of the Political Action Committee (PAC) to the legislature. Another form of advocacy is legal representation. Having a lawyer who actually speaks for you is not only an asset, but in today's litigious society, a necessity.

In a positional negotiation the Other's job, goal and compensation are focused on driving the price of raw materials down, while the seller's is to provide value to the customer and to extract part of that value for their organization. Regrettably, some sales organizations' compensation systems are incompatible with that goal and do not reflect incentives for extracting value. So who can serve as an advocate for sales in a supply or product/service acquisition? The list is extensive; technology, the end user, operations, executive leadership and compliance departments, just to name a few. I am still amazed that sellers do not fully exploit advocacy. Remember, the way procurement discourages advocacy is to limit or deprive sales from accessing their organization. If you are on the procurement side, understand that granting access to your organization may undermine your leverage and weaken your ability to manage pricing discipline.

This can ultimately keep the procurement function from reaching their goals and objectives. That being said, this approach may be of greater service to your organization.

Make Intelligent, Planned Offers and Concessions

WARNING

Neither hard, inflexible, unbending adherence to a position nor flagrant capitulation can build a durable resolution

Concession making, like questioning, should not be a random event. It should be planned and intelligent in that it should strive to trade things of lower value for things of higher value. Remember that value is perceived, so what you might think is of low value might actually be of high value to the Other and raise their expectations. Concessions should have a strategy behind them. If they do not, they tend to be unpredictable, which leads to confusion and distrust. Concession making is a process that heuristically attempts to discover the expectations of the Other. Heuristics are a trial and error based process, so go slow and be deliberate. The following are a few strategies and tactics used to reach an end and determine the Other's reality:

Shock and Awe – Some cultures will test you by offering or asking for incredibly high or low prices, or challenges that have startling new news. If you flinch or react involuntarily to the offer, then they know that they have exceeded a threshold of credibility. They then quickly gloss over the offer and make another offer that has a little more credibility but is still out of the ball park. The strategy here is two-fold; first, to see if you react to the outrageous offer, and second, to let you know that there will be substantial time spent on bargaining and give and take. By sending the latter signal, they are testing your resolve to the process and hoping that you'll want to just get it done, cut to the chase, and accept the over the top offer.

WARNING

Always anticipate the unexpected from the Other

Avoid Telegraphing – Telegraphing sends predictable signals or patterns to the Other. Most telegraphing is subconscious to the doer, but can have very bad consequences on the results of a negotiation. As an example, if I am a buyer and set my expectations in a negotiation for an end price of $5000 and the seller list price is $5400, my initial offer is $4500. What are my options? If I were to telegraph, my progression of offers might look like this.

> $4500, $4600, $4700, $4800 ... $5000 or
> $4500, $4550, $4600, $4650 ... $5000 or
> $4500, $4525, $4550, $4575 ... $5000

Why is this approach telegraphing? The smaller the increments of concession, the more protracted the negotiation. With an end price, the buyer has not signaled anything other than the next concession will be the same increment as the previous.

CAUTION

When negotiating, be consistent but not predictable. Consistency builds trust; predictability makes you vulnerable to being exploited

What if, or Inflated Requirements – A seemingly innocent way of determining the negotiating space is to do the "what if?" It works like this. I start off by saying I need this quantity and ask for the corresponding price. You respond with a price. Then I start the what if process by asking what if I buy 2 times the quantity, 3 times and so on. You would respond with a price for each corresponding volume. What have I accomplished?

By your responses to my quantity breaks, I now have insight to your cost structure. You are willing to deal at the price for the highest quantity that I demanded, and I want that price. So how do you deal with this approach? How can you civilly respond to someone who is obviously trying to get a concession? Try this. Ask what volume they are willing to commit to today. Put a string on your responses. Build policies and procedures, like approval processes, that make it difficult to get discounts for lessor quantities. Say, "If you issue a purchase order for that quantity I can..."

A variation on this approach is pervasive in the new product world. Say I develop a new product with sales projections. I need to do product costing, so the potential volumes that I quote are astronomically high. I need a cost of raw materials pricing for steady state manufacturing. I ask you to project pricing for the opportunity at the end state. What can you do?

Several options are possible. One is tier pricing; as volumes increase the price drops commensurately. Another technique is to offer a rebate based upon achieving certain levels of purchase by the customer. They usually have a percentage of sales rebated in either money or product after reaching a certain level of performance. In more sophisticated agreements, these rebates can define multiple levels of volume with corresponding rebates. They are usually reconciled yearly, quarterly, or monthly. Be careful with rebates. They are problematic in that if the given level is not reached, but very close, you may creep from a lower tier to a higher tier unless you practice a discipline structure of administration. From experience, this can set up a contentious dynamic.

Law of Diminishing Returns – Let's go back to our telegraphing example. How can we send a strong signal that we are near the end of our concession making and that any further concessions will not merit the time spent, or the law of diminishing returns? How abut this as an approach to the same situation as before, where our target under heavy duress is $5000 and we opened at $4500.

$4500, $4600, $4650, $4675, $4687.50, $4693.75, $4696.875, ...

What is this concession making pattern saying that the telegraphing examples are not? It's saying that the return on the investment of time just isn't there. The concessions are pointing to the end of the line.

Eventually in the year 1,000,000 the price will asymptotically approach $5000, but is it worth it?

Opening Offers: Asking for More Than You Expect – To avoid the first meaningful concession pitfall, here's some good advice. Depending on if you are buying or selling, start lower or higher than where you want to eventually settle. Generally speaking, the more you ask for, the more you get. Let's apply that principle to opening offers.

Depending if you are buying or selling set your opening offers to a point slightly above or below the ridiculous threshold. Don't negotiate on behalf of the Other. Depending on the value (cost/price versus performance/benefit) that you're offering, have an opening demand that approaches but does not exceed the realm of reality. Once you exceed the elastic limit of reality, you're credibility breaks down and you will quickly find yourself in a hole, and that limit will vary from person to person because people are different.

Never Make the First "Meaningful" Concession

"Life cannot subsist in society but by reciprocal concessions."

-- Samuel Johnson

All positional negotiations must involve a degree of give and take, but the question is, how much is each party willing to move? That is the process of discovery and what positional negotiations are all about. A skilled negotiator always assesses the situation and anticipates what they believe to be the negotiating space, but the assessment is usually based on assumptions of the Other's position, strengths, vulnerabilities, expectations and urgencies. That's why the first offer, which usually is some concession or 'give,' is so critically important. It is usually driven by a combination of our expectations and what we believe are the Other's expectations.

This first round of 'give and take' is wrought with risk. Your actions are being driven by assumptions, estimates and conjecture. How do we determine what might be meaningful? What does meaningful really mean? Who determines what's really meaningful? By making a low-ball opening offer, can you actually encourage the Other? Let's look at these questions one by one, but first let's be clear that the expectations of the Other are what drives what is meaningful, not our expectations.

How do we determine what might be meaningful? As stated earlier, in the early stages of a negotiation we have lots of untested assumptions, estimates and conjecture. The more we plan and anticipate, the more precise our intelligence of the Other will be. The best way to determine what's meaningful to the Other is to have them tell us, without realizing what they are giving away. This is accomplished through skillful questioning cast in a problem-resolving context, not a negotiating context. Trust and rapport are crucial if you are to get honest information from the Other. If these elements are not present, the best strategy is to go slowly and talk around, but never make a concession. At this phase of the negotiation, what we might consider to be a concession that has little to no value might have the opposite effect on the Other.

WARNING

Never, ever make a gratuitous concession. Make people work to receive any concession. If you don't make them work, it will encourage them to ask for more

What does meaningful really mean, and who determines it? Meaningful is what resides in the expectations and the needs of the Other. Their assessment, needs, desires, and perceptions of value create meaning. If a concession signals that their expectation will be reached, then you have made a meaningful concession in the mind of the Other. This could be true even though it was a low-ball opening offer. Your concession may have encouraged the Other, if their expectations were low. A meaningful concession signals to the Other that their expectations are going to be met and that there may be more to gain. That's the dangerous part. Once expectations are met or exceeded, few people recalibrate new expectations. Most people go for more, pushing to see how much more they can get. The irony of the situation is that it was our meaningful concession that triggered a change in the Others expectations. It may not be a new concrete expectation, but it is now certainly higher than before.

CAUTION

Whenever possible, put a sting on your concessions. It makes them conditional so that if the Other accepts your offer, you get something in return. Since the offer is conditional, if it's not accepted, it's off the table

Unilateral concessions are generally a bad strategy. Strive to make any concession conditional. That is, put a string on the concession, so if it is not accepted you can pull it back, like a yo-yo. Unilateral concessions are gratuitous in that they are given without consequence. Strings on concessions can take the form of time-bound offers, reciprocal concessions or contractual commitments.

NOTE

When asked to make a concession, ask for equitable consideration in return

Sing The Company Song Loud and Proud

"A lie told often enough becomes the truth"

- Vladimir Lenin

How do businesses get people to take action to buy their products and services? They advertise. Advertising as we know it grew with industrialization. In 2010 it was estimated that the United States alone spent about $140 billion on advertising. The worldwide advertising estimate for the same year was around $467 billion. Why do companies advertise? Because it works!

So how can we apply the tenets of advertising to the practice of negotiation? We live in a world where we are continuously bombarded with messages and thirty-second sound bites. The keys to advertising are the consistency of message and frequency of exposure to it. In a negotiation, we are trying to persuade the Other to adopt our views of reality and visa-versa. The intent of the Company Song is to make our messages at the top of the Others mind. Here are some important lessons that we can apply to the Company Song from the Advertising Industry:

- ***People have to hear your message seven times before they remember it.*** You may have heard a different number, but the exact number isn't important. What's Empire Carpets Toll Free Number? 800-588-2300. When Empire was only in Chicago the number was 312-588-2300. What *is* important in negotiations is that you have to repeat yourself. You'll have to say it to the Other a lot.
- ***Stick with the Song much longer than you think.*** Why do you think Dunkin Donuts used the same ad campaign and tag line "America Runs on Dunkin" for so long? Or BMW is the "Ultimate Driving Machine"? It takes time for these to sink in.
- ***Use multiple media to give the same message.*** Don't be afraid to put the same basic information into your visuals, follow up communications, executive communications, communications by your team members to the Other's team, emails and subsequent calls. It will help enforce the song even when you are not there to sing it.
- ***Leave information up for much longer than you think.*** How long does the message have to be in front of the Other? Longer than you think.
- ***Repeat messages many more times than you think necessary.*** How many times do you have to send your message on Twitter or Facebook before your average follower even sees it once? It takes repeated efforts to get the song stuck in the Other's head.

Build A Series Of Three or Four Message That Make Your Point

"If you have an important point to make, don't try to be subtle or clever. Use a pile driver. Hit the point once. Then come back and hit it again. Then hit it a third time –
a tremendous whack."

- Winston Churchill

Decide on three similar messages that capture the essence of what you want the Other to understand about the negotiation. Then craft each these messages into a succinct sentence. Don't be wordy or curt. Always answer the 'so what' question; what's the impact on the Other? Create two or three versions of the message. Playing the Broken Record can be irritating, but slightly changing the nuance of the message will take the edge off.

Let's look at an example. Say that we are going to attempt to negotiate a 10 percent price increase with our automotive customers. The three messages that I want to communicate are that we are making a bet on technology as our differentiator, that because of depressed pricing and rising costs the business is becoming unattractive, and that we are the only supplier that has manufacturing capability in the region for very sensitive, short shelf-life products.

Crafting the sentences in writing:
1. We have been and will continue to invest over $1,000,000 per year in R&D to create next generation, compliant products for you.
2. The current rising costs and falling prices have made this business relatively unattractive for our owners.
3. Unlike our offshore competition, our short supply chain and domestic manufacturing can assure you will have your product when and where you need it.

Create variations on each sentence. Take the first sentence, for example:
4. We continue to invest over $1,000,000 per year in R&D to create next generation, compliant products for you.

5. Our investment in R&D will provide new green products for you.
6. The vast majority of our R&D efforts are focused in the automotive market.
7. We need this price increase to invest in R&D and provide you with what you need.

Repeat The Message Frequently
Look for opportunities to sing the company song. Repetition, consistency and tying the message back to a benefit for the Other are absolutely essential. Don't be timid. If you think that you're singing the song too often, then you're probably singing it at the correct frequency. Make sure that all the members of your team, including management, can sing the song. Don't wing it; practice it. Simulate what might happen in a meeting with the Other. If people only remember 10 percent of what they heard, you can increase the odds of getting your message heard through repetition.

Lets go back to the second Principle of a *Mindful Manipulation*: "Relationship and Gain." Singing the company song might impact the relationship, but if you are in front of the Other to make your case for gain, it will be a necessary trade. It may be uncomfortable and feel unnatural, but the company song does get the message across. You know that your message has been transmitted when the Other says, "OK, I hear you loud and clear," or something to that effect.

Know When to Fold 'em

Lastly, the difference between a professional gambler and an amateur is to know when to quit. This is applicable to negotiations on two levels. First, as a negotiator, you must be able to recognize when a deal is not going anywhere that is favorable to you. Second, as a sales person, you should be able to tell when a deal isn't going to happen at all. You must know the signals that warrant you cutting your losses and swallowing your pride. The first deals mostly with working out the deal, the second understands if there is really a deal to be had. Negotiating is the challenge in the first and selling in the second.

If your negotiating default is gain over relationship, trust your hard wiring. It will be your safety valve. But if your default is relationship, you will tend to try to salvage a deal by trading gain for relationship. This is a slippery slope. If you sense that the deal is going in that direction, ask is the juice worth the squeeze?

As salespeople, we tend to work hard to get business, go the extra mile and do what it takes and all of the other 'can do' clichés. That behavior can easily backfire on us. In a negotiation, the Other can exploit us through our own investment of sweat equity, our commitments to our management or our need to close the deal. In this case, continuing down the path of commitment and concession without reciprocity in kind should be a warning to you. Salespeople also tend to be optimists. At times we can hold on to a deal that is never going to happen due to our own positive outlook, either because the deal is on a grand scale or is a pet project of someone superior to us. Sometimes, we need to recognize that our best option is to back away and cut our losses.

Recognize that selling (*if* we will be doing business), and negotiation (*how* we will be doing business), consumes resources, time and energy. Stick with the higher probability of success deals. Play the odds. Long shots are called that for a reason.

Chapter Seven: Best Practices After Negotiation

Document All Agreements

Once you have completed your agreement, document it and get a signification from the Other that it has been accepted. Oral contracts are usually very difficult to enforce. For simple transactions such as buying or selling a used car complete a bill of sale specifying if a warranty of any kind is excluded or included. On more complex deals more legal formality may be required. On legal agreements, make certain that remedies or consequences for breach are specified. This action makes it more difficult for someone to simply not honor an agreement. A word of caution, if you have remedies in the agreement, then you always should be prepared to exercise them.

Competent experienced legal counsel is an absolute necessity. Don't let your old grade school buddy Anthony or your cousin Vinnie handle things because you know them. Make sure they know what they're doing too. Placing business with friends and relatives invariably backfires. In the long run you don't get what you pay for and the relationship usually suffers.

Sleep with One Eye Open - Monitor Progress

Periodically check to see if the agreement is progressing as intended. Have objective measures that can tell you if it is working as you had planned.

Enforce Agreements

If someone is not performing as agreed, use the remedies specified in the agreement. If you are not prepared to use them, why have them? At a minimum have your lawyer write a letter. If the Other is playing games this tactic may flush it out.

Be Prepared to Renegotiate

If things have changed significantly, you may want to renegotiate an agreement. It doesn't do much good to hold someone to a deal that will either financially damage them or force legal action. Always weigh your options. Winning in court may wind up losing financially.

Part IV: Final Thoughts

Things do not change; we change.

-- Henry David Thoreau

Within today's context, ***Mindful Manipulation*** may seem counterintuitive because it is largely contrary to conventional wisdom, but that's what makes it so effective. Please understand that inevitably, humans continue to evolve or devolve and things will change; the music of life will change and a new beat will emerge. That will require us to modify the dance to match this new beat. Therefore, practicing Mindful Manipulation will need to morph.

In the future, I see the realm of negotiation advancing in seemingly opposite directions: the science of information technology and the art of detecting deception and lies. The use of technology will only become more pervasive, leading to more machines and less human interaction. Reading people faster and more accurately will become a more formidable craft, since less time will be spent face-to-face. Quickly discovering an involuntary response that is always indicative of someone telling a lie or displaying critical emotions and then developing technology or skills to sense it. Absent the implications of the future, these Principles will help you negotiate better for this foreseeable future, but they must change to match a new reality.

Part V: Resources

Psychometric Instruments
    Myers Briggs Type Indicator (MBTI)
    DiSC
The Planner
Case Study – Relationship versus Gain

Psychometric Instruments

The Myers-Briggs Type Indicator (MBTI)

The Myers-Briggs Type Indicator (MBTI) is an internationally recognized personality inventory based upon the psychological theory of C. G. Jung (1921-1971). Isabel Briggs Myers and Katharine Briggs' purpose in developing this list was to transform Jung's theory into an understandable and useful tool in people's lives. MBTI uses four pairs, or four sets of opposites. According to Jung's theory, these four pairs are believed to reflect psychological and mental dispositions.

The score for each of the four pairs is calculated based upon participants' forced responses to each of the questions. The dominant opposite is the one with the net highest score. The score is an indication of the participants' clarity of the preference for that opposite in that particular pair. The combination of dominant dipoles indicates personality type or preferences.

There are 16 possible personality types using the four dichotomies, or paired opposites. The type is not simply a combination of the results of the dominant opposite for the four pairs, but goes further and looks at how the preferred dimensions of the four pairs interact with each other. It's a classic case where the whole is greater than the sum of its parts. We will discuss this aspect later in the book as well.

A type is determined based on how you answer the questions. The higher the score on a particular dimension means the greater the clarity of preference. Clarity is not the same as behavior. Clarity simply means that there was a strong consistency of response in the way you answered the questions within a pair. Only the participant can validate the results of the instrument. Factors like your state of mind, physical well being, where you completed the instrument, and distractions you may have had during its completion can influence the instrument's results. Ideally, the participant should complete the assessment in their 'shoes-off self' state-of-mind, free of distractions and other detractors.

Personality type is usually established early in a person's life. It remains relatively constant over the span of a lifetime. However, in rare instances, a life-changing event may shift the degree of clarity and maybe the preferences themselves, yielding a different personality preference.

MBTI attempts to measure innate personality preferences. These preferences may not translate directly into behavior. Behavior can arise from either of two sources: innate or learned. Learned behavior, if reinforced, can dominant a person's behavioral pallet and subjugate their innate preferences. Personal preferences are just that, preferences. They answer the question, what is my unconscious default reaction? Learned behavior is not bad; if complimentary, learned behavior is great. It provides perspective and helps to avoid blind spots.

According to Kroeger and Thuesen, each of us develops a preference early in life and sticks with it. The more we practice those preferences (intentionally or unintentionally), the more we rely on them with confidence and strength. That doesn't mean we're incapable of using our non-preferences from time to time. In fact, the more we mature, the more our non-preferences add richness and dimension to our lives. However, they never take the place of our original preferences. So, Extraverts never become Introverts, and vice versa.

The MBTI is reliable across both gender and culture. The interpretation and framing of the results of the instrument usually need to be modified to accommodate cultural conditions and yield richer insights. A woman is not required to be a Feeler, someone who considers people in the decision making process, by definition, nor a man a Thinker. All gender bias has been removed from the current version of the instrument. Cross culturally, the instrument has proven to be reliable and repeatable throughout the world.

As mentioned earlier, there are four sets of pairs measured with the MBTI. They are Extrovert (E) or Introvert (I), Sensing (S) or iNtuitive (N), Thinking (T) or Feeling (F), and Perceiver (P) or Judgmental (J).

Let's dive into each of these dimensions, highlighting some key indicators of preference:

Source of Energy

The E/I dichotomy has a tremendous impact on How We Gather Information. Extroverts (E) are energized by the external world. They thrive on being with people. They tend to talk to think, or think out loud. Extroverts tend to let their energy flow out into the environment. They may become aware of their reliance on the outside environment for stimulation, and therefore have an eagerness to interact with the environment. As a result, Extroverts are dubbed 'action oriented'. Sometimes in the extreme, this behavior may be classified as impulsive. Nonetheless, Extroverts are usually open to new experiences, sociable and good communicators.

Introverts (I) prefer to recharge themselves in thought. They need to be able to go inside and think. As opposed to their Extrovert counterparts, Introverts think to talk. Introverts tend to absorb environmental energies. They attempt to be reflective, maintain focus and ponder non-trivial issues. They tend to be contemplative, and enjoy their privacy. They are much more able to be alone with themselves than an Extrovert.

Clue for Determining Extroverts and Introverts –
Out There and In Here (Differences between E's and I's)
– Extroverts tend to be more gregarious and animated in their communication style, while Introverts act more subdued and detached.
– Extroverts tend to talk louder than Introverts
– Extroverts talk to think where Introverts think then talk
– Extroverts repeat and exaggerate their points, Introverts tend to understate them
– Extroverts tend to talk more than Introverts

Sources of Perception

The S/N dichotomy determines our preference for What Kind of Information We Gather. Sensors (S) are perceivers of the conscious state. Sensors define life by what is. They deal with the here and now and are present in the moment. They tend to focus on their five senses to define reality. They are described as realists, have acute powers of observation and good memories for facts. Sensors live in the moment defined by data.

iNtuitives (N), according to Jung, are perceivers of the unconscious. Intuition refers to the perception of possibilities, meaning and relationships by way of insight. Intuition allows us to gain meaning outside of what is visible. iNtuitives can synthesize seemingly unrelated events into a pattern that may predict future occurrences. They may be described as imaginative, future oriented, theoretical, abstract and creative. Intuitive are 'big picture' people.

Clue for Determining iNtuitives and Sensors –
Gut Feel versus Data (Differences between N's and S's)
- Sensors may be more concrete; iNtuitives more abstract.
- Sensors prefer dealing with specifics and details; iNtuitives prefer concepts and the 'big picture'
- Sensors enjoy dealing with 'what is', the reality of the hear and now; iNtuitives like to explore the realm of the possible and 'what can be'
- Sensors tend to deconstruct an event or problem to its components; iNtuitives search for the meaning within the context of the event or situation

Sources of Judgment
The T/F dichotomy influences How We Balance Relationship and Gain. Thinkers (T) make decisions based upon logic. They tend to rely on the principle of cause and effect relationships. They strive to be objective and impersonal in their decisions. Thinkers tend to be neutral and impartial. They attempt to subjugate biases, desires, beliefs and values to the quality of the decision, and detach the impact of the decision from the people making it and the people affected by it. Thinkers strive for fairness and justice, objectivity, criticality, analysis, and attempt to be dispassionate in their demeanor. Time is viewed as a linear continuum, here we take the learning of the past, apply it to the present and connect it to the future. Their default setting is to the gain side of the Relationship/Gain continuum.

Feelers (F) use rational function, as do Thinkers, but with a different set of criteria. Feelers use relative value and merit of the issues in their decision-making heuristic. Feelers tend to be more subjective than Thinkers because they use both personal values and group values in the process. Feelers tend to be in touch with the feeling of others much more than Thinkers. Feelers are concerned with the human aspects of a decision rather than the technical aspects. Feelers will focus on the impact a decision has on the people who will be affected by it. Therefore, Feelers generally will trade gain for relationship.

This dichotomy is the most critical and greatly impacts the negotiated outcome. Without learned behaviors tempering the situation, Thinkers, the T's, logically deduce that the appropriate course of action is to get as much as you can. The Feelers, F's, will invariably lean to the relationship side to keep harmony and protect the personal side of the equation.

Clue for Determining Feelers and Thinkers –
Lead with the Heart versus Use Your Head (Differences between T's and F's)
- Feelers tend to feel their feelings, Thinkers want to analyze and understand them.
- Thinkers want precision and objectivity; Feelers try to promote accord and fairness.
- Feelers concern themselves with a decisions impact on others; Thinkers look at the 'if ... then' consequences of a decision.
- Feelers are more variable and apply subjectivity based upon the situation; Thinkers seek to be consistent in decisions
- Thinkers tend to be more linear in their thinking; Feelers more heuristic.

Orientation or Attitude to the World Outside
The P/J dichotomy has particular effect in determining How Much Information Is Needed to Make a Decision. A Judging (J) attitude is characterized by a need to make decisions, seek closure, plan events and organize things. The operative descriptors for Judging people are structure and order. An easy way to spot a Judger is to observe their work area. If the area is neatly organized and tidy, there is a good chance that the person that you are observing has a Judging

preference. A clean desk with no extraneous paraphernalia is a dead giveaway.

A Perceiving (P) attitude is one that is attuned with incoming information. People with this attitude are referred to as spontaneous, adaptable, curious, and open to what is new and changeable. Their quest is to take in new information as much as possible so that nothing important is missed. Their ability to deal with ambiguity and not be troubled by time is a hallmark of Perceivers' behavior. 'P' can also stand for piles. A classic trait of P's is to stack things into piles. It's not that they are disorganized; it's their way to organize with minimal structure.

Clue for Determining Judgers and Perceivers –
Structured versus Adaptable (Differences between J's and P's)
– Judgers tend to focus on the one right answer; Perceivers usually can see multiple solutions to a situation.
– Judgers are driven by time and schedule; Perceivers usually don't wear watches, and if they did it wouldn't be set to the correct time, because time isn't a driver.
– When asked a question, Judgers will be decisive and answer it straightaway; Perceivers are likely to respond to your question with a question of their own.
– Judgers drive conversations, projects and tasks to a conclusion; Perceivers move from topic to topic, project to project and task to task easily and without completion, which gives the impression to non-Perceivers of randomness or eccentricity.

In summary, the four MBTI dichotomies are inextricably linked to the four critical dynamics that effect negotiated outcomes. The **Source of Energy**, the **E/F** preference pair, greatly affects **How We Gather Information**. How we give, get and share information. The **Sources of Perception**, the **S/N** preferences, filter **What Kind of Information We Need to Make a Decision**. The **Sources of Judgment**, or the **T/F** dichotomy, influence **How We Balance Relationship and Gain**. Lastly, **Our Orientation or Attitude to the World Outside**, driven by the **J/P** pair, determines **How Much Information We Need to Make a Decision**.

Traditional learned negotiating behaviors, conventional strategy, tactics and countermeasures ignore these dynamics and only prepare the negotiator to protect their self-interests. We must expand our understanding to include how we and the Other gather information, use information to make a decision, balance relationship and gain, and determine how much information is needed to make a decision. These dynamics are at the very heart of what effects negotiations. This understanding can help transform the zero-sum, positional, fixed pie arena of negotiation to one with more equitable, durable and sustainable results. This will yield mutual benefits, balanced equity and more civility. Albeit counterintuitive, mastery of the traditional negotiating skills is required to effectively capitalize on this knowledge anchored to a deeper understanding of people's intrinsic preferences.

In the next few pages, we will present the MBTI (Myers-Briggs Type Indicator) Typology as it applies to negotiating. It's a simple tool. If you know your MBTI type, look it up. Find your type and see if it fits you.

Type	Descriptor	Strengths	Liabilities	Cues
ENTJ	Follow Me Default: Gain	– Generates lots of logical solutions – Out-of-the box thinker – Makes opinion known – Decisive	– Can miss critical details – Ideas may be too complex – May have trouble with authority – May be overwhelming – Not inclusionary – May make heat-of-the-moment decisions – Can mislead self – May be inflexible	– Talks to think – Deals mainly with concepts, avoids details – Values objectivity over subjectivity – Quick to make up their mind
ENFJ	Convincing John Default: Relationship	– Resolves conflicts – Usually good communicator – Motivational – Makes opinion known – Decisive – Has a people perspective	– Tends to decide based on own biases – Has a hard time staying neutral, can get sucked into the problem – May be overwhelming – Not inclusionary – May make heat-of-the-moment decisions – Can mislead self	– Talks to think – Deals mainly with concepts, avoids details – Considers people issues above the bottom line – Quick to make up their mind
ESTJ	Company Guy Default: Gain	– Traditional thinker – Plays by the principles – Dependable – Makes opinion known – Decisive – Concrete	– Predicable – May not be an innovator – Usually short term thinker – May be overwhelming – Not inclusionary – Finds it difficult to conceptualize – May be inflexible	– Talks to think – Deals mainly with facts, concepts are a waste of time – Values objectivity over subjectivity – Quick to make up their mind
ESFJ	Smooth Operator Default: Relationship	– Traditional thinker – Plays by the principles – Dependable – Makes opinion known – Decisive – Has a people perspective	– Predicable – May not be an innovator – Usually short term thinker – May be overwhelming – Not inclusionary – Acutely sensitive to peoples feelings	– Talks to think – Deals mainly with facts, concepts are a waste of time – Considers people issues above the bottom line – Quick to make up their mind

Type	Descriptor	Strengths	Liabilities	Cues
ENTP	So Many Challenges, So Little Time Default: Gain	– Generates lots of logical solutions – Out-of-the box thinker – Quick on their feet	– Can miss critical details – Ideas may be too complex – May have trouble with authority – Likely to talk too much – May talk in circles – Finds it difficult to accept differing perspectives – Can be a perfectionist	– Talks to think – Deals mainly with concepts, avoids details – Values objectivity over subjectivity – Slow to decide in order to make the best decision –
ENFP	Life is Good Default: Relationship	– Resolves conflicts – Usually good communicator – Motivational – Quick on their feet – Defends underdogs	– Tends to decide based on own biases – Has a hard time staying neutral, can get sucked into the problem – Likely to talk too much – May talk in circles – Finds it difficult to accept differing perspectives	– Talks to think – Deals mainly with concepts, avoids details – Considers people issues above the bottom line – Slow to decide in order to make the best decision
ESTP	Fire, Ready, Aim, Woops Default: Gain	– Can deal with ambiguity – Good in crisis – Resourceful – Quick on their feet – Concrete	– Unpredictable – May lose energy when crisis passes – May not consider the consequences of their – Likely to talk too much – May talk in circles – Finds it difficult to conceptualize – Can be a perfectionist	– Talks to think – Deals mainly with facts, concepts are a waste of time – Values objectivity over subjectivity – Slow to decide in order to make the best decision
ESFP	Life in the Here and Now Default: Relationship	– Can deal with ambiguity – Good in crisis – Resourceful – Quick on their feet – Defends underdogs	– Unpredictable – May lose energy when crisis passes – May not consider the consequences of their behavior – Likely to talk too much – May talk in circles – Acutely sensitive to peoples feelings	– Talks to think – Deals mainly with facts, concepts are a waste of time – Considers people issues above the bottom line – Slow to decide in order to make the best decision

Type	Descriptor	Strengths	Liabilities	Cues
INTJ	Pursing the Perfect Solution Default: Gain	– Generates lots of logical solutions – Out-of-the box thinker – Gets more information than they give – May be perceived as a good listener	– Can miss critical details – Ideas may be too complex – May have trouble with authority – May not appear to be engaged fully – May make heat-of-the-moment decisions – Can mislead self – May be inflexible	– Thinks before talking – Deals mainly with concepts, avoids details – Values objectivity over subjectivity – Quick to make up their mind
INFJ	Caring Dreamer Default: Relationship	– Resolves conflicts – Usually good communicator – Motivational – Gets more information than they give – May be perceived as a good listener – Has a people perspective	– Tends to decide based on own biases – Has a hard time staying neutral, can get sucked into the problem – May not appear to be engaged fully – May make heat-of-the-moment decisions – Can mislead self	– Thinks before talking – Deals mainly with concepts, avoids details – Considers people issues above the bottom line – Quick to make up their mind
ISTJ	Plays According to the Principles Default: Gain	– Traditional thinker – Plays by the principles – Dependable – Gets more information – May be a good listener – Concrete	– Predicable – May not be an innovator – Usually short term thinker – May not appear to be engaged fully – Finds it difficult to conceptualize – May be inflexible	– Thinks before talking – Deals mainly with facts, concepts are a waste of time – Values objectivity over subjectivity – Quick to make up their mind
ISFJ	Count On Me Default: Relationship	– Traditional thinker – Plays by the principles – Dependable – Gets more information than they give – May be perceived as a good listener – Has a people perspective	– Predicable – May not be an innovator – Usually short term thinker – May not appear to be engaged fully – Acutely sensitive to peoples feelings	– Thinks before talking – Deals mainly with facts, concepts are a waste of time – Considers people issues above the bottom line – Quick to make up their mind

Type	Descriptor	Strengths	Liabilities	Cues
INTP	Putting All of the Pieces Together Default: Gain	Generates lots of logical solutions Out-of-the box thinker Doesn't shoot from the hip Can be a perfectionist	– Can miss critical details – Ideas may be too complex – May have trouble with authority – May come across as aloof – Finds it difficult to accept differing perspectives	– Thinks before talking – Deals mainly with concepts, avoids details – Values objectivity over subjectivity – Slow to decide in order to make the best decision
INFP	The Consummate Idealist Default: Relationship	Resolves conflicts Usually good communicator Motivational Doesn't shoot from the hip Defends underdogs	– Tends to decide based on own biases – Has a hard time staying neutral can get sucked into the problem – May come across as aloof or detached – Finds it difficult to accept differing perspectives	– Thinks before talking – Deals mainly with concepts, avoids details – Considers people issues above the bottom line – Slow to decide in order to make the best decision
ISTP	Doing What's Happening Now Default: Gain	Can deal with ambiguity Good in crisis Resourceful Doesn't shoot from the hip Concrete	– Unpredictable – May lose energy when crisis passes – May not consider the consequences of their behavior – May come across as aloof or detached – Finds it difficult to conceptualize – Can be a perfectionist	– Thinks before talking – Deals mainly with facts, concepts are a waste of time – Values objectivity over subjectivity – Slow to decide in order to make the best decision
ISFP	Being in the Moment Default: Relationship	Can deal with ambiguity Good in crisis Resourceful Doesn't shoot from the hip Defends underdogs	– Unpredictable – May lose energy when crisis passes – May not consider the consequences of their behavior – May come across as aloof or detached – Acutely sensitive to peoples feelings	– Thinks before talking – Deals mainly with facts, concepts are a waste of time – Considers people issues above the bottom line – Slow to decide in order to make the best decision

DiSC

DiSC deals with only two behavioral sets, not four dimensions of preference like the MBTI. DiSC is a behavioral instrument, not psychological. It measures behavior, not preference or personality. Like MBTI, its results can have tremendous applicability to the negotiating process. DiSC is also highly culturally sensitive in that behaviors tend to closely follow societal norms. If being active is not appreciated by the culture, then the major tend to act passively.

The graphic below summarizes the DiSC profile. At its core, there are two sets of behavioral dipoles that are measured by the user: Task versus People and Active versus Passive. Based upon the response to questions both polarity and strength of that polarity are established. One set of dipoles is Active versus Passive, and the other is People versus Task. You can usually get insight to a person's DiSC by watching their behavior and listening to them. It's a kind of personality short hand for people watching.

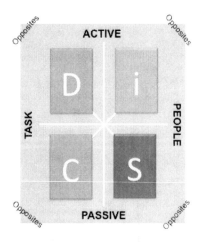

If my behavior describes me as having a Task/Active bias, I would be classified as a 'D'. D stands for Dominance. People with this behavior pattern tend to be driven and results-oriented. They speak fast and generally are economical with words. They usually are direct, sometimes blunt, and aren't warm fuzzy people. They enjoy challenges and are highly competitive. The D will do what it takes to win in a negotiation. They may not be focused on defeating others, but they will if necessary. Their nature may set up a contentious environment.

People who have an Active/People profile are referred to as 'I'. They are influencers. They see themselves as persuasive and leaders. Like the D, they speak forcefully, energetically and rapidly, but they do not share the cold prickliness of the D. They tend to be warm and charismatic. They are more informal than the D, but have a strong ego, so don't try to run them over. From a negotiating perspective, the 'I' will attempt to convince you. Their talkative nature may tend to divulge too much information during the negotiation. They will tend to trade gain for relationship because of their need to be people pleasers.

Passive/People profiles are designated 'S' for Steadiness. They tend to be what in Spanish is referred to as 'Sympatico'. Good listening skills and introspective thinking are behavior hallmarks. They tend to speak slowly and softer than the 'D' and 'I' profiles, but they share the warmness and friendlier nature of the 'I'. Expect them to be calm, methodical, and attentive listeners. Don't force a quick response, don't interrupt them and don't mistake their willingness to go along as a sign of satisfaction or agreement. They generally get more information than they give, and because of their passive deliberate style, can be excellent negotiators. Because of their people (relationship) orientation, they will look for a mutual win sometimes at their own expense.

Passive/Task behavior pattern, called 'C's for Conscientious, tend to follow processes and principles and observe standards and norms easily. They work and talk at a slower pace, and pride themselves on being competent. Expect them to want a lot of information, and to respond logically. Don't be too personal or informal, don't get too close to them and don't be disorganized in appearance or thought process. They can be very tough negotiators since they require facts and are passive, so the information balance will usually be in their favor. They are logical and able to debate. They will test you and what you say. They, like the 'D', tend to be more on the formal, cold prickly side of the equation. They will readily trade relationship for gain.

To finish up describing our graphic, the strength or dominance of the behavioral pattern can be determined two ways. First, the distance from the center; the further from the center your behavior is plotted, the stronger the behavior. Second, the farther from adjacent profiles your results indicate; the strong and more pure the profile. If you find yourself approaching another quadrant, you probably have a dominant/subordinate type. This means your behavior tends to be influenced by an adjacent behavioral trait. Pay particular attention to which of the traits are least present in your profile. This can be your blind spot and presents a possible vulnerability. Generally, the profile diagonally opposite your primary will be the people to whom you have to pay attention. They represent the behavioral area where you have no common ground. These are the people that you will generally have the hardest time building trust and rapport and ergo negotiating successfully.

Should you desire to explore this instrument further, simply Google DiSC and it will generate a number of options to take the instrument on line. Feedback is almost instantaneous.

Negotiating Pluses:
Focused on Results
Fact Driven
Strength of Personality
Logical

Negotiating Plus
People Like Them
Persuasive
Generally Dynamic

Negotiating Pitfalls:
Ego May Get in the Way
May Piss People Off
Can Be Myopic

Negotiating Pitfalls
May Be Too Trusting
Overly Optimistic
Doesn't Like Details
Trusts "Gut Feel"

Default: Gain

Default: Relationship

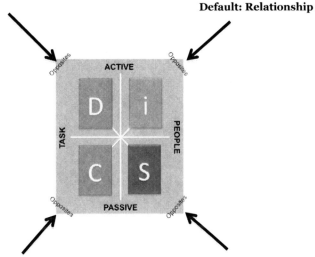

Negotiating Pluses:
Follows Principles
Fact Driven
Gets Information
Not Transparent
Negotiating Pitfalls:
May Be Too Precise
Overly Analytical
May Get Lost in Details

Default: Gain

Negotiating Pluses:
Amiable
Caring
Careful
Gets Information
Negotiating Pitfalls:
May Be Too Trusting
Overly Sincere
May React Too Slowly

Default: Relationship

The Planner

HAVE A FALLBACK POSITION

Assess Leverage

What are the key *sources* of LEVERAGE and LIMITATIONS in this negotiation?

> Consider the situation, personal skills, brand identity, time constraints, personal authority and responsibility, technology, price, cost, product performance, perceived value, competition, service, information, relationship history, management expectations, etc.

Based upon the key *sources* of LEVERAGE and LIMITATIONS in this negotiation, is there a clearly dominant participant?

Based upon the key *sources* of LEVERAGE and LIMITATIONS in this negotiation and each participants EXPECTATIONS, is it likely an outcome will be reached?

Create a Fallback Position

What is/are our FALLBACK POSITION(S)?
(Alternative courses of action if this negotiation fails)

What do we EXPECT as a result of this negotiation?

What does THE OTHER likely EXPECT as a result of this negotiation?

Separate Needs and Wants

What are OUR ABSOLUTE NEEDS (Must-Haves, rank ordered)?

What are OUR WANTS (Nice-to-Haves, rank ordered)?

What are THE OTHER'S NEEDS (Must-Haves, rank ordered)?

What are THE OTHER'S WANTS (Nice-to-Haves, rank ordered)?

Based on the above WANTS and NEEDS, what will OUR OPENING POSITION be?

Based on the above WANTS and NEEDS, what do we anticipate THE OTHER'S OPENING POSITION will be?

Goal, Strategy and Consequences

What is the Goal of this Negotiation?

Anticipate the Goal of the Other:

What is your strategy to achieve your Goal?

Anticipate the Strategy of the Other?

What are the BEST, WORST and MOST LIKELY outcomes of this negotiation?

What are the Consequences of executing this strategy?

What are the unintended consequences or collateral damage of executing the strategy?

ANTICIPATE

Assess Differences

Using Hofstede's rankings create a Cultural Landscape of the similarities and differences between or among national cultures.

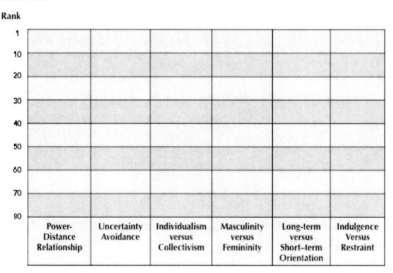

Culturally (Nationality)
    Reinforce   **Avoid**

Create a Cultural Landscape of the similarities and differences between or among organizations.

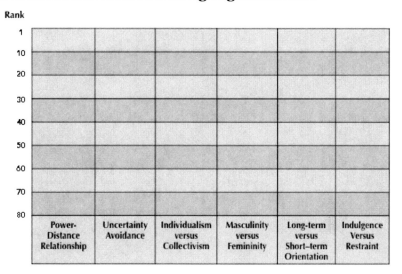

Organizationally (Corporate Culture)
Reinforce   Avoid

Generationally
       Reinforce   **Avoid**

Gender Issues
       Reinforce   **Avoid**

Preferences and Behaviors
     Reinforce   **Avoid**

Type Casting:

For each negotiator, including you, your team and the Other team, estimate or identify the following:

My Team

Negotiator	Me		
Type/Temperament			
DiSC			
Watch out for ...			
Leverage ...			

Their Team

Negotiator	Their Lead		
Type/Temperament			
DiSC			
Watch out for ...			
Leverage ...			

Implications: Reinforcing and Mitigating Actions

Personal Motivators Assessment

Evaluate the Other's personal needs for each of the following criteria from high to low. Using a difference color or mark assess you own needs versus the same criteria. Look for areas of similarity and difference. Assess the impact on the negotiation.

Need to	High		Medium		Low
Build relationships					
Win					
Avoid risk					
Get things done					
Have data					
Understand the concept					
Be respected					
Be heard					
Maintain harmony					
Save face					

What are the possible impacts of the personal motivator differences and similarities on this negotiation?

Business Motivators Assessment

Evaluate the Other's business needs for each of the following criteria from high to low. Using a difference color or mark assess you own needs versus the same criteria. Look for areas of similarity and difference. Assess the impact on the negotiation.

Need to	High		Medium		Low
Maintain a long term relationship					
Be perceived as the Winner					
Not to be perceived as losing					
Achieve financial incentive					
Justify the results to the Other's management					
Execute functional responsibilities					
Maintain authority					

What are the possible impacts of the Business motivator differences and similarities on this negotiation?

What are the financial and career incentives tied to this negotiation for the Other?

What is the fiduciary functional role that the Other must play?

Recognizing Blind Spots:
Given my cognitive preferences, what four things do I need to keep in mind during the negotiations?

     1.

     2.

     3.

     4.

DO A REALITY CHECK

As a negotiating team complete the format below. Use post-its in blocks A, B and C. Then assess your team's competitive advantage in block D.

Reality Check

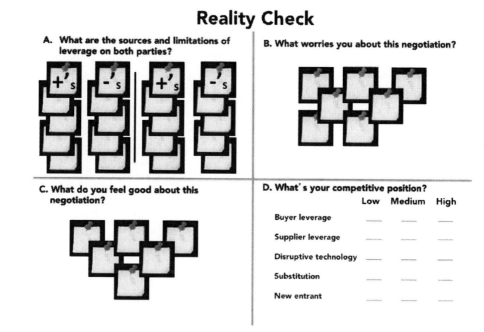

What are the implications of the Reality Check? Create reinforcing and mitigating actions to strengthen your position.

Existing Information

What information exists – i.e. what is known by whom?

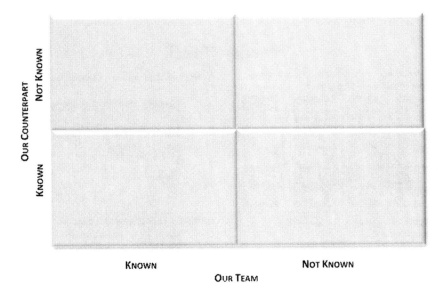

Information GAPs

The GAP is the created by difference between the desired and actual states of information. What is our information GAP.

Value Our Information

What is the value of information, known to only us?

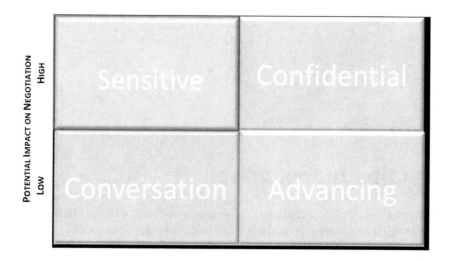

Definitions:

Confidential – Information that is not shared under any circumstances

Sensitive – Information that can be shared with extreme caution and under duress in return for valuable information from the Other

Advancing – Information that is shared to advance the relationship in return for information from the Other, if needed

Conversation – Information that can be shared which has no bearing on the negotiation

Implications: Reinforcing and Mitigating Actions

Providing Information:

Confidential Information: What information that we possess will we not provide under any circumstances?

Sensitive Information: What information that we possess will we provide – if we obtain information in return?

Advancing Information: What information that we possess will we provide to advance the conversation?

Conversational Information: What information that we possess will we provide and likely receive nothing in return?

Complete the following Information Trade-off tool

What We Can Give	If, We Get

<u>TEST</u>

Fill Information Gaps
A deeper drill of what was identified earlier.

What information that we don't have is critical to obtain before the negotiation starts?

What information that we don't have is critical to obtain once the negotiation starts?

What information that we don't have is irrelevant to the negotiation?

What questions can we ask to fill in our information gaps – either information we don't have or assumptions we have made that require verification?

Information Gap	Provocative Question

Ask Questions

Ask open-ended questions to obtain strategic information:
-   **Why?**
-   **What?**
-   **How?**
-   **Tell me more...**

Ask closed-ended questions to obtain factual / tactical information:
-   **Who?**
-   **How many?**
-   **How much?**
-   **Which?**
-   **Where?**
-   **Is? – Leading to yes/no answers**

Test and summarize with closed-ended clarifications:
-   **So, your position is...**
-   **Let me see if I understand your position...**
-   **What I hear you saying is...**

Propose conditionally:
-   **What would your position be if we could...?**
-   **If we offered "this," could you offer "that?"**
-   **If you were to offer "this," what would you need in return?**
-   **Under what conditions could you accept "this?"**

Use provocative questions:
-   **What if we are unable to agree to "this?" – Speculate as to the outcome**
-   **Why is "this" important to your company? – Personal Opinion**
-   **Is there an alternative solution that you see to "this" particular issue? – Analyze**

Develop Other Questions Here:

EXECUTE

Develop an Opening Offer:

Is there a strategic advantage to providing the opening offer, or do you want the Other to make the opening offer?

Document Control:

If the negotiation will result in a contract or other written documentation, is having control of the document critical? What is the plan to maintain document control, if applicable?

Expectation Setting:

For the overall negotiation, what is your Opening Offer, Target Range and Walk Away value for each of the negotiable items? Are there any non-negotiable items?

Negotiable Items:

	Opening Offer	Target Range	Walk-away
1.			
2.			
3.			
4.			

Non-Negotiable Items

1.

2.

3.

4.

Concession Planning:

Prior to each round of negotiations, what are your best case, likely case and worst-case outcomes for each negotiable item, as well as a attaching a string on any concession for that negotiation round?

Round One:

Item	Opening Offer	Target Range	Walk Away	String

Round Two:

Item	Opening Offer	Target Range	Walk Away	String

Round Three:

Item	Opening Offer	Target Range	Walk Away	String

Build Advocacy:

Identify Possible Advocates:

Who	Why	How	Lead

Social Events: Where, Why, Who, When?

Contact Schedule: When and How?

Messages to Build Relationships:

Compose a "Company Song:"

Our three or four CONSISTENT MESSAGES are:
    1.

    2.

    3.

    4.

How to Say the Same Thing Differently:
    1.

    2.

    3.

    4.

Create a Control Plan:

Possible Risks to the Agreement:

Impact to the Deal if They Occur:

Mitigating Actions:

Definition of Non-compliance:

How to Monitor Compliance:

Actions to Take to Remediate a Non-compliant Situation:

A Case Study

How Some Salespeople Trade Gain for Relationship

Recently I said the following to a client, "Your customer facing people are not working for you. They are working for your customers. They tend to focus on keeping the customers happy at your expense. This results in much of your company's profit being left on the table. They are good with people and have pleasing personalities. It's in their nature. Conventional negotiating situations put these people in predicaments well outside their comfort zone and they are ill equipped to handle them."

The following case study is offered to exemplify this point. It deals with the results of a primer on negotiating that I delivered for that client on the last day of each of the workshops. These simulations were conducted globally for a multinational corporation. Given the same scenario, the results vary widely and the gain/relationship default figures predominantly in the outcomes. The results of a negotiation simulation were both unexpected and rather dramatic. During the course of the workshops there were over 250 separate, mostly one-on-one simulations completed. Leading up to the negotiation simulation the participants learned to create and extract value from the products and services being sold to the customer, not merely to meet a competitive price. The instructions advised the participants that the incremental value that the customer would receive from using the sellers' product versus the competitor's product was about four dollars or euro per kg. This was above the targeted success/failure-selling price of sixteen dollars or euro per kg. The currency denomination was contingent on the geographic region that the workshop was held. Euros and dollars were assumed to have a one-to-one exchange rate. It is important to note that the sellers in the simulation had a dominant position. The sellers did not know the exact extent of their dominance. Essentially, the buyers were at their mercy.

The participants were both commercial and technical. The commercial personnel, sales and marketing were always assigned to play the role of the seller. The DiSC instrument was used as part of this workshop to illustrate a difference in behavior. The salespeople involved in the simulation would be best described as mature, technically oriented, relationship-focused and highly experienced salespersons. Their DiSC profile was predominantly Influence, whose default gain/relationship trade-off is Relationship. Their actual compensation was mainly based on salary, plus a minor variable component tied to actual performance. Technical or logistics people played the role of procurement. In contrast to the sellers, their DiSC profiles were predominantly D's and C's, Dominance and Conscientious. Both have a default gain/relationship trade-off of gain default. The sales cycle was typically repeated business to the same group of customers. New sales occurred by displacing a competitor's product, gaining incremental volume through the customers' organic growth or new applications at an existing customer. The risk associated with losing one of these larger customer's business grossly outweighs the reward of incrementally raising the product price to the customer. The primary customer interface is the procurement functions. Because of the size of the customers spend; the sales team is dealing with a commodity manager. Procurement tended to be the primary decision maker and point of contact for most salespeople in this company.

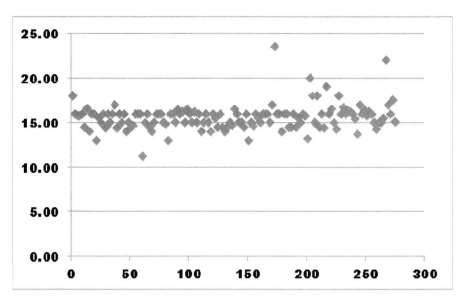

The graph above depicts the results of the simulations, price agreed by from each simulation from low to high. Reviewing the results, there is a large cluster around sixteen (16) dollars or euro as an agreed to a price, but there is also about 50 percent of the agreements that are less than the targeted success/failure point for receiving variable compensation. The simulation agreement extremes ranged from a low of eleven fifty (11.50) per kg to a high of twenty-three twenty-five (23.25) per kg. The extreme lows and highs maybe indicative of participant's skill, reaction to high-pressure, competitive situations and/or the cognitive preference default.

Case Study Conclusions:
- The vast majority of the sales people traded gain for relationship
- Value (pricing above sixteen per kg.) was extracted in less than 10 percent of the total simulations
- 50 percent of the simulations failed to meet the minimum success failure mark
- Most opening offers from sales were at or about 16 dollars or euro per kilo, which is near the success/failure point. They don't leave room to negotiate
- Most simulations tended to wind up around the targets set by management
- Participants viewed selling and negotiating as two separate activities
- If the rewards and consequences changed so to would the results
- Bottom line profitability is affected 866,000 units (dollars or euro) for each one unit of currency change in the final price
- Very few of the sellers attempted to take advantage of their powerful position in this negotiation.
- Most sellers assumed that the volume was a superior gain than price.

Mindful Manipulation is an avant-garde, unconventional and counterintuitive look at the ancient practice of negotiating. It is driven by understanding the Other's perceptions and expectations, influencing them through civil, consistent and purposeful behaviors to create advantageous negotiated results. Mindful Manipulation is a hybrid approach that links four value driven principles with the time tested practices of traditional negotiating. Mindful Manipulation strives for win-win resolutions, but is pragmatic and recognizes the need for a suboptimal win-lose fallback. Practicing Mindful Manipulation produces better, more durable, equitable and balanced results.

Bibliography

Alinsky, Saul D., *Rules for Radicals,* New York; Random House (1971)

Atkinson, J. W., *A Theory of Achievement Motivation,* New York: John Wiley & Sons (1974)

Carrere, S., and Gottman, J.M., (1999). Predicting Divorce among Newlyweds from the First Three Minutes of a Marital Conflict Discussion, *Family Process, Vol. 38(3),* 293-301;

Carrere, S., and Gottman, J.M., (1999). *Predicting the future of marriages,* In E.M. Hetherington (Ed.) Coping with divorce, single parenting and remarriage: A risk and resiliency perspective, 3-22

Carrere, S., Buehlman, K.T., Coan, J.A., Gottman, J.M., Coan, J.A., and Ruckstuhl, L., (2000). *Predicting Marital Stability and Divorce in Newlywed Couples,* Journal of Family Psychology, 14(1), 42-58

Coupland, D., *Generation X,* New York: St Martin's Press (1991)

Doyle, M. and Strauss D., *How to Make Meetings Work,* New York: Berkley Books (1976)

Fisher, R. Ury, W., *Getting to Yes,* New York: Penguin (1991)

Fisher, R., Kopelman E. Schneider, A. K., *Beyond Machiavelli,* Cambridge: Harvard (1994)

Forni, P. M., *Choosing Civility,* New York: St Martin's Press (2002)

Falcoa, H., *Say it Like a Woman – Why the 21st century negotiator will need the female touch,* World Business May, 2006

Gale, B., *Managing Customer Value*, New York: Simon & Schuster (1994)

Garreau, Joel, *The Nine Nations of North America*, New York: Avon Books (1981)

Gladwell, Malcolm, *Blink*, New York, Little, Brown and Company (2005)

Grant, Adam M., *Give and Take*, New York: Penguin Books (2013)

Greene, R., *The 48 Laws of Power,* New York: Penguin Books (1998)

Haidt, Jonathan The Righteous Mind: Why Good People Are divided by Politics and Religion. New York, NY: Pantheon.

Harvey, J. B., *The Abilene Paradox and Other Meditations on Management*, New York: Lexington (1988)

Hofstede, Geert, *Culture's Consequences*, London: Sage (2001)

Hofstede, Geert, Hofstede Gret Jan, Minkov, Michael, *Cultures and Organizations: Software for the Mind*, New York: McGraw Hill (2010)

Janis, I. L., *Groupthink*, 2d ed., Boston: Houghton Mifflin (1982)

Joy, N. and Kane-Benson S. *"Selling Is a Woman's Game: 15 Powerful Reasons Why Women Can Outsell Men"*.

Karrass, C. L., *Give & Take*, New York: Crowell (1974)

Karrass, C. L., *The Negotiating Game*, New York: Crowell (1970)

Karrass, C. L., *In Business As In Life – You Don't Get What You Deserve, You Get What You Negotiate,* Los Angeles: Stanford Street Press (1996)

Kroeger, O. and Thuesen, J. M., *Type Talk*, New York: Delta (1988)

Leary, Kimberlyn, Pillemer, Julianna and Wheeler, Michael *"Negotiating with Emotion"* January-February 2013, Harvard Business Review

Mayer, D and Greenberg, *H. M., "What Makes a Good Salesman,* July-August 2006, Harvard Business Review

Machiavelli, N., *The Prince,* New York: Barnes & Noble (1994)

Massey, M, The Massey Triad Video Program: *What You Are Is Where You Were When, What You Are is Not What You Have To Be, What You Are Is Where You See,* Enterprises Media (1986)

Malkiel, B, *"A Random Walk Down Wall "- 10ᵗʰ Edition,* New York: Norton (2011)

Myers, I. B., McCaulley, M. H. Quenk, N. L. and Hammer, A. L., *MBTI Manual,* Palo Alto: Consulting Psychologist Press (1998)

Nierenberg, Gerard I., *Fundamentals of Negotiating*, New York: Hawthorn (1973)

Pease, A., Pease B., The Definitive Book of Body Language, New York: Bantam (2006)

Peters, T. J. and Waterman, .R. W., *In Search of Excellence*, New York: Warner Books (1993)

Porter, M. E., *Competitive Strategy*, New York: Free Press (1998)

Poundstone, William, *Prisoner's Dilemma* New York: Doubleday (1992)

Pradel D. W., Riley Bowles, H., McGinn, K. L., *When Does Gender Matter in Negotiation?*, Harvard Business Review: November 2005,

Sandberg, Sheryl, and Scovell, Nell, *Lean In: Women, Work and the Will to Lead*, Alfred A. Knopf, New York (2013)

Talley, J. L., Problem Solving 2.0, www.problemsolving2.com

Thaler, R. H., *Nudge: Improving Decisions about Health, Wealth, and Happiness – 8th edition,* New York: Penguin (2009)

Tolle, E, *A New Earth,* London: Plume (2005)

Tversky A. and Kahneman, D. *Framing of Decisions and the Psychology of Choice,* Science, New Series, Volume 211, Issue 4481 (Jan 30, 1981) 453-458

Ury, William, *Getting Past No*, New York: Bantam Books (1991)

Waldman, Katy, *Negotiating While Female: Sometimes It Does Hurt to Ask,* Slate.com, March 14, 2014

Wikipedia: The Free Encyclopedia. Wikimedia Foundation Inc. Updated 22 July 2004, 10:55 UTC. Encyclopedia on-line. Available from http://en.wikipedia.org/wiki Internet.

Wolfe, I. S., Geeks, Geezers, and Googlization, Lancaster: Xliberis (2009)

Index